The Shadow of Slavery:
Peonage in the South

1901-1969

PETE DANIEL

Oxford University Press

LONDON   OXFORD   NEW YORK

OXFORD UNIVERSITY PRESS

London   Oxford   New York
Glasgow   Toronto   Melbourne   Wellington
Cape Town   Ibadan   Nairobi   Dar es Salaam   Lusaka   Addis Ababa
Delhi   Bombay   Calcutta   Madras   Karachi   Lahore   Dacca
Kuala Lumpur   Singapore   Hong Kong   Tokyo

LIVERPOOL POLYTECHNIC
LIBRARY SERVICE

Accession number

011210/44

Class number

331.542097 DAN

© 1972, 1973 by The Board of Trustees of the University of Illinois
Library of Congress Catalog Card No. 73-83234
First published by University of Illinois Press
Reprinted by special arrangement with University of Illinois Press
First issued as an Oxford University Press paperback, New York, 1973
Printed in the United States of America

TO BONNIE

Contents

Preface

Out of the ashes and ruins of the Civil War the shadow of slavery once more crept over the South. Even as some black Southerners tried to achieve political power, civil rights, and personal security during Reconstruction, many laborers became mired in the quicksand of debt. Black educator Booker T. Washington, usually soft-spoken on economic and social issues, observed in 1888 that the "colored people on these plantations are held in a kind of slavery that is in one sense as bad as the slavery of antebellum days." Washington spoke of the system of debt that pervaded the South, a system that grasped the black man, that "binds him, robs him of independence, allures him and winds him deeper and deeper in its meshes each year till he is lost and bewildered."

At the turn of the twentieth century the federal government acknowledged that the labyrinth of local customs and laws which bound men in debt was peonage, and an 1867 federal statute, aimed at abolishing a similar system in New Mexico, outlawed debt servitude. The federal government timidly moved against peonage, slowly penetrating some of the maze and confusion of the Southern labor system, but it continually failed to end peonage. The dread of debt still hangs heavy upon the land. When a Southerner says, "I ain't beholden to no man" or "I don't owe nobody," the words have an uneasy assertiveness. Owing in the South often led to imprisonment, beating, or even death. Though most rural laborers in the South moved about with freedom, seeking an escape from poverty and debt, some men, especially black sharecroppers and immigrants, lacked that freedom.

Peonage in the South was complex, confusing; customs and laws intertwined. Planters probably purposely made few distinctions between their legal rights as employers and what had grown into custom, into peonage. In time peonage came to resemble a series of imaginative western movie scenarios; ranch gangs too rough for the local authorities to control, ranchers with imperial dreams for the county, towns in the hands of toughs who dominated the well-meaning but impotent sheriffs, minor characters intimidated or killed by the villains, a federal marshal riding into town to restore order. No script for peonage, however, has a scene with a hero riding into the sunset—which is to say, the violent and frontier-like customs of the South triumphed. Quite different from the silver-screen tone of most U.S. history, peonage defeated righteous men, withstood them, endured.

Nor was peonage limited to the Southern states, for it occurred to some extent in the North. But it was the Southern brand of peonage that resembled in some ways similar labor systems that emerged in Mexico, Latin America, and the Philippines. Indeed, the term *peón* originated from Spanish, from a term that originally meant foot soldier but that came through popular usage to mean a man indebted to an employer. Evidently peonage flourishes best in a primitive capitalistic economy that is adjusting its labor system. After the abolition of the *encomiendas* in Latin America, for example, peonage emerged as a transitional state between slave and free labor. In the Philippines slavery and peonage existed simultaneously as the Spanish adjusted existing slavery to fit plantation agriculture. The Philippines, Latin America, and the American South contained transitional labor systems, high illiteracy rates, a rural and isolated environment, an inviolate power structure, and corrupt or corruptible local law-enforcement officers. In the Philippines the system oppressed mostly children, in Latin America Indians, and in the Southern United States blacks.

Perhaps a close examination of peonage in other countries would reveal more parallels, yet such an analysis lies beyond the scope of this study. Whether peonage in the South grew out of slavery, a natural and perhaps unavoidable interlude between bondage and freedom, or whether employers, perhaps with paternalistic motives, distorted laws and customs to create debt servitude, most Southerners quietly accepted peonage. To the employer peonage was a way to control laborers; to the peon the system, as Booker T. Washington suggested, was bewildering. The alternatives open to the peon were absurd: remain quietly; run away and be pursued, shot, or beaten; or kill the employer and risk lynching.

This book is in part the record of an American failure—the inability of federal, state, and local law-enforcement officials to end peonage. Perhaps these men were convinced that the progression of successful yet inexorable court cases signified that peonage was dying out, or possibly they were traduced by the notion of American innocence that precluded slavery by definition, or more likely they were simply blinded by institutional apathy. In the end, federal, state, and local institutions failed to guarantee some workers a most basic right: the freedom to move about and seek higher wages, to rise from grinding debt to a better life.

This study is more an attempt to re-create the neglected world of peonage than to assign fault or to belabor theories. Failures of the past are only ghosts of the present. But if a form of slavery yet exists in the United States, as so much evidence suggests, then the relevant questions are: Why? And by whose irresponsibility?

Louis R. Harlan, who directed this study (originally my doctoral dissertation), patiently read and re-read the manuscript and added any literary merit that the study may possess. Raymond W. Smock contributed his unique criticisms to my work and is especially responsible for many ideas in the following pages. Bonnie Sullivan Daniel took my rough chapters and organized them into an intelligible body of material. August Meier made numerous suggestions concerning organization and focus, and Mary R. Berry added her suggestions regarding legal matters. Steven A. Channing suggested the present organization of Chapter V and offered numerous stylistic suggestions for the manuscript. Dan T. Carter, Horace Samuel Merrill, Herman Belz, and Aubrey Williams also contributed suggestions on style and organization. I sincerely appreciate the suggestions from these scholars. The American History Seminar at The Johns Hopkins University criticized Chapter II, and in general I wish to express my thanks to Professor David Donald for the year of fruitful research and writing provided by my National Endowment for the Humanities Fellowship in Afro-American Studies. The faults that remain in this study come from my stubbornness about taking good advice, and not from the lack of it.

Donald Mosholder, who works in the Justice Department Records at the National Archives, revealed the peonage collection to me and with his staff painstakingly screened out the forbidden material. His patience with my demands has been extraordinary. Searching other repositories for peonage material has taken me to the Library of Congress manuscript collection, and I wish to thank the staff there for its cooperation, as well as the staffs at Howard University, the New York Public Library, and Tuskegee Institute. Herbert Aptheker made his personal papers on peonage available and granted me an interview. S. M. Hay, Clerk of Newton Superior Court in Georgia, sent me copies of the trial transcripts in the *Williams* and *Manning* cases and supplied useful information on the participants. The staff of the Federal Records Center at East Point, Georgia, made microfilm available for several cases. James P. Woods III helpfully provided me with photocopies of material used in Chapter VIII. It has been a pleasure to deal with the cooperative archivists throughout the country who have made this research so enjoyable, and I give the numerous staff members my appreciation for their help.

The History Department of the University of Maryland encouraged this study in many ways, especially by relieving me of my assistantship duties in the spring of 1969. My work on the Booker T. Washington Papers at the University of Maryland gave me valuable experience in techniques of editing and research. And long ago David L. Smiley at Wake Forest University gave me a vision of history and confidence in myself, and I now give him my appreciation.

Many people have no doubt been bored by my endless discussion of peonage. To those many coffee companions at the Library of Congress, the National Archives, and elsewhere I offer my apologies and my gratitude. In addition to those mentioned by name above, Dennis Burton, David Goldfield, James B. Lane, Leslie B. McLemore, and Walker Rumble gave me understanding, companionship, and criticism that made this study better and my life bearable.

Preface to the Paperback Edition

Though this book was first published in May 1972, the continuation of significant peonage cases makes an addition imperative. After eight years of inactivity, the Justice Department in 1972 prosecuted four cases of involuntary servitude and presently has two cases pending trial and several complaints under review. Meanwhile, in a letter to the author dated April 25, 1973, the Justice Department reported that "the number of servitude complaints received by the Justice Department has been increasing in recent years, 19 having been received in 1970, 30 in 1971, and 54 in 1972. Most of these have involved migrant laborers." Only one of these cases has been resolved, *U.S.* v. *Campbell and Harrison;* the two black defendants were sentenced to three years' imprisonment on May 15, 1972. The irony of blacks enslaving whites led *Esquire* magazine to list the case in its Dubious Achievements for 1972. The other cases are either being appealed or have not come to trial.[1]

The most recent of these cases seems the most significant. Two men were arrested on March 16, 1973, by local authorities in Homestead, Florida, for allegedly holding twenty-eight black migrant workers in peonage. Labor contractor Joseph L. Brown, who was indicted by a federal grand jury the next day, was "seized as he walked to his car, a 1973 Cadillac, clutching a bag containing $43,786 in cash." The facts were familiar. One migrant, Semmey Smith, testified that "when it come to settlement day, he said I owed him $26 'cause he give you a place to stay and the like. All the money goes back to him." The "place to stay" was a nine-foot square pillbox; the diet consisted of "sardines, pork and

---

[1] *U.S.* v. *John Miller, et al.; U.S.* v. *Willie Charles Simmons; U.S.* v. *Jack Simmons, Jr.; U.S.* v. *Walter Taylor, et al.;* and *U.S.* v. *Joe L. Brown.*

beans and bread. And a little buttermilk." Smith stated that he had "wanted to leave," but Brown "said he'd beat me, hurt me bad. So I stayed." The workers lived in fear and suffered from malnutrition. Brown's arrest came only a week after typhoid had broken out in a similar migrant camp.

Joseph L. Brown, like most men indicted for peonage in migrant labor camps, was a labor contractor. His $43,786 and new Cadillac can easily be accounted for. Brown's crew picked about 1000 buckets of tomatoes a day, and the workers were supposed to get 25¢ of Brown's 85¢ per bucket; thus Brown made $600 a day in addition to what he was taking illegally from the workers who never saw the money they earned.

Cesar Chavez in California and the Rural Legal Services in Florida have attacked the exploitative contractor system. In California, however, the International Brotherhood of Teamsters is well on the way to destroying Chavez's power, and the crucial issue is not wages but union hiring halls that eliminate contractors. Even if Chavez has not run the hiring halls efficiently, as the Teamsters and growers have charged, his program eliminated the exploitative contractors. And if Joseph L. Brown typifies how contractors "deliver" pickers cheaply, it is understandable that growers prefer such contractors and why the Teamsters have such leverage in winning contracts. In Florida there has already been a bill introduced into the legislature to prohibit union hiring halls. Peons have no lobby.[2]

Whether Chavez wins or loses his contracts in California, or the Rural Legal Services manages to indict a few more contractors in Florida, there will still be peonage. So long as contractors exploit pickers, growers furnish laborers miserable housing, local officers ignore conditions, state authorities condone the system, federal agents act only when there is a complaint, Congress investigates but fails to legislate effectively, and so few citizens care about the human cost of food, there will be peonage.

May 1973   P.D.

[2]*New York Times,* March 17, 1973, p. 12; April 29, 1973, p. 17.

The Shadow of Slavery

CHAPTER I

The Blind Goddess

The scream and profanity exploded from a shanty near where two men were talking, and as they watched, a child and her parents materialized in the doorway. Behind them holding a pistol stalked J. O. Elvington, a naval stores operator from nearby Otter Creek, Florida. As the two groups converged on that February 6, 1901, morning, Elvington informed the owner of the turpentine farm where they stood that the man at gunpoint, George Huggins, had left his turpentine farm while owing him $40.[1] Elvington threatened that "he would compel Huggins to return to his service, or kill him."[2] Huggins, attempting to gain the sympathy of the two men, related that he had recently arrived in Florida from South Carolina, hired as a cooper, "but on his arrival he had been compelled to live in a structure formerly occupied by horses and mules." Huggins's wife added that Elvington's farm was "unhealthful," a complaint that brought forth more profanity from Elvington.[3] Terrorized, Huggins begged his employer to pay the debt, but he refused, so Elvington, "after capturing a negro man and woman, whom he claimed were indebted to him, compelled Huggins and his family to return to his farm."[4]

As the procession of debtors disappeared down the road, thirty-one-year-old Fred Cubberly, a U.S. commissioner from nearby Bronson,

[1] Fred Cubberly to Charles W. Russell, Dec. 18, 1906, Box 083, Classified Subject Files of the Department of Justice, National Archives, Washington, D.C., Record Group 60. Hereafter cited according to file, folded file (ff), or box number, Dept. of Justice, NA, RG 60.

[2] Cubberly to John Eagan, May 30, 1901, ff 10719–01, ibid.

[3] Cubberly to Russell, Dec. 18, 1906, Box 083, ibid.

[4] Cubberly to Eagan, May 30, 1901, ff 10719–01, ibid.

who was visiting the farm, was incredulous. He had heard that such forced labor was a common practice throughout the turpentine area of Florida, but this incident vividly illustrated the illegality and barbarity of the system. Cubberly was born in Missouri, and his family had moved about extensively before settling in Florida when Fred was sixteen years old. He had studied law, and in 1898 he had set up a practice at Bronson, near the northwest coast of Florida. Cubberly saw that "Elvington had no warrant or process from a court for the arrest of Huggins, and at the time of making the arrest did not claim to be an officer."[5] Obviously such forced labor stood outside the law, but Cubberly could think of no state or federal law that applied. But unlike countless other men who had passively observed such incidents, he began searching the federal statutes. "I found the peonage laws and shortly after mentioned them to Mr. Eagan U.S. Attorney for this district," he recalled. "He advised me, after considering my statements, to send in a test case."[6]

Cubberly got the first glimpse of what would be the test case a week after the episode at the turpentine farm. While waiting for a train in Gainesville, Cubberly saw "three armed men in the waiting room." He talked to the men "and came to the conclusion that they were 'man hunters' from Georgia on an expedition to my home county, (Levy)." His hunch proved correct. Several days later James R. Dean, a naval stores operator, called on Cubberly and told him "a most remarkable story of a raid on his camp by these men from Georgia, assisted by a local deputy sheriff."[7]

Dean explained that on February 11 three armed men, accompanied by Deputy Sheriff W. E. Yearty, had roused him before dawn. Samuel M. Clyatt led the intruders, and he charged that several of his former employees had left owing him money and that "he proposed to take the men to Georgia in order to make an example of them; that he always went after men who ran away from him."[8] Dean offered to pay what the

5 Harry Gardner Cutler, *History of Florida, Past and Present, Historical and Biographical*, 3 vols. (Chicago and New York, 1923), III: 234–35; Helen Cubberly Ellerbe to author, Apr. 27, 1971.
6 Cubberly to Russell, Dec. 18, 1906, Box 083, ff 10719–01, Dept of Justice, NA, RG 60. See also Eagan to William B. Sheppard, Aug. 20, 1896, Appointment and Credentials Files, ibid.
7 Cubberly to Russell, Dec. 18, 1906, Box 083, ibid.
8 Ibid.

workers owed and keep them employed at his still, and Clyatt allowed him to pay off the debts of two of the blacks. Clyatt insisted, however, that he wanted to make an example of Will Gordon and Mose Ridley. Dean summoned the two blacks, and Clyatt put handcuffs on them. One of the blacks "refused to put his hand in the cuff, and Mr. Clyatt threw his gun on him and made him put his hand in." Will Gordon protested that he did not owe Clyatt any money, but Clyatt, manifesting the Southern employer's prerogative, again raised his gun and threatened that other men had left owing him money, "and I always found them and they paid me."[9]

Cubberly informed U.S. Attorney John Eagan that Clyatt's actions seemed to be an ideal case for testing the constitutionality of the 1867 federal peonage statute, and they began preparation. By mid-June Eagan had accumulated evidence showing that what he conceived to be peonage existed throughout the turpentine area. Such incidents "are almost every day occurences in this locality," wrote Cubberly. "The scarcity of labor, causing the naval stores operators, to advance money to negro laborers, who work a few days and then leave, to hunt some other victim."[10] W. O. Butler, an attorney from nearby Pensacola, provided Eagan with additional details on how the peonage system worked. Where Cubberly had faulted black laborers for leaving their jobs, Butler explained that the blacks were at the mercy of still owners and local law-enforcement officers. With officers and owners joined in their vicious pact, black laborers found themselves "held by these turpentine men in a worse state then when they were slaves." An owner advanced his employee some goods, Butler wrote with unsure spelling, "and then that negroe never gets out of debt I care not what may be his earnings." The blacks were then "held at the muzzle of a gun," worked on skimpy rations, "and when he happens to do anything that does not suit them they are tied up and beat most out rageously." Butler believed that the system had become so ingrained that it was "dangerous" for anyone to attempt to aid the victims.

Butler mentioned the case of a black who had spent two years attempting to work out a $40 debt. Realizing that he was only falling deeper into

[9] Transcript of Record, p. 14, *Clyatt* v. *United States*, 197 U.S. 207, copy in ff 10719–01, ibid.

[10] Cubberly to Eagan, May 30, 1901, ibid. Negro, according to the custom of the day, was not capitalized.

debt, the man left and went to another town, only to have some men from his former employer force him to return. Before arriving back at the turpentine still, however, the black was beaten "most terribly, and is now lying at this man Still very sick from the wounds that he received from these people, beside being held in bondage." This case, Butler lamented, "is just one instance among a large number out in this section, and there seems to be no remidy, for it is just useless to try one of these men before a J. P. out here in which a negroe is prosecuting a white man for beating him." Butler explained that not all the justices of the peace were corrupt "but it comes very near it," and, in fact, if a black appeared in a court there it would lead to his murder. "I know that the negroe in ma[n]y instances is much to blame and should have a little flogging," he concluded, "yet this way of saying to a man you owe me and g-d-d you, you have got to stay here and work until you pay me what you owe me which the por negroe never does, because they will not let him pay them his account, and as a result they keep him and work him right on." Butler, like other informers later on, offered his information in confidence, and he advised Eagan that "if it should be known that I have written you as I have there are some of my own friends who would condem me for it."[11]

Armed with the complaints of Cubberly and Butler and having investigated the cases himself, Eagan wrote to the attorney general of the United States on July 13, 1901, formally announcing that proceedings were under way to test the peonage statute. He enclosed the 1891 Florida law providing that a laborer could be imprisoned for leaving a job while owing money, explaining that local law officers usually omitted the court procedure and simply returned the laborer directly to his employer. The justice of the peace would issue a warrant and "a constable or sheriff" would "forcibly deliver [the] laborer to the possession of the employer who made the complaint, and the employer held him in his service until his claim, including all costs and charges of the proceedings, are worked out." Eagan then explained what he knew of the federal peonage statute, adding that he had no knowledge of a case argued under the law.[12]

11 W. O. Butler to Eagan, June 29, 1901, ibid.
12 Eagan to Attorney General, July 13, 1901, ibid. There had earlier been a federal case argued under the peonage statute of 1867. In *United States* v. *Eberhart*, 127

On November 21, 1901, a grand jury promptly indicted Clyatt for peonage, and he stood trial on March 24, 1902, in Tallahassee. At the trial James R. Dean told the story of Clyatt's visit to his turpentine farm. Then H. S. Sutton, sheriff of Levy County, testified that he had been informed some weeks earlier of Clyatt's plans and was prepared to aid him in serving his papers. Obviously the return of the laborers to Georgia from Florida necessitated some kind of extradition proceedings, but the sheriff testified that he did not know that he lacked the power to serve the papers prepared by a justice of the peace in Georgia. "It has been the universal custom and practice of the turpentine men in Georgia and Florida to go and take negroes whenever they wanted to in this way," the sheriff admitted. "I did not know until now that I had no right to serve warrants issued in another state."[13]

Deputy Sheriff W. E. Yearty did not question the warrants either, for he admitted that he "could not make out what they were for, as I had left my spectacles at home and it was night, but I knew they were made out by an officer in Georgia." Yearty then contradicted Dean's account of the arrest, stating that he had put the handcuffs on the two blacks and "they did not resist." He went on to say that the arrested men rode in a buggy with him and begged him to allow them to return to Georgia with Clyatt instead of going to jail for "gaming" as the warrants charged. Yearty quickly turned over the handcuffed blacks to Clyatt and evidently excused them from the charges levied against them.[14] The collaboration between Clyatt and the local law-enforcement officers, and especially the officers' either disregard for or ignorance of the letter of the law, typified peonage in the South.

E. T. Ford, one of the men who assisted Clyatt, substantiated Yearty's story. He further testified that the only reason he took the trip to Florida was to help protect Clyatt, who had a feud with a laborer on the Dean farm named Davis. He admitted knowing that Clyatt was going for the employees and "that his going, and going armed, was because of the ex-

---

F. 252 (C.C. Ga. 1899), a federal court decided that there was no peonage involved in the case because no system of peonage had been proven. The case, however, was not reported until much later. The law that Eagan enclosed was probably Florida *Laws* 1891, c. 4032.

[13] Transcript of Record, pp. 16–17, *Clyatt* v. *United States*, 197 U.S. 207, copy in ff 10719–01, Dept. of Justice, NA, RG 60.

[14] Ibid.

pected difficulty with Davis."[15] Once on the train Ford removed the handcuffs and allowed the two blacks to ride in the "second-class coach." "I never saw Gordon and Ridley any more after they got off the train at Tifton, and we took them to the defendant's house," Ford concluded.[16]

John Eagan's closing argument for the government was "one of the most eloquent speeches ever delivered in the Federal Court at this place," declared a Jacksonville newspaper.[17] The jury had heard enough to convince it that Clyatt was guilty of peonage, and Judge Charles Swayne sentenced Clyatt to serve four years in the federal penitentiary.[18] Eagan informed the attorney general of his victory in this "first conviction, so far as we know here, under the law." The victory was somewhat blunted by Clyatt's appeal to the U.S. Circuit Court of Appeals on a writ of error. Nevertheless, Eagan reported that the case had "attracted a great deal of interest, and if the law that we contend for is sustained by the Court of Appeals it will have a salutary effect in protecting negro laborers, particularly, in this section of the country."[19] There was another consideration that had somehow been overlooked, for witness Ford had not seen the two blacks since they arrived in Tifton, Georgia, and neither had anyone else. They had mysteriously disappeared.[20]

After many delays the Circuit Court of Appeals heard the case on March 13, 1904, and certified the leading questions to go before the U.S. Supreme Court on a writ of certiorari.[21] During the interlude between the conviction of Clyatt and the hearing before the Supreme Court neither Clyatt nor the Justice Department was idle. Though John Eagan had died in the meantime, the concern over peonage persisted as numerous cases continued to erupt in Florida and other Southern states. Though George Huggins, the first victim of peonage discovered by Fred Cubberly, unaccountably disappeared (as had the two blacks in-

15 Ibid., p. 20.

16 Ibid., p. 19.

17 (Jacksonville) *Florida Times-Union and Citizen*, Mar. 27, 1902; clipping in ff 10719–01, ibid.

18 Transcript of Record, p. 8, *Clyatt* v. *United States*, 197 U.S. 207.

19 Eagan to Attorney General, Mar. 18, 1902, ff 10719–01, Dept. of Justice, NA, RG 60.

20 Eagan to Attorney General, Apr. 3, 1902, ibid.

21 Eagan to Attorney General, May 1, 24, 1902, Jan. 3, 1903; William B. Sheppard to Attorney General, Dec. 5, 1903; Attorney General to Sheppard, Dec. 9, 1903; William Wirt Howe to Attorney General, Mar. 19, 29, 1904, Box 083, ibid.

volved in the Clyatt case), J. O. Elvington eventually pled guilty to the charges against him and was fined $1,000.[22] Other complaints documented the fact that Clyatt's conviction had not stopped the practice of peonage.

While the Justice Department prosecuted other peonage cases, the turpentine operators and lumbermen united to preserve their debt-labor system. In Tifton, Georgia, headquarters of Clyatt's turpentine operation, the sawmill association held a meeting to raise funds to fight the case before the Supreme Court. As U.S. Attorney Alexander Akerman reported, the sawmill men reasoned that unless they "were permitted to control their labor as they saw fit, without any interference from the federal authorities, they would be unable to carry on the saw mill business." The *Atlanta Constitution* reported that the meeting raised $5,000. Before the case reached the Supreme Court, Fred Cubberly estimated that naval stores men had raised $90,000 to fight the case.[23] The alarm that seized the turpentine and logging industries was understandable, for their labor force consisted mostly of indebted blacks who were becoming recognized by the law as peons.

While Clyatt's defenders prepared their case for the Supreme Court, another group of employers was attacking the peonage statute from a different direction. Simultaneously with Clyatt's indictment, Robert W. Lewis and two cohorts were indicted for forcing George Walker, a black worker, to return to Lewis's farm and work out a debt. The three-count indictment also included a charge that Walker was beaten. When a motion to quash the indictments failed, Lewis asked for a writ of habeas corpus, claiming that no law of the United States had been involved and that the U.S. Circuit Court "has no jurisdiction of any offense charged in the indictments." The Circuit Court disagreed on April 12, 1902, denying the writ and ruling that Lewis had to stand trial for peonage.[24]

That peonage should suddenly emerge as an issue is at least partially

[22] Cubberly to Russell, Dec. 18, 1906, Box 083, ibid. For additional peonage complaints, see Grand Jury Report, Western Division of Northern District, Florida, March, 1904; J. N. Stripling to Attorney General, Dec. 21, 1903; Attorney General to Stripling, Jan. 11, 1904; Attorney General to William B. Sheppard, Oct. 25, 1904, and other complaints in ff 10719–01, ibid.

[23] Akerman to Attorney General, Apr. 14, 1904; *Atlanta Constitution*, Apr. 12, 1904, clipping in ff 10719–01; Cubberly to Russell, Dec. 18, 1906, Box 083, ibid.

[24] *In Re Lewis*, 114 F. 963 (C.C. Fla., 1902); Eagan to Attorney General, Apr. 3, 1902, ff 10719–03, Dept. of Justice, NA, RG 60.

explained by the temper of the times. During the first few years of the twentieth century the United States experienced the beginning of the Progressive era. Somehow the boy scout enthusiasm of President Theodore Roosevelt personified a new reform spirit, as many men set out to do good deeds. In the South this movement had a peculiar thrust. Instead of seeking the economic democracy preached by some Populists or attacking abuses unmasked by muckrakers in the North, Southern Progressives attacked some of the more grotesque social conditions still existing in the South, such as child labor, convict-leasing, and illiteracy.

But Southern progressivism contained both a contradiction and an illusion, for at the same time that whites were "progressing," Southern blacks were becoming more depressed under the sanction of segregation by the U.S. Supreme Court, increasing violence, state disfranchisement laws, deteriorating race relations, and the North's willingness to abandon the effort to moderate Southern race policies. The rhetoric of reform convinced some Southerners that there was indeed progress, but there was a contradiction; black Southerners did not share the benefits. While there was progress if measured by smokestacks, spindles, and editorials, poor blacks and whites continued to be ground against the mudsill of a diseased society. Like running on a treadmill, reformers rushed breathlessly to pass good laws, while the not-so-healthy poor either stood still or fell behind. If peonage was any measure, progress was an illusion, a journalistic and political invention that successfully clouded economic and social reality.

Like lynching, whitecapping, intimidation at the polls, and shooting on sight, the peonage system uncovered by Fred Cubberly represented but one aspect of the violent South. Some areas of the South had not moved very far from the frontier in either appearance or custom, as individualism combined with illiteracy, provincialism, economic frustration, and racism. Lynching exorcised real and imagined affronts to Southern womanhood, while providing entertainment; whitecapping drove off black landowners and business competitors; intimidation at the polls deprived blacks of control over those who ruled them; and, for special problems, there was murder.[25] As Fred Cubberly observed, "It

---

[25] See Wilbur J. Cash, *The Mind of the South* (New York, 1941), pp. 75–76, 112–41, 312–14, 424–29; C. Vann Woodward, *Origins of the New South* (Baton Rouge, 1951), pp. 158–60; Sheldon Hackney, "Southern Violence," *American His-*

is but a step from the evasion of the Fifteenth Amendment to an actual violation of the Thirteenth Amendment."[26] Peonage, a practice that gave employers complete control over their laborers, practically reinstituted slavery. Vestiges of the system had been visible since the Civil War, yet it was only in 1901 that any legal action was taken to combat the practice. By 1901 Southern society had reached the point where a debt-labor system characterized by violence and the corruption or acquiescence of local police officers was openly tolerated. In a section of the country characterized by illiteracy and poverty, vulnerable victims were in profusion, and most of the peons were black.

Peonage infected the South like a cancer, eating away at the economic freedom of blacks, driving the poor whites to work harder in order to compete with virtual slave labor, and preserving the class structure inherited from slavery days. The Progressive political surgeons might occasionally perform a successful operation, cutting out a lump of peonage from the body of the South and declaring the patient well; but the disease was in the vitals, manifesting itself in lynching, whitecapping, convict-leasing, disfranchisement, and segregation. To carve out all the diseased parts could mean death to the patient. So self-proclaimed Progressives fought against peonage while employers battled to preserve it, but the condition of the masses remained unchanged.

Even as peonage cases were mushrooming throughout the South, the *Clyatt* case became increasingly important, for its backers sought to test the constitutionality of the 1867 federal peonage statute. If the statute were held unconstitutional, the men in the turpentine camps could practice peonage with no threat of federal prosecution. Sensing the desire of the Justice Department to hang their entire peonage offensive on the success of the *Clyatt* case, turpentine distillers and sawmill operators employed two Georgia politicians, Senator Augustus Oc-

torical Review 74 (Feb. 1969), 906–25; William F. Holmes, "Whitecapping; Agrarian Violence in Mississippi, 1902–1906," *Journal of Southern History* 35 (May 1969), 165–85.

[26] [Fred Cubberly,] "Peonage in the South," *Independent* 55 (July 9, 1903), 1616. Though this article was unsigned, Cubberly admitted that he wrote it (Cubberly to Russell, Dec. 18, 1906, ff 10719–01, Dept. of Justice, NA, RG 60). The editors explained: "The writer of the following article is a resident of the South, thoroughly familiar with what is known as peonage, and to some extent personally interested in the peonage prosecutions. For reasons in no way discreditable to himself, he prefers that his name shall not be published."

tavius Bacon and Congressman William G. Brantley, to defend Clyatt.[27] Ex-Confederate Bacon allowed Brantley to carry the burden, and the younger man took up his responsibilities with a vengeance.

Congressman Brantley, paying no heed to his Progressive colleagues, molded his defense of Clyatt on the historical development of the peonage statute and on states' rights. On March 28, 1904, long before he argued the case in the Supreme Court, Brantley outlined his forthcoming defense on the floor of Congress. Tracing the legislative history of the peonage statute, he explained that the Senate debate in 1867 had only concerned peonage in New Mexico and that the ultimate legislation was chiefly aimed at preventing the U.S. Army from returning New Mexican peons to their masters.[28] Brantley noted that most senators in 1867 knew little of peonage, and he drove that point home. Indeed, during the short 1867 debate on peonage senators had joked about their own private debts and revealed that none of them knew the workings of the system. They finally did agree that peonage was a "disgrace" and that a federal statute should prohibit it.[29] Neither the senators in 1867 nor Brantley in 1904 apparently knew of a New Mexican statute passed in January, 1866, that legally ended peonage in New Mexico.[30]

Yet the bill had passed, and Brantley had to concern himself with the law, not solely with the intent of the legislators. The statute outlawed peonage both in the territories and in the states of the Union. It abolished "the system known as peonage," as Brantley carefully pointed out, but the law also outlawed "all acts, laws, resolutions, orders, regulations, or usages" that would allow peonage to exist.[31] Relying on a states' rights

27 William G. Brantley to Attorney General, Oct. 29, 1904, ff 10719–01, Dept. of Justice, NA, RG 60.

28 U.S., Congress, House, *Congressional Record*, 58th Cong., 2nd sess., 1904, 38, pt. 4:3898–3900.

29 U.S., Congress, Senate, *Congressional Globe*, 39th Cong., 2nd sess., 1867, 78, pt. 3:1571–72.

30 Robert W. Larson, *New Mexico's Quest for Statehood, 1836–1912* (Albuquerque, 1968), p. 20.

31 14 Stat. 546. "*Be it enacted by the Senate and House of Representatives of the United States of America in Congress assembled*, That the holding of any person to service or labor under the system known as peonage is hereby declared to be unlawful, and the same is hereby abolished and forever prohibited in the Territory of New Mexico, or of any other Territory or State of the United States; and all acts, laws, resolutions, orders, regulations, or usages of the Territory of New Mexico, or of any other Territory or State of the United States, which have heretofore estab-

argument, he stated that the federal government had jurisdiction in states only when there was a system of peonage upheld by state statute. "So far as the States are concerned," he reasoned, "the act is directed specifically against them as States; the only individuals it is directed against are the individuals in the Territories. . . . An individual acting as an individual and independently of any law, regulation, or usage maintained or enforced by his State or Territory," Brantley triumphantly concluded, "could not be guilty of 'peonage.' "[32]

It was simple enough to Brantley, who added that "the same rule applies to peonage that applies to slavery; and the rule as to slavery being, if there is no law to authorize it there is no slavery; it necessarily follows, if there is no law to authorize 'peonage,' there is no peonage." He strengthened his argument by correctly noting that "Congress has never passed a law providing punishment for slavery or for involuntary servitude in those terms." The reason that no federal slavery law had been passed after the Civil War, he concluded, was because no state had set up a system of slavery; therefore there was no necessity for such a law.[33] Brantley's argument inadvertently revealed what many Justice Department investigators were coming to realize: namely, that individuals acting on their own volition could hold laborers in slavery, for there was no state or federal statute that prohibited it. The federal

---

lished, maintained, or enforced, or by virtue of which any attempt shall hereafter be made to establish, maintain, or enforce, directly or indirectly, the voluntary or involuntary service or labor of any persons as peons, in liquidation of any debt or obligation, or otherwise, be, and the same are hereby, declared null and void; and any person or persons who shall hold, arrest, or return, or cause to be held, arrested, or returned, or in any manner aid in the arrest or return of any person or persons to a condition of peonage, shall, upon conviction, be punished by fine not less than one thousand nor more than five thousand dollars, or by imprisonment not less than one nor more than five years, or both, at the discretion of the court.

Sec. 2. *And be it further enacted*, That it shall be the duty of all persons in the military or civil service in the Territory of New Mexico to aid in the enforcement of the foregoing section of this act; and any person or persons who shall obstruct or attempt to obstruct, or in any way interfere with, or prevent the enforcement of the act, shall be liable to the pains and penalties hereby provided; and any officer or other person in the military service of the United States who shall so offend, directly or indirectly, shall, on conviction before a court-martial, be dishonorably dismissed [from] the service of the United States, and shall thereafter be ineligible to reappointment to any office of trust, honor, or profit under the government."

[32] U.S., Congress, House, *Congressional Record*, 58th Cong., 2nd sess., 1904, 38, pt. 4:3900–3901.

[33] Ibid., p. 3902.

peonage statute served as the only instrument to combat forced labor, but only when an employer held his labor because of debt did the peonage statute apply.[34]

Clyatt v. *United States* finally reached the Supreme Court in December, 1904. When Brantley and Bacon answered the three main questions of whether returning a man to work out a debt violated the peonage statute, both argued along the lines of Brantley's oration before the House of Representatives. Brantley's states' rights argument dealt with the second point that questioned whether peonage could exist in the absence of supporting state law. The third question, however, supplied Clyatt's defenders with a strong point, for Bacon asked if the "acts and conduct of [the] defendant as charged in the indictment constitute the offense of holding, arresting, or returning to a condition of peonage."[35] The indictment had charged that Clyatt did "unlawfully and knowingly return one Will Gordon and one Mose Ridley to a condition of peonage."[36] Brantley then argued that the only thing that could be proven was an unlawful arrest, not peonage. No one had seen Gordon or Ridley after their return to Tifton, Georgia; therefore no one could prove that they had been returned to a condition of peonage.[37]

The Justice Department, eager for a conviction in this major case, presented two briefs, both signed by Attorney General William H. Moody. To the Justice Department the case represented more than just Clyatt's conviction. As the briefs pointed out, since Clyatt's conviction "more than a hundred cases have been prosecuted by the Government and carried to a final determination under this section." Attorney General Moody, who made an oral argument, pointed out the conditions that led to peonage and the helplessness of the victims because of local law-enforcement officials. "We think that we may truthfully say that upon the decision of this case hangs the liberty of thousands of persons, mostly colored, it is true," he apologized, "who are now being held in a condition of involuntary servitude, in many cases

[34] See *Annual Report of the Attorney General, 1911* (Washington, 1912), p. 27; Russell to Attorney General, Feb. 14, 1907, file 50–162–2, Dept. of Justice, NA, RG 60.

[35] Brief for Plaintiff (by A. O. Bacon), p. 63, *Clyatt* v. *United States*, 197 U.S. 207.

[36] *Clyatt* v. *United States*, 197 U.S. 209.

[37] Brief for Plaintiff (by W. G. Brantley), p. 7, *Clyatt* v. *United States*, 197 U.S. 207.

worse than slavery itself, by the unlawful acts of individuals, not only in violation of the thirteenth amendment of the Constitution, but in violation of the law which we have here under consideration."[38]

Such arrests of laborers, Moody continued, were nothing less than peonage. The employer could "always maintain an action to recover damages because of the breach of such contract, but could never compel a specific performance."[39] Such compulsion was peonage. In the supplemental brief the government answered the inevitable sectional charges that the federal government had been guilty of attacking the Southern states. "The verdict in this case, and other like cases, resulted from the combined action of southern judges, southern prosecuting officers, and southern grand and petit juries," the government argued. The federal government had simply supported its Southern employees. Finally, Attorney General Moody attacked what the defense argued was only Southern custom. "Get a settlement! We shall see what getting a settlement means," said Moody indignantly; "it means collecting the debt or taking the body of the debtor." Moody then dealt with the charges that no return to peonage had been proved. "The offense was completed if they had never done a day's work after the return, or if they had escaped on the way to Georgia, or if they had been rescued, or had died," he concluded.[40]

Three months later, on March 13, 1905, Justice David J. Brewer delivered the opinion of the Supreme Court. He found the legal origins of peonage in an 1857 New Mexico case, *Jaremillo* v. *Romero*. The case had begun when Mariana Jaremillo allegedly left the employ of Jose de la Cruz Romero while owing him $51.75 that had been advanced to her. Though the case had turned on technicalities, it had also explored the history as well as the definition of peonage. Kirby Benedict, who had become chief justice of the New Mexico Supreme Court in 1858, wrote the opinion and traced the history of the institution from its Spanish origins to the time when the United States occupied New Mexico. In 1846 the United States found a large class of persons called peons who were not "of any particular color, race, or caste of the inhabitants." They all had one binding characteristic, the decision read; "all were in-

[38] Brief for Defendant, pp. 2–3, ibid.
[39] Ibid., p. 37.
[40] Supplemental Brief for Defendant, pp. 38, 40, 42, ibid.

debted to their masters." Moreover, once the peon got into debt, he could not leave the employ of his master or, like a slave in the Southern United States, he could be pursued and placed again in servitude. If a master decided he wanted a peon on another estate, he could pay the man's debt and take him.[41] In short, once a man became indebted, he could be bought and sold much as a slave; his debt migrated with him. Complaining of the ease with which Romero held Mariana Jaremillo, Judge Benedict observed with keen foresight that it is "easy to perceive how any person whosoever within the territory may be made a debtor and sent into servitude, should an unscrupulous man and an ignorant and faithless prefect or probate judge devise mischief together."[42] Mariana Jaremillo had gone free in this case, not because peonage was outlawed but because no debt could be proved.

After reviewing the legal history of peonage, Brewer answered Brantley's states' rights argument. "We entertain no doubt of the validity of this legislation, or of its applicability to the case of any person holding another in a state of peonage, and this whether there be municipal ordinance or state law sanctioning such holding." Then the Court proceeded to construe the peonage statute. The acts prohibited by the statute were "holding, arresting, returning," the court stated. It then clarified the three terms. The law was violated when a laborer was held in peonage, arrested with the intention of placing him in peonage, or returned to peonage after having escaped such a condition.[43] In Clyatt's case, the opinion continued, the indictment charged that Clyatt returned Gordon and Ridley to a condition of peonage. The court ruled, however, that "there is not a scintilla of testimony to show that Gordon and Ridley were ever theretofore in a condition of peonage." Though the Court obviously disapproved of Clyatt's excursion into Florida, it held that "it is the imperative duty of a court to see that all the elements of his crime are proved, or at least that testimony is offered which justified a jury in finding those elements." Because the testimony did not reveal that the two black laborers had been held in peonage prior to their arrest or afterward returned to a condition of peonage, the Court ruled that

[41] *Jaremillo* v. *Romero*, 1 N.M. 194.

[42] Ibid., p. 203. See also Henderson K. Yoakum, *History of Texas*, 2 vols. (New York, 1856), I:262–63.

[43] *Clyatt* v. *United States*, 197 U.S. 218–19.

the lower court had erred by not directing the verdict for Clyatt, and it ordered a new trial for Clyatt.[44]

The case, however, did not escape the censure of Justice John Marshall Harlan. He refused to go into the technical details of the case but dissented, stating that enough testimony existed to prove that Clyatt was guilty of violating the statute. He pointed out that the Court admitted that there was enough evidence to prove that Gordon and Ridley were taken against their wills "back to Georgia to work out a debt." Furthermore, he continued, it was "conceded that peonage is based upon the indebtedness of the peon to the master. The accused admitted to one of the witnesses that the negroes owed him," Harlan argued. "The accused made no objection to the submission of the case to the jury," he concluded, "and it is going very far to hold in a case like this, disclosing barbarities of the worst kind against these negroes, that the trial court erred in sending the case to the jury."[45]

Though the Clyatt case required a new trial because the charges in the indictment were not proven, the government had successfully tested the constitutionality of the peonage statute. Peonage cases that had been suspended during the Clyatt litigation proceeded.[46] Peonage clearly fell under federal jurisdiction, and though there was no federal law against slavery, lynching, whitecapping, or murder, the Clyatt decision opened the door to federal enforcement of the 1867 peonage law. The Justice Department immediately instructed U.S. attorneys to draw their indictments more in keeping with the evidence, yet no massive assault on peonage began.[47] The cases that did arise usually came from the individual initiative of local Justice Department employees or because of especially outrageous circumstances.

Despite the legal rhetoric, the whereabouts of Will Gordon and Mose Ridley remained unsolved. As the Justice Department continued the case against Clyatt, the victims of the case remained absent. In 1906

[44] Ibid., p. 222. See also Robert K. Carr, *Federal Protection of Civil Rights: Quest for a Sword* (Ithaca, 1947), 51n, 78–79.

[45] *Clyatt v. United States*, 197 U.S. 223. See also Edward F. Waite, "The Negro in the Supreme Court," *Minnesota Law Review* 30 (Mar. 1946), 259–60.

[46] See Warren S. Reese, Jr., to Attorney General, Dec. 20, 1904, Jan. 3, 1905; Attorney General to Reese, Jan. 6, 1905, ff 5280–03, Dept. of Justice, NA, RG 60.

[47] Attorney General to Alexander Akerman, Mar. 14, 1905, ff 10719–01, ibid. See also Sheppard to Attorney General, May 7, 1906, ibid.

William B. Sheppard, U.S. attorney at Pensacola, urged that the case be nolle prosequi (dropped) because the witnesses could not be found, and without them a new trial was useless. But he was overruled by the attorney general. A year later Sheppard again requested that the cases be dropped. Finally, on May 18, 1909, more than eight years after he had drawn the original indictment, Fred Cubberly, who had secured a position as U.S. attorney, requested that the cases be dropped, and the Attorney General assented.[48] This final irony—that Clyatt never went to jail and that the witnesses disappeared—typified peonage prosecutions in the United States. Perhaps the black poet Langston Hughes had such a case in mind when he wrote:

> That Justice is a blind goddess
> Is a thing to which we poor are wise:
> Her bandage hides two festering sores
> That once, perhaps, were eyes.[49]

[48] Attorney General to Sheppard, June 4, 1906; Sheppard to Attorney General, Jan. 30, 1907; Cubberly to Attorney General, May 18, 1909; Attorney General to Cubberly, June 2, 1909, ibid.

[49] *New Masses* 7 (Aug. 1931), 15.

CHAPTER II

The Vortex of Peonage

At the beginning of the twentieth century the South resembled a backward colony, poverty-encrusted and dependent on Northern capital. If the urban Southern elite were the colonial sycophants of the North, then the poor whites were the unconscious subjects of the rural Southern elite. Southern blacks, stuck in the center of this web, lacked both a political voice and an economic stake. Peons existed at the core of concentric circles of oppression, their entire world circumscribed by exploiters. Defrauded of their wages and deprived of mobility either by threats that they could not legally move until their debts were paid or by actual force, they lived in the vortex of peonage.[1]

Peonage in the Southern United States grew out of the labor settlement following emancipation. Because of the tremendous upheaval after freedom, both Southern planters and the federal government believed that blacks needed close supervision. Even before the war ended, a contract system emerged as one way to create a stable labor force.[2] Lacking

[1] Recently two Ph.D. dissertations have probed the subject of peonage from different angles. Howard Devon Hamilton devotes large segments of his "The Legislative and Judicial History of the Thirteenth Amendment" (Ph.D. diss., University of Illinois, 1950) to the technical problems surrounding the institution, giving an excellent account of the origins of state laws, the changes in the U.S. Code regarding peonage, and the technical treatment of court cases. Less useful is William Delmer Wagoner, "The Non-Free Worker in Post-Civil War American History" (Ph.D. diss., University of Texas, 1961). Relying exclusively on published sources, Wagoner also makes numerous errors in definition and interpretation. Neither study used the Justice Department papers on peonage.

[2] See Thomas Wallace Knox, *Camp-Fire and Cotton-Field: Southern Adventure in Time of War* (New York, 1865), pp. 364–69; William S. McFeely, *Yankee Stepfather. General O. O. Howard and the Freedmen* (New Haven and London, 1968), pp. 149–65.

peonage = Legacy of slavery

land or capital of their own, blacks had little choice but to sign yearly contracts. These agreements at first continued some of the practices of slavery, such as providing medical care and requiring the employer's permission to leave the plantation. Even as Southern state legislators attempted to reinstitute a form of slavery through state vagrancy laws, contracts, and black codes, the U.S. Army seemingly agreed with such a program, for troops often returned errant blacks to plantations.[3]

As military control became less strict in the South, a labor pattern emerged. Most blacks signed annual contracts. Improvident, they took advances on their expected share of the crop. When settlement time came the next fall, the laborers often discovered that their share of the crop did not cover what they owed the supply merchant or the planter. Some sharecroppers signed for another year, attempting to get ahead; others moved on. The system was typified by mobility, but some planters demanded that workers remain until they had worked out their entire debt, and when planters used indebtedness as an instrument of compulsion, the system became peonage.

Documentary evidence of peonage in the nineteenth century remains sketchy, for few observers were familiar with what constituted peonage. Yet from travelers' accounts, official reports, congressional hearings, and other sources, there is strong evidence that peonage was no twentieth-century invention.[4] Certainly the conditions that would allow such

[3] One Freedmen's Bureau agent wrote in 1865 that "I have refused to approve any contract which does not obligate the employer to furnish all Medical attention" (Spencer Smith to Col. C. Cadle, Dec. 9, 1865, Letterbook 154, subcommissioners letters sent, Sept. 1865–Apr. 1866, Bureau of Freedmen, Refugees, and Abandoned Lands, NA, RG 105). Smith later wrote that most blacks were keeping their contracts and those who did not he sent "back and tried to explain to them the necessity of Complying in letter and in Spirit with their obligations of their contracts" (Smith to Cadle, Jan. 25, 1866, ibid.). Smith predicted in the spring of 1866 that "unless Something is done to compell the Planters to comply with Part 1 Gen order no. 12 that hundreds of Freedmen will come out in debt to the employer at the end of the year without receiving any compensation" (Smith to Cadle, Mar. 10, 1866, ibid.). During the next several years grievances from both freedmen and planters grew. Planters sold their crops with no notice to black laborers, and they occasionally assaulted the laborers. And freedmen violated their contracts. See Monthly Reports from Montgomery, Alabama, Box 34, ibid.

[4] For example, see Whitelaw Reid, *After the War. A Tour of the Southern States, 1865–1866* (New York, 1965), p. 85; John Pilsbury to Carl Schurz, July 24, 1865, quoted in *Senate Executive Documents*, 39th Cong., 1st sess., 1865–66, no. 2, p. 51; Sidney Andrews, *The South since the War* (Boston, 1866), p. 371; Frances Butler Leigh, *Ten Years on a Georgia Plantation since the War* (London, 1883), p. 84; William Pickens, *Bursting Bonds* (Boston, 1923), pp. 13, 25, 29–30; Booker T.

a system of bondage to develop had persisted in the South. The Southern white employer would not voluntarily relinquish the control over black laborers which he had experienced during the days of slavery. Furthermore, the violence that characterized twentieth-century peonage had a long history in the South. Poverty, illiteracy, and low cotton prices combined with traditional racism and violence to enervate the Southern masses. The seeds of peonage grew well in social and economic soil so fecund with oppression.

Nor was the American South the only location that experienced the emergence of peonage as an aftermath of slavery. Mexican peonage emerged after the abolition of slavery and continued despite constitutional sanctions prohibiting it. After the laborers, mostly Indians, were freed from slavery, plantation owners advanced them money, and they fell into debt much as had the blacks following emancipation in the South. Though Mexican peons were indebted to their masters, they claimed proprietary rights to the land that they tilled. As in the South, there was little opportunity to escape. Peonage also flourished in the Philippines, where American efforts to end it in the early twentieth century failed because the legislature, composed of many large landowners, refused to pass the necessary legislation. Philippine peonage also grew out of a slave system, but the primary victims were children who were sold by parents to cover debts. Peonage or similar debt servitude has existed throughout the world.[5]

Peonage that existed throughout the American South was most obvious in three patterns. First, the cotton belt from the Carolinas to Texas and including the Mississippi Delta supplied most peonage complaints, a testimony to the enduring plantation system. Second, the turpentine areas of northern Florida, southern Georgia, Alabama, and Mississippi furnished numerous peonage complaints. Third, for a relatively brief time railroad construction camps became the scene of peonage. Peonage

---

Washington to George Washington Cable, Oct. 8, 1889, Washington Papers, Howard University, Washington, D.C.; George K. Holmes, "The Peons of the South," *Annals of the American Academy of Political and Social Science* 4 (Sept. 1893), 67.

[5] See George McCutchen McBride, *The Land Systems of Mexico* (New York, 1923), pp. 30–34; Dean Conant Worcester, *The Philippines Past and Present* (New York, 1930), pp. 509–43, and *Slavery and Peonage in the Philippine Islands* (n.p., 1913). See also Stanley H. Udy, Jr., *Organization of Work* (New Haven, 1959), pp. 85–86. Besides giving a working definition of peonage, Udy describes peonage among pearl fishermen in Arab lands.

incidents plotted on a map would appear as an intersected right angle. One leg of the angle would extend from Florida to Mississippi through the turpentine belt, while the other leg would begin at the lower Mississippi River and extend northward along the river through Louisiana, Mississippi, and Arkansas. The intersecting line would begin in Mississippi and extend outward through the cotton belt to South Carolina, with scattered cases spread throughout the South.[6] Though the areas and occupations varied, peonage maintained a deadening consistency.

Because peonage was frequently isolated in the backcountry, no clear estimate of its extent is possible. A. J. Hoyt, who had spent years investigating whitecapping and peonage, estimated in 1907 that in Georgia, Alabama, and Mississippi "investigations will prove that 33 1/3 per cent of the planters operating from five to one-hundred plows, are holding their negro employees to a condition of peonage, and arresting and returning those that leave before alleged indebtedness is paid."[7] Hoyt's estimate received further documentation from other investigations. Cases reported in Alabama from 1903 to 1905 show that peonage existed in nearly every county. In 1905 a U.S. attorney in Alabama noted that twenty-five complaints needed investigating and sixty-three peonage and whitecapping cases were still on the trial docket.[8] A Florida citizen complained in 1907 that "Slavery is just as much an 'institution' *now* as it was before the war."[9]

Nearly every scrap of evidence suggested that peonage lay heavy on the land. "It is estimated that within the past year from 1500 to 2000 men have been illegally held in peonage," reported a Texas newspaper in 1910. Warren Reese, Jr., an Alabama district attorney, discovered in 1910 that there was much more peonage still existing in Alabama than he had suspected. "I had imagined that the vigorous prosecutions of these cases in the District for the last ten years had virtually stamped it out, but I find that though this is to some extent true in the Northern por-

6 This generalization emerged from a tabulation of complaints and cases from 1901 to 1945.
7 Hoyt to Attorney General, Feb. 4, 1907, file 50–162–1, Dept. of Justice, NA, RG 60.
8 Julius Sternfield to Attorney General, Sept. 18, 1905, ff 5203–03, ibid. See also Warren S. Reese, Jr., to Attorney General, Feb. 25, 1905, ibid.; Reese to Attorney General, July 3, 1912, file 50–119, ibid.
9 J. D. Lucas to John E. Wilkie, Apr. 11, 1907, file 50–162–6, ibid. Italics in original.

tion of the District, in the Southeastern portion of the District, more particularly in Coffee and Henry Counties, this practice is quite extensively carried on."[10]

Peonage continued because it was an institution that had deep roots in history and in custom; it was the extreme manifestation of the social, legal, and economic ills of the South. A South Carolina newspaper in 1910 admitted that Joshua W. Ashley's peonage acquittal "was not at all surprising, for while everybody knows that he is guilty it is equally well known that he is not any more guilty than scores or perhaps hundreds of other men." The editorial noted that public sentiment agreed that "it would hardly be an act of justice for him to be convicted and punished for doing a thing which so many other people have been doing."[11] Public support of peonage made investigations difficult and convictions rare. Southern sentiment acquiesced in or approved of peonage, either because people did not see anything wrong with it (the resemblance of peonage to slavery perhaps evoked fond memories) or because the practice was shrouded in overtones of legality and made respectable by the approval of community rulers. Southerners effectually nullified the peonage law.

Peonage formally emerged at the beginning of the twentieth century when Fred Cubberly uncovered the 1867 statute. When child labor, illiteracy, and regulation of corporations became the crusader's cry, peonage loomed as a throwback to slavery or colonial bondage or even to medieval serfdom, a Gothic horror.[12] The more reformers chopped at the underbrush of peonage, the more it seemed to grow and to envelope the South. By 1920 each Southern state was enmeshed in a tangle of virtually countless cases and complaints.

Southern landlords and credit merchants, fighting against financial

[10] Unidentified clipping in file 50–385, Feb. 7, 1910, ibid.; Reese to W. R. Harr, July 22, 1910, file 50–102, ibid.

[11] *Anderson Daily Mail*, Apr. 29, 1910, clipping in file 50–357, ibid.

[12] See Lewis C. Gray, *History of Agriculture in the Southern United States*, 2 vols. (Gloucester, 1958), I:342, 350–51; Abbot Emerson Smith, *Colonists in Bondage* (Chapel Hill, 1947), pp. 28, 68–78, 119–22, 233, 264–78; Richard B. Morris, *Government and Labor in Early America* (New York, 1965), pp. 315–22, 354–63. In two excellent articles Richard B. Morris revealed that peonage-like practices and the custom of selling laborers from jail continued until the Civil War. See Morris, "White Bondage in Ante-Bellum South Carolina," *South Carolina Historical and Genealogical Magazine* 49 (Oct. 1948), 191–207; "The Course of Peonage in a Slave State," *Political Science Quarterly* 65 (June 1950), 238–63.

ruin and lack of capital, were notorious for their exploitation of the tenant class. In theory the sharecropping system in the cotton belt offered a poor agrarian worker the opportunity to become a farmowner. Successful years sharing a crop with a landowner might enable the man to save his money and eventually make a downpayment on his own acres. If he survived the usurious rates of credit at the crossroads store and received a fair settlement when the crops were sold, he might even pay off his farm completely, escaping the cycle of debt. That, at least, was the theory. Some men did manage to climb the agricultural ladder from sharecropper to owner. There was another direction that the sharecropper could go, however, for beneath the cropper's bare life peonage existed. The cropper and the peon did the same work. Cotton and tobacco needed constant care from the early spring plowing through the summer chopping to the harvest in the late summer and fall. The financial settlement came only when the crop had been marketed, if at all.

The line that divided the cropper from the peon was a thin but crucial one. It depended on the compulsion that forced a man to remain on a plantation year after year. Sometimes planters discounted the inflated and partly fictitious bills that the croppers owed. For example, one planter might claim that a cropper owed him $300 but let a neighboring planter have him for $150. The second planter continued to record the indebtedness as $300. This practice, nailed as it was to the high interest rates prevailing through the cotton and tobacco areas, kept the workers in constant debt. Yet harsh as this system was, it did not constitute peonage. Peonage occurred only when the planter forbade the cropper to leave the plantation because of debt. If, at settlement time, the planter told his cropper that he remained in debt and could not move from the plantation, then the system became peonage. Peonage rested on debt, but the debtor had to be restrained for the legal definition to be fulfilled. Some planters were paternalistic in extracting forced labor, while others used threats and violence, and, as reflected in their complaints, only the most abused laborers sought relief.

Another kind of peonage grew out of the corruption of local law-enforcement officials. This type of peonage differed from the more formal convict-lease system. That equally abusive system usually existed as a statewide operation, and convicts were often divided up among the mine operators, large businessmen, and planters of the state. Peonage, on the other hand, originated from local jails and often existed in the absence of supporting laws. Moreover, convicts leased by the state were bound out not because of a debt but because they were serving terms in the penitentiary. The local laws and customs that permitted peonage were tied to debts, real and fictitious. Except in local court-approved contracts with prisoners, which were similar to state convict-lease systems, men bailed out of local jails had squared their debts to society by allowing an employer to pay their fines. Both systems, however, were characterized by brutality and violence.[13]

By the dawn of the twentieth century, peonage in the Southern cotten belt was a confusing mass of customs, legalities, and pseudo-legalities. Nearly every Southern state legislature had passed a contract-labor measure that in many ways resembled the black codes of Reconstruction. Under such laws, discussed at length in the *Alonzo Bailey* case below, a laborer who signed a contract and then abandoned his job could be arrested for a criminal offense. Ultimately his choice was simple: he could either work out his contract or go to the chain gang.

Though state and local laws favored employers, much peonage stemmed from custom, not law. Local police in the cotton belt would arrest black laborers, hold them in jail until the planter arrived, and then allow the employer to deal with the prisoners as he would. In a letter to Litie James and her two sons in 1912, for example, B. C. Barganeer bluntly informed them, "You know that you all owe me and I will make you all pay it." She refused to return, however, and the three blacks went to jail in Mobile, Alabama, arrested on a warrant sent by Barganeer from Butler County. Not satisfied with her choice, Barganeer traveled to the Mobile jail and demanded that all three return. After a long negotiation she and her two sons did return, but the three blacks never stood trial for any offense. They concluded the settlement informally with no aid from a court and became peons. Despite the presentation of Barganeer's threatening letter, a U.S. commissioner dismissed the case, and two U.S. attorneys agreed "that it would not be wise for the Government to pursue this prosecution any further."[14]

[13] See Dan T. Carter, "Prisons, Politics and Business: The Convict Lease System in the Post-Civil War South" (M.A. thesis, University of Wisconsin, 1964).
[14] Statements of Litie James, Sam James, and Ed James, Apr. 6. 1912; B. C. Barganeer to Lydie James, Jan. 5, 1912; Reese to Attorney General, Apr. 29, 1916; Wil-

Some contracts negotiated through the bars of a jail cell placed restrictions on the movement of workers even after they had arranged for the planter to pay the bail and were free of their obligation to the state. One South Carolina case illustrated the extremes of the system. After a laborer had been shot while leaving a plantation, evidence showed that the man had been guarded, placed in a stockade, and worked under the gun. The contract he signed after a trumped-up arrest actually provided for this treatment. It gave the planter "the right to use such force as he or his agents may deem necessary to require me to remain on his farm and perform good and satisfactory services." The contract also gave the planter "the right to lock me up for safe keeping," and even provided that the expense of bringing the fugitive back, should he try to escape, be docked from his wages.[15] Such informal contractual arrangements forced black workers to labor much as they had before emancipation.

Though the informal agreement with prisoners seemed exploitative enough, the formal, court-approved contract with prisoners proved even more vicious. Once a prisoner became indebted, he was sucked into the swirl of peonage. When Ed Rivers, a black man, was convicted of petit larceny in a Monroe County, Alabama, court, he drew a $15.00 fine and $43.75 in costs. Rivers then entered into a contract with J. A. Reynolds to work nine months and twenty-four days at $6.00 per month to pay the fine. He signed the contract in court before Judge I. B. Slaughter on May 4, 1910. Rivers left his job and on June 6, 1910, again appeared in Judge Slaughter's court and received an additional fine of one cent and $87.05 in costs for violating a "criminal contract." At this point Gideon W. Broughton, a neighboring planter, made a contract with Rivers calling for fourteen months and fifteen days of labor at $6.00 per month.[16]

---

liam H. Armbrecht to Attorney General, May 20, 1912, file 50–116, Dept. of Justice, NA, RG 60.

15 *Atlanta Constitution*, Feb. 17, 1901, p. 12. For a large sample of the petty nature of the offenses that allowed peonage to flourish, see the fines and contracts in Box 12, Correspondence of U.S. Attorneys and Marshals, NA, RG 118. For example, on Nov. 15, 1909, Mary Jackson, for using abusive language, was fined $10 plus $25.10 costs and hired out as a farm hand for eight months and eleven days at $4 per month.

16 Grand Jury report, U.S. District Court, Southern Division of Southern District, May term, 1911, *U.S. v. Reynolds*, 235 U.S. 133, copy in Federal Records Center, East Point, Georgia. Hereafter cited as FRC, Georgia. See also *U.S. v. Reynolds*, 235 U.S. 139–46.

The impossibility of escaping the spiral of imprisonment became apparent when Rivers fled from Broughton after only several days of work. Rivers this time drew a fine of $300.00 and $112.80 costs, and, undoubtedly because the men who had been working him saw that he would not remain on a farm even when threatened with continual arrest, he went to the chain gang for a year. When he appeared fresh from a turpentine camp, he came before a grand jury with "shackles riveted on his legs." Had Rivers chosen jail when he first pled guilty to petit larceny, he would have served only about two months. William W. Armbrecht, U.S. attorney in Mobile, Alabama, pointed out that many of the fines were less than $1 in such cases, and the courts did not really consider the crimes serious. Armbrecht, whose nomination for the post of U.S. attorney had been opposed by a large number of blacks who objected to his lily-white Republicanism, concluded that "the prosecution is not instigated with any idea of up-holding the majesty of the law, but with the idea of putting these negroes to work."[17] A native of Mobile who had once been vice-president of a utilities and railroad company in Meridian, Mississippi, Armbrecht became interested in this form of peonage and arranged a test case, securing the cooperation of some Monroe County landowners. "I am informed by Special Agent Bruff," Armbrecht wrote to the attorney general, "that certain citizens of Monroe County are willing that the Government should make a test case, provided that if the defendant is convicted a fine only be imposed." If the case for the government proved successful, he noted, the planters in Monroe County "will abandon the custom."[18]

After Rivers lost an appeal to a federal district court, the U.S. Supreme Court heard the case and handed down its decision on November 30, 1914. The Court observed that Rivers could have been continually rearrested and kept in perpetual peonage. Had Rivers served his sen-

[17] Armbrecht to Attorney General, June 10, 1911, file 50–106, Dept. of Justice, NA, RG 60. See also Armbrecht to Attorney General, Mar. 24, 1911, ibid.; T. P. Jones to President, Jan. 26, 1904; Philip Joseph to President (petition enclosed), Jan., 1904. James L. Pittman, on the other hand, stated that Armbrecht's appointment "would not be objectionable" (Pittman to President, Jan. 11, 1904, Box 30, Appointment and Credentials File, NA, RG 60).
[18] O. L. McKay to P. C. Knox, Jan. 4, 1904, Box 30, Appointment and Credentials File; Armbrecht to Attorney General, Mar. 24, 1911, file 50–106, ibid. For more details of the arrangement, see Armbrecht to Attorney General, Oct. 27, 1911; Oliver D. Street to Attorney General, Dec. 4, 1913; Armbrecht to A. D. Pitts, Apr. 5, 1915, file 50–106, ibid.

tence, the Court continued, his punishment would have been lighter than provided in the contract that he signed. "This contract must be kept," the decision read, "under pain of rearrest, and another similar proceeding for its violation, and perhaps another and another. Thus, under pain of recurring prosecutions, the convict may be kept at labor, to satisfy the demands of his employer." The law violated the Thirteenth Amendment, the Court concluded, and it reversed the judgment of the district court.[19]

Forced labor permeated the cotton belt and reached into South and North Carolina. Peonage was difficult to identify, for in some cases it rested upon law that later became unconstitutional, as in the *Reynolds* case, while in other cases it was based upon some pseudo-law that the illiterate peons dared not challenge. Indeed, local customs of labor control characterized peonage. Somehow Southerners, so upset lest there be no check on the federal government, failed to see that some check was also necessary on local government. The eternal Southern preoccupation with minority rights halted at state and race lines; actively apathetic local officials failed to protect peons.

Though some plantation owners used the loose system of bail laws and contracts to secure peons, most complaints from the rural South charged that coercion, not laws, kept the victims at their jobs. The peons told their stories best. Joe Roberson of Adrian, Georgia, wrote that "I am a negro of course while I am I dont think white government offercers should Let white men work negroes as slaves I have ben working 16 months with Mr J Lit Price and I just cant get a way." Roberson owed $40, but he had not made a contract with his employer, so he complained; "I am in no contract with Mr Price he only taken his gun in his hand and say negros let me have the work."[20] From Lexington, Georgia, a man signing his letter "Doctor" Watkin complained that "I want something done with Mr. M. V. Appling," for the white man "met me on the 9 day of January an shot at me twice and trid to make me hier to him and I told him I wont and I cant stand such treatment." A man in Magnolia, Mississippi, reported that his boss kept the laborers

19 *U.S.* v. *Reynolds*, 235 U.S. 150. For comment on the case, see Waite, "The Negro in the Supreme Court," p. 268; "Violations of Federal Peonage Laws by State Statutes," *Virginia Law Review* 2 (Feb. 1915), 385–90.

20 Joe Roberson to Judge, Aug. 15, 1912, file 50–326, Dept. of Justice, NA, RG 60. Many complaints lack correct grammar and spelling.

in slavery and "rids with his pocket full of guns and a large stick a cross his saddle and he is cursing and beating."[21] In each case the Justice Department promised to send an agent to investigate the complaint, but there remains no evidence of prosecution.[22]

The distinction between peonage and slavery was often blurred. From Grapeland, Mississippi, Clara Please warned her husband that "i Dont no when i Can get there Because the White peopeers is watching me So They is trying to keep me here and they are watching for you ont to the River on the Kate Adam and they Say if you cane Dom Om the Boat the are gonng to Hang you to the telephone pose and Brake your neck and Dont you Came Don Here Darling." In another case Mary Ella Foster asked federal officials in Jackson, Mississippi, to rescue her husband. He was in Flora County, and "he is up their and is work as a slave and wont come home to me and my children he is with a man by name of Duncan Towns and wont let him come home to surport me and my children and dont get enoth to sen me a Penny and he Beat me up mity bad when i was up and he thought that i would died and he sen me home to mama." Henry Holifield of Forrest, Mississippi, wrote that his wife lived on another plantation, where the boss "told har to write an tell me to com Back that he would not hurt me." Returning, Holifield faced a pistol, and then the boss "tid my han behind me and put a chin on mi nack Card the chan up to the raftel and the Chan was so tit untell it lake to charke me to def But i prade to the lod to hep me an so he did."[23] Although the Justice Department responded to these complaints by promising investigations, there remains no evidence of successful prosecution.[24]

The violence that attended peonage sent tentacles of dread throughout the entire black community. From Richton, Mississippi, William Moffett wrote to his sister that he could hardly bear the waiting. The

[21] Doctor Watkin to F. Carter Tate, Jan. 10, 1911, file 50-202; J. S. Daniels to U.S. Attorney in Washington City, D.C., Feb. 1, 1915, file 50-326, ibid. See also Charles Herman to Attorney General, June 17, 1912, file 50-233, ibid.

[22] Attorney General to U.S. Attorney, Macon, Ga., Aug. 27, 1912, file 50-236; Attorney General to F. Carter Tate, Jan. 25, 1911, file 50-202; William Wallace, Jr., to John E. Laskey, Feb. 9, 1915, file 50-326, ibid.

[23] Clara Please to William Please, May 17, 1912, file 50-312; Mary Ella Foster to W. S. Hill, June 22, 1915, file 50-331; Henry Holifield to J. W. George, Apr. 17, 1915, file 50-327, ibid.

[24] W. E. Storrs to Attorney General, July 2, 1912, file 50-312; Wallace to Hill, June 24, 1915, file 50-331; Wallace to Robert C. Lee, Apr. 27, 1915, file 50-327, ibid.

white folks, he wrote, "took a colored man out last night and tied him to a tree and blindfolded him and they beat him until the blood run down on the ground and they shot they guns till the people thought war had began and the people went today and looked at where the blood soked in the ground, and I am afriad my time next I cant sleep at night when I go to bed so do Some thing at once and get me away from this place." But again the Justice Department apparently took no action.[25] It was the fear that a beating or death was the reward for leaving a plantation that kept many laborers quietly at work.

A Justice Department official reported in 1910 that an employer made an example of a black worker who had tried to free his sister from peonage. The employer "took Wes Mosely with him and drove out to this farm, went into the house caught Lath Horne, and dragged him out in the yard and began to beat him over the head with his pistol." The report continued that the two white men "then threw Lath Horne in the Buggy and drove over into Houston County into a Cemetery and there beat him to death, with their pistols and the end of a buggy line with a metal rope eye snap on the end of it."[26] Emory Speer, a native of Monroe County, Georgia, presided over the peonage trial. At age sixty-two Speer still exhibited the vigor that had enabled him to become champion of the mountain whites of Georgia in the late 1870s and early 1880s. "After hearing the evidence, I had a strong impression that they were guilty," he wrote to the Justice Department, "but for the first time within my experience of twenty-five years as Judge, I fear there was a miscarriage of justice in the verdict. The accused were acquitted."[27] After defeating the peonage charge, the accused men had fled the state in order to avoid standing trial for murder in the state courts.[28]

A victim of lawlessness usually turns to the nearest law-enforcement officer, but peonage victims found this avenue blocked. County sheriffs, constables, justices of the peace, and sometimes federal officials aided in

[25] William Moffett to Mattie Durr, Jan. 31, 1917; J. W. George to Attorney General, Feb. 28, 1917, file 50–127, ibid.

[26] E. L. Clyatt to Robert L. Storrs, June 28, 1910, file 50–188, ibid.

[27] Speer to Attorney General, July 8, 1910, file 50–188, ibid. Speer's letter gives a thorough review of the federal laws regarding peonage and conspiracy. He urged the Attorney General to prosecute crimes of violence and peonage, for he reasoned that "the consequences will be very grave if crimes of this character are permitted to go unwhipped of justice."

[28] Clyatt to Robert L. Storrs, June 28, 1910, file 50–188, ibid.

preserving the nightmare world of peonage. King Moore, held in a Vienna, Georgia, jail, appealed to Judge Speer for help. "This man that Had me put in Here he Rape my wife," his tale began. Moore had heard his wife scream, rushed to her aid, and found that his boss "had her just bleeding and had a Pistol drawn on Her." Moore then told his boss that he would not stay on the farm any longer. That night, according to his complaint, he started to Macon to get help from Speer, but a crowd of white men stopped him and threw him into jail, threatening to lynch him if he made any trouble. Local police charged Moore with "assault with intent to murder and for forgery," an investigator reported, but added that there was no proof of any peonage violation. The agent admitted that "there may be irregularity in the performance of their duty on the part of state officers," but he did not think the federal government had jurisdiction in the case.[29]

Local law-enforcement officials, secure in their isolated domains, accepted the customs that encouraged peonage. Sam Sadler, a Negro from Hartwell County, Georgia, had refused to work out a debt claimed by J. D. Matheson. The local sheriff, Matheson, and Matheson's son took him from his home and then to jail. There the sheriff and the chief of police held pistols on Sadler as the younger Matheson beat him. One of them asked, "Now, will you promise to go back and work out what you owe us?" The group of tormentors warned Sadler not to tell about the beating or they would drown him in a nearby river.[30] Such collusion between local police and planters was common throughout the South.

Justices of the peace also contributed to peonage by cooperating closely with employers. Much of the local corruption throughout the rural South thrived on the apathy of white Southerners, but in an unusually frank grand-jury report citizens in Jefferson County, Alabama, condemned the justice-of-the-peace system, calling it a "disgrace to civilization." They concluded that it would be better if the jurisdiction of the justices "were limited to marrying negroes who live twenty miles or more from the court house." Noting that the dockets of the justices

[29] King Moore to Speer, Oct. 6, 1911, file 50–215; Arthur H. Codington to Attorney General, Nov. 1, 1911, file 50–216, ibid.

[30] H. H. Sanders to Tate, Jan. 8, 1912; Tate to Attorney General, Jan. 11, 1912; Sanders to Tate, Jan. 8, 1912, file 50–224. There are numerous charges of complicity of local officials in peonage complaints; for example, see L. D. Miller to Alexander Akerman, Jan. 27, 1912, file 50–226; Tom Stephens to Secretary of Interior, Sept. 1, 1917, ff 5240–03, ibid.

of the peace had been padded, the grand jury charged that this practice "would convict many of them for peonage should the federal government choose to enforce its laws against them." The report also held that justices had pocketed fine money instead of paying it to the county treasury.[31] Complaints against justices of the peace were common throughout the South. Thus, from the lowest local official to the highest state and federal officials, peons customarily found no champion. The men who actively pushed peonage cases, such as Fred Cubberly and Emory Speer, were exceptional.

Federal employees often displayed a similar apathy or acquiescence which troubled their superiors. In 1907 Attorney General Knox subtly warned a U.S. marshal in Florida that it "would be a source of deep regret to me to receive reports of lukewarmness" regarding peonage investigations. In 1910 Judge Emory Speer, perpetual champion of the peons, cautioned an assistant U.S. attorney about his attitude. "This, permit me to observe," reprimanded Speer, "is not the careful investigation which I requested." He then outlined what he wanted the local Justice Department official to do.[32]

A case near New Orleans in 1912 raised the question of racial prejudice, but the attorney's reaction could have been simply frustration. A black man named Ed Sanders had allegedly been held in peonage; at the trial the jury could not agree on a verdict. Complaining of the failure of the government's case, Charlton R. Beattie, U.S. attorney in New Orleans, explained to the Attorney General that the "accused have strong influences behind them, and the witnesses on behalf of the Government are principally negro witnesses and I do not believe that a conviction can be secured in a second trial." Beattie advised the attorney general to drop the case. "If, as you state," replied Assistant Attorney General W. R. Harr, "the witnesses on behalf of the Government are principally negroes, this fact is not a sufficient reason for failing to further prosecute this case." Beattie denied that the race issue was his

[31] Grand jury report, criminal court of Jefferson County, Alabama, Sept., 1911, copy in file 50–112, ibid. See also M. A. Waring to Justice Department, Oct. 23, 1915, file 50–370, ibid.

[32] Attorney General to John F. Horr, Jan. 16, 1907, file 50–162–2; Speer to Robert L. Storrs, June 14, 1910, file 50–188, ibid. See also Mingo Norfleet to Justice Department, Nov. 21, 1911, June 21, 1912, file 50–223; Charlton R. Beattie to Attorney General, Jan. 8, 1912, file 50–280, ibid.

primary motivation and successfully argued that the case be dropped.[33]

Beattie was not the only U.S. attorney who was frustrated, for Southern juries were not sympathetic with peons. Throughout the South federal officials made a persistent complaint that juries rarely found guilty verdicts in peonage cases. Helping try a Mississippi case, U.S. Attorney William H. Armbrecht reported that his failure to secure a conviction came from the "prejudice of juries in the South against the enforcement of peonage laws, and the fact that white men contradicted the testimony of the negro witnesses for the Government." Later Armbrecht made much the same observation from Mobile, Alabama. "I cannot understand why an indictment was not found," he complained, "except that, the country members of the Grand Jury in that section of Alabama are not disposed to find true bills in cases of peonage."[34] After presenting what he thought to be an airtight case, a Justice Department official in Florida explained that he had failed to secure a conviction because "it is generally understood in this section that no white jury will convict a white man for anything he might do to a negro." A U.S. attorney in Shreveport, Louisiana, reported that a severe case of peonage had ended in a hung jury as one of the jurors refused to join the other eleven in conviction. In another instance a judge exhibited "an intense and active bias that was exceedingly hurtful and prejudicial to the prosecution."[35]

The root of the peonage problem was anchored in the long-practiced abuse of black laborers, and until that custom disappeared or lost public support the frustrations would continue. Several judges became so upset at the injustice in their own courtrooms that they lectured peonage offenders. Emory Speer, district judge of the southern federal judicial district of Georgia, once charged a jury by telling them of the nature of peonage. "No other crime is so subtle in its operation, more destructive in its results than that which degrades the public conscience, until it can tamely and without protest witness the unlawful slavery of the citizen." Four years later, in 1909, Speer was still speaking out against

[33] Beattie to Attorney General, Mar. 21, 1912; Harr to Beattie, Mar. 27, 1912; Beattie to Attorney General, Mar. 29, 1912; Harr to Beattie, Apr. 11, 1912, file 50–277, ibid.
[34] Armbrecht to Attorney General, July 16, 1913, file 50–307; Armbrecht to Attorney General, Dec. 22, 1908, file 50–92, ibid.
[35] A. J. Hoyt to Charles J. Bonaparte, June 18, 1907, file 50–162–4; M. C. Elstner to Attorney General, Apr. 20, 1910, file 50–302; G. W. Pickle to Attorney General, Mar. 13, 1907, file 50–376, ibid.

peonage. "I gravely fear that a great deal of oppression is being exercised by the unscrupulous upon many obscure, and therefore so helpless," he wrote to the attorney general, "that unless there can be afforded relief under the statutes denouncing peonage it may result in a condition which will be a reproach to our civilization."[36]

Likewise, Federal Judge William B. Sheppard, who had earlier fought peonage as a U.S. attorney, became irate when a Florida jury failed to find the defendants guilty in an especially brutal case of peonage. "This man is guilty of peonage," he told them plainly. When a victim bared his back in the courtroom, showing scars from a beating, Sheppard said that it suggested "the most rabid stories of the hardships of the slave before the civil war." In this case the peon masters, finding the Justice Department on their trail, spirited the victim off to Cuba to rid themselves of his embarrassing presence. The fugitive immediately found a person who spoke English, was directed to the U.S. embassy, poured out his story, and later returned home to testify—in vain.[37]

Nearly always the class lines were clearly drawn. The peon, at the bottom of the economic and social scale, battled the men of wealth and power at the top. As Speer informed the Justice Department in 1911, the destruction of peonage would give "more hope to the humble classes than anything of a similar character the administration could accomplish."[38] For example, Edward J. McRee, a Georgia state representative, maintained a gigantic part-convict, part-peonage camp. He and his family controlled the local law officers, dominating the poor.[39] Another Georgian, James M. Smith, was the source of a series of peonage complaints flowing from Oglethorpe County. He once ran for governor of Georgia, and, as one neighbor complained, "is a very wealthy man, and boats of the fact that he is able to buy his justice to suit himself."[40] U.S.

[36] *Savannah Press*, Mar. 20, 1905, clipping in file 50–10719–01; Speer to Attorney General, Sept. 16, 1909, file 50–184, ibid.

[37] Unidentified clipping ca. Aug. 25, 1913, in file 50–97, ibid. See also E. J. Parsons to Attorney General, Feb. 16, 1910; E. S. Thigpen to Attorney General, Mar. 12, 1910, ibid.

[38] Speer to Attorney General, Mar. 20, 1911, file 50–222, ibid.

[39] *New York Evening Post*, June 18, 1903, p. 7. See also "Peonage in Georgia," *Independent* 55 (Dec. 24, 1903), 3079–80; *New York Times*, May 6, 1903, p. 1; "Servitude for Debt in Georgia," *Outlook* 74 (June 27, 1903), 486. Many instances of the McRees' peonage practices came to light. Typical was the case of two black youths reported in "Peonage in Georgia," p. 3080.

[40] G. H. Lee to George Wickersham, Sept. 6, 1909, file 50–183, Dept. of Justice,

Senator Joseph F. Johnston of Alabama expressed disbelief to the attorney general that three white men from Brantley, Alabama, were guilty of peonage. One of the men, he advised the attorney general, was a banker, and his business would suffer if a peonage trial ensued. He wanted a quiet hearing before a U.S. commissioner instead of a grand-jury investigation.[41]

The case that first attracted Fred Cubberly's attention in 1901 was not the only case involving white peons. Besides immigrants who entered the Southern labor force in large numbers around 1906, some native Southern whites fell victim to peonage. An anonymous informer from Florida complained in 1914 that O. H. Eastus, a poor white, had been jailed because he owed his employer. He got out of jail only when he agreed to work out his debt.[42] Jim Knight, a South Carolina white, complained that Robert E. Taylor held him in peonage. According to Knight, Taylor had made "threats and notices both verbal & written forbidden me to leave his place and any one giving me a home or work to do." A preliminary investigation proved Knight's complaint valid; yet three weeks later he complained again, "R. E. Taylor is still holding me." Knight's case apparently ended with a promise that a special agent would be sent to investigate.[43]

A Georgia incident in 1911 caused much concern for Arthur H. Codington, assistant U.S. attorney in Macon. J. F. Smith, a wealthy resident of Baxley, had secured seven young white laborers from east Tennessee to work on his plantation, promising them $1.25 a day. The young workers soon discovered that their wages were less than promised, and they were in debt to Smith long after they thought they had paid out. They ran away but were apprehended in Savannah. There they were chained by the neck, threatened with imprisonment unless they returned to the Smith farm to work out their debts, and returned to Baxley in the "colored coach." The case was heard in Speer's court,

---

NA, RG 60. See also Bill Fulton to Tate, Dec. 27, 1911, file 50–225; J. D. Lucas to John E. Wilkie, Apr. 11, 1907, file 50–162–6, ibid.

[41] Joseph F. Johnston to Wickersham, Jan. 17, 1913, file 50–120, ibid. See also S. J. W. Timms to Dept. of Justice, Nov. 30, 1913, file 50–247; Ernest F. Cochran to Attorney General, Oct. 17, 1908, file 50–357, ibid.

[42] No signature to Speer, Nov. 1907, file 50–182, ibid.

[43] Knight to Jude Smith, Mar. 19, 1914; W. D. Sullivan, Jr., to Francis H. Weston, Apr. 6, 1914; Knight to Weston, Apr. 7, 1914; Weston to Attorney General, Apr. 9, 1914; William Wallace, Jr., to Weston, Apr. 11, 1914, file 50–369, ibid.

and the men, including the conspiring justice of the peace and constable, pled guilty and drew fines. Codington explained to the attorney general that this case "is a fair example of the method frequently utilized for the arrest and return of laborers." Until this case, he wrote, "the abuses have been chiefly of negroes, but this case illustrates clearly how readily they might be extended to white men of excellent character." Then he outlined the nature of the system. "A pliant judicial officer, a subservient and cruel petty arresting officer, and a man of wealth and influence utilizing both, made this an excellent case for example." Evidently there were other cases that Codington knew of. "In the country counties, not well penetrated by railroads, violations of the peonage statutes are apparently worse than in others."[44]

In rare cases blacks would cooperate with whites to place black laborers in peonage. Two black men, one a doctor, took a black girl on a "pleasure trip" to Valdosta, Georgia, "manufactured a claim against her for medical services," and sold her to the infamous McRee family. Appearing in Speer's court, they received a lecture and a fine. "I am afraid if you had remained in Africa," reprimanded Speer, "that you both would have become leaders of bands of slave catchers, who swoop down on the unprotected kraals of the Hottentots or Congo and seize the defenseless people and bear them off and sell them into slavery."[45]

Most peonage complaints originated in the cotton belt, but, as the *Clyatt* case illustrated, peonage also existed in the turpentine-producing area of the South. Though the work was different, the manifestations of peonage were similar. The census of 1910 listed 27,211 men and 316 women as turpentine workers; almost 25,000 of this number worked in the turpentine area along the borders of Florida, Georgia, and Alabama.[46] "The pioneer citizens of fifty years ago who moved into the West with their families and household goods," wrote turpentine expert Albert Pridgen, "... did not find conditions more raw and difficult than the modern turpentine producer who moves into a new territory." Pridgen, contributing to a work publicizing the turpentine industry, gave an excellent account of the work in the forests. Ideally, the man who began a

44 Codington to Attorney General, Apr. 17, 1911, file 50–222, ibid.
45 Unidentified clipping enclosed in Speer to Attorney General, Mar. 27, 1905, ff 10719–03, ibid.
46 U.S. Bureau of the Census, *Thirteenth Census of the United States: 1910*, Occupational Statistics. Compiled from Table 35, pp. 52–107.

turpentine operation searched for 200 acres of pine trees; such a large stand necessarily existed away from the main routes of transportation and population. The work, usually heavy and exhausting, continued throughout the year. During the winter the trees had boxes or cups cut into them to catch the gum. In the spring as the sap began to run some men collected the gum, while others chipped the trees, exposing fresh wounds in the trunk from which the sap could drain. The chipped streaks were V-shaped; after a succession of assaults on the tree it re-sembled a downward-plunging arrow, its gummy feathers misplaced on the point. Chipping and gum-collecting continued from the first week of March until late October, and workers lugged large, heavy barrels about the forests, dipping the gum from the boxes and pouring it into large vats. The distilled gum yielded spirits of turpentine and rosin. Be-cause the trees began to lose their productivity after several years, the turpentine operators continually searched for new sites for their stills.

Pridgen, writing in 1921, complained that labor had become increas-ingly difficult to secure and to hold. While complaining of the insecure labor supply, Pridgen inadvertently outlined what probably caused the labor shortage. Continuing his pioneer analogy, he wrote that gambling dens substituted for schools and churches. The food consisted of "corn-bread, bacon, black coffee, and an occasional treat of baking powder biscuits."[47] Another writer claimed that this diet had to be supplemented by local squirrels, opossums, raccoons, rabbits, and fish.[48] Laborers, dis-enchanted with such primitive conditions, often fled in search of other jobs. Like Samuel Clyatt, other employers pursued the fugitives, forc-ing them to return and work out what they owed—sometimes a largely fictitious bill exaggerated by high interest rates.[49] The savagery and lawlessness duplicated frontier conditions; violence and peonage be-came a standard way of life in the turpentine woods. As one old-timer recalled, the turpentine industry was "outlaw work carried on by outlaws."[50]

Had there been no peonage, life in the turpentine camps would have

[47] Albert Pridgen, "Turpentining in the South Atlantic Country," in Thomas Gamble, ed., *Naval Stores* (Savannah, 1921), p. 104.
[48] Nollie Hickman, *Mississippi Harvest, Lumbering in the Longleaf Pine Belt, 1840–1915* (University, Miss., 1962), p. 150.
[49] Pridgen, "Turpentining in the South Atlantic Country," pp. 103–4; Hickman, *Mississippi Harvest*, pp. 50, 139–50, 243.
[50] Quoted in Hickman, *Mississippi Harvest*, p. 147.

been miserable enough. Peonage added its brutal stamp, and it was widespread. Special Agent A. J. Hoyt wrote to the attorney general in 1906 that the more he investigated in Florida "the more convinced I am that peonage exists in every section of this State, especially in the turpentine districts." He reported that every week local Justice Department officials received complaints of peonage. During the first twenty years of this century, Florida loomed as one of the primary offenders.[51]

The bleak turpentine forests encircled men who fell victim to practices resembling those in the rural agricultural areas. Once in the woods, men bought their food and supplies from the company commissary. Often a laborer would sign a contract, receive advances on his pay, and begin buying his goods from the commissary. Agent Hoyt revealed in 1906 that provisions cost "at least one hundred per cent. more than when purchased with money from a regular dealer, and, in some instances, I have discovered where they even exact one thousand per cent. profit for the goods sold to these employees." If a man attempted to escape from this situation, the owner would pursue him, charge him with some trivial offense, and then pay his bond (charging it to his account), and take him back to the camp; the longer a man remained in the camp, the more indebted he became.[52]

As immigrants entered the turpentine forests in large numbers around 1906, they discovered alarming brutality. Sometimes, instead of making verbal threats, the woods riders (foremen) merely suggested consequences. At a hearing before a U.S. commissioner an interpreter, F. C. Benjamin, reported that each morning the foreman "took out his revolver and loaded it with bullets before us and we were afraid." Other foremen were more direct. Immigrant worker Iacomo Corrado testified that his foreman prodded him to work with a pistol, saying, "If you do not go on to work, I will shoot you, and if you run away, I will go after you and get you and put you in jail." This proved no idle boast, for Corrado revealed that some men fled one night and "the next morning I saw them with a guard on horseback with a gun, bringing them back." When asked why he did not leave these miserable conditions, the witness replied, "First, I had no money; second, I did not know the road;

51 A. J. Hoyt to Attorney General, Sept. 26, 1906, file 50–162, Dept. of Justice, NA, RG 60. See also Hickman, *Mississippi Harvest*, pp. 141–44.

52 Hoyt to Attorney General, Aug. 28, 1906, file 50–162–1, Dept. of Justice, NA, RG 60.

and third a man threatened me with a gun every time I try to leave."[53]

The violence that immigrants faced was probably part of the daily life of the turpentine workers. Having been lured to isolated May-town, Florida, by the glittering promises of New York labor agents, two of a group of immigrants recorded their experiences in statements given to Justice Department officials.[54] The owner "gave us a cabin without any furniture in it and about eight men were to sleep on the floor," Bennie Rubenstein reported. His friend Mike Fink noted that in his cabin "there was no furniture at all, the floor was torn up and it was filthy with dirt." Attempting to get better conditions, the immigrants refused to work, but "*the foreman showed us his pistol and guns and the whip.*"[55] Kirt Sanders, an ex-sailor foreman who sported a skull-and-crossbones tattoo, claimed "I am a special policeman here, I have a right to shoot anyone who runs away."[56] The "special policeman" often beat the men and also played deadly games with them. The two men fled and headed down the railroad track, avoiding sentries posted along the way. After they had reached a train station far away from Maytown, Sanders accosted them with a pistol. "He began to count, 'One, two'—we were afraid," Rubenstein admitted.[57]

The Justice Department, spurred by publicity and diplomatic pressure, acted to end immigrant peonage. Blacks suffered the same conditions but received less sympathy. The black peons in turpentine camps experienced the same dread as those in the cotton belt. One black woman, Gertha Haigs, escaped from a turpentine still and made her way with her baby to the railroad station at Galliver, Florida. As she stepped up to the train, her former employer grabbed her, charged her with some petty offense (though he had no warrant), and carried her back to the still. Before arriving at the still, however, he whipped her and said, "Now you had better keep your damned mouth shut or I will do you

---

[53] Statement of Bennie Graubart, Aug. 20, 1906, file 50–162–8; testimony of F. C. Benjamin and Iacomo Carrado, in testimony taken at commissioner's hearing, *U.S. v. J. Lynch*, Sept. 1, 1906, file 50–162, ibid.

[54] For a brief description of the case, see Charles W. Russell, *Report on Peonage* (Washington, 1908), pp. 8–12.

[55] Statement of Bennie Rubenstein, n.d.; statement of Sam Fink, n.d., file 50–162–8, Dept. of Justice, NA, RG 60. Italics in original.

[56] Statement of Rubenstein, ibid. For a description of Sanders, see A. J. Hoyt to Attorney General, Dec. 28, 1906, file 50–162–2, ibid.

[57] Statement of Rubenstein, n.d., file 50–162–8, ibid.

worse." The man claimed that she still owed him money, though she had already worked for nine months to pay for her railroad ticket.[58]

Two U.S. attorneys gave a succinct description of the turpentine system that illustrates its similarity to cotton-belt peonage. A desirable laborer was paid only a fraction of his wages, but when he attempted to leave "he will be arrested on some charge such as carrying a concealed weapon or other charge of that character and unless he agrees to stay at the Camp he will be put in jail on such charge." As one Negro reported, it was not the money that the still owner wanted in his case, because the boss stated that "he did not want the money but he wanted the damn negro."[59]

By 1906 the construction of railroads that crossed desolate mountains or water attracted immigrant laborers, and many of these men became victims of peonage. Thus, as in the turpentine camps and in the Mississippi Delta, immigrants were sprinkled into the existing labor force. Many of the new lines had to cross the wastes of Florida, the keys, or circumvent the mountains in other areas of the South; these were unpopulated and barren areas. Railroading, like farming and turpentine camps, required stamina. Clearing the right-of-way, grading the road bed, and carrying the heavy cross-ties and rails called for strong backs. Moreover, there was little diversion in the barren camps, except what the men could manufacture in the way of card games and liquor.

In some instances the conditions were so dire and the pay so poor that men attempted to flee, but foremen threatened and finally forced workers to remain at work. One case, perhaps as typical as any peonage case could be, involved forty Greeks who went to Punta Gorda, Florida. There on the Florida west coast they found a miserable camp, inadequate lodging, and no access to freedom. Eight of the party finally fled down the river and hired a boatman to row them across.[60] Before U.S. Commissioner H. L. Crane the Greeks poured out their grim story in broken English. The Justice Department sent the experienced A. J. Hoyt to ascertain the conditions there and verify the immigrants' story. Hoyt described the beds and concluded that "no hard working man or boy, can do an honest days work with such rest as he gets in these

[58] Statement of Gertha Haigs, Oct. 31, 1916, file 50–178, ibid.
[59] H. S. Phillips and Fred Batts to Attorney General, Oct. 2, 1913, file 50–175; Jack Richburg to Attorney General, Sept. 10, 1908, file 50–163, ibid.
[60] Joanis A. Mbousa et al., statement, Jan. 24, 1907, file 50–162–2, ibid.

bunks." Walking out the back door he confronted a swarm of flies. "I did not believe that it was possible that there would be so many flies at this time of the year," he said. The drinking water came from a ditch and was "nearly as red as blood." The foremen carried guns, he noted, allegedly to kill the wild game of the area. "In my opinion," Hoyt concluded, "this is the most gigantic condition of peonage that has ever come to light."[61]

Random complaints of peonage came from the mountainous country in Tennessee and North Carolina. One such case involving black laborers arose over the practices of Oliver Brothers Construction Company. After rumors had drifted from the railroad camp that peonage existed there, an investigator approached the camp. Downriver from the camp he talked to a man who lived nearby and asked him if the fishing was good in the river. The man replied, yes, but "no one around there would eat the fish now. I asked him why and he said the river was full of dead negroes." They came from the railroad camp upstream, the man informed the agent. Though most of the evidence pointed to peonage, the case resulted in a mistrial.[62]

From the cases that somehow surfaced (and there were many that did not), the magnitude of peonage throughout the South was appalling. Peonage complaints poured in, even though 2.6 million blacks could not read or write in 1900.[63] If only the literate or semiliterate complained, certainly many other peons languished, mute and invisible, in the forests, mountains, and cotton belt of the South.

Among the broken-backed cabins of the cotton belt, the forsaken turpentine farms, and barren railroad camps, peons scratched out their complaints. A network of conditions encircled them, however. The separate and unequal Southern education system prepared many men for lives as peons. Racial and class customs among Southerners, rooted

[61] A. J. Hoyt to John M. Cheney, Jan. 27, 1907, file 50–162–2, ibid.

[62] Henry E. Thomas, daily report, Sept. 8, 1906, ff 44463, ibid. See also William Muller to W. H. Hoot, Sept. 6, 1913, file 50–174; *Atlanta Constitution*, Jan. 7, 1910, clipping in file 50–185; R. M. Hall to Casey Todd, Apr. 1, 1912, file 50–115, ibid. The federal government was successful in prosecuting E. H. Benson, superintendent of the Barker Chemical Company at Port Inglis, Florida. Seventeen Italians had been held in peonage (unidentified clipping ca. May 8, 1907, file 50–162–4, ibid.). For a survey of similar cases, see A. J. Hoyt to Attorney General, May 7, 1907, ibid.

[63] Woodward, *Origins of the New South*, p. 400.

in a myth-enshrouded antebellum past, dulled community senses to daily crimes against the poor of both races. Juries and sometimes judges balked at finding a white man guilty of holding a laborer in peonage. Local law-enforcement officers, obsequious to the wealthy, served as a fugitive-slave force. Federal officials either acquiesced, made token efforts to prosecute peon-masters, or joined the futile battle to eliminate peonage. Trapped in this web of exploitation, the peon was a submerged reminder of the myth of the New South—a myth of racial harmony and industrial and educational advances. But peonage was the undistorted mirror reflecting the social, economic, political, and legal scars that defaced the South.

CHAPTER III

An Experiment in Leniency

Coosa and Tallapoosa counties are located northeast of Montgomery, Alabama, in the hill country that rolls gently southward into the black belt. The counties take their names from the rivers that run through them, forming at their confluence near Montgomery the Alabama River, which traces the heart of the Alabama black belt. The main settlements in the two counties, dating from the 1830s, grew out of Indian trading-posts; sawmilling, mining, and cotton-farming customarily furnished occupations for most inhabitants. The hill country, unlike the black belt, maintained a predominately white population, characterized by small farms and occasional sparsely populated settlements.[1]

An explosion of peonage cases in these Alabama counties in 1903 furnished a view of peonage in microcosm. Thomas Goode Jones, Civil War hero and twice Democratic governor of Alabama in the 1890s, eventually presided over the peonage trials in the federal district court in Montgomery. Nothing in Jones's past hinted that he would push so hard to abolish peonage. His recent appointment by Republican President Theodore Roosevelt to a federal judgeship followed an anti-labor past. He had called out the militia and the Pinkertons to crush the 1894 Alabama strikes and had been an attorney for the Louisville and Nash-ville Railroad. Even the fact that the peons were mostly black did not deter Jones, who in the 1901 suffrage convention in Alabama had argued that whites should give the Alabama black man "all the civil rights that will fit him to be a decent and self-respecting, law-abiding and intel-

[1] WPA, Federal Writers' Project, *American Guide Series, Alabama* (New York, 1941), pp. 337–38; Francis G. Caffey to editor, July 22, 1903, published in *New York Evening Post*, July 25, 1903, p. 5.

ligent citizen."[2] Whatever motivated Jones, he took the lead in assaulting peonage, gathering support from the Justice Department and the self-anointed "best Southerners," or patricians. Jones had, it seems, left some of his Bourbon heritage behind and imbibed the Progressive era remedy of gathering facts, exposing corruption, and expecting automatic self-correction as men became educated to their failures. By exposing peonage and bringing the accused offenders to the dock of justice, he thought that the disease would cure itself.

Just as Jones represented the juxtaposition of the Southern past and present, so also did the Northern press. Oswald Garrison Villard, grandson of abolitionist William Lloyd Garrison, led an editorial crusade that would have gratified his grandfather as he attacked the neo-slavery of peonage through the columns of the *New York Evening Post*. Other Northern journals covered the Alabama peonage cases and, like their abolitionist predecessors, vied for the most atrocious stories to set before their readers. Time and again the press crusade revived the theme that the Negro question should be a federal problem because the Southern states seemed unwilling and powerless to correct abuses. President Theodore Roosevelt, using the federal peonage statute, agreed with this theory and pushed the peonage cases with his executive power, an avenue of attack denied him in the case of lynching. Seemingly miscast in a role of civil rights advocate, Booker T. Washington quietly entered the cases as an informer to the Northern press.

After secret service agents at the request of Jones made tentative reports on peonage in April, 1903, U.S. District Attorney Warren S. Reese, Jr., of Montgomery responded in revulsion, reporting to the attorney general that he had "lived in this State my entire life of thirty seven years and I never comprehended until now the extent of the present method of slavery through this peonage system." Reese seemed genuinely surprised to learn that in Coosa and Tallapoosa counties "reputable men, most of them holding official offices such as justice of the Peace, Deputy Sheriffs, Sheriff and Mayor of a small town" were involved in the cases.[3] Reese's report on Coosa and Tallapoosa counties,

---

[2] Woodward, *Origins of the New South*, pp. 262, 266–67, 339, 383, 463; *Dictionary of American Biography*, s.v. "Jones, Thomas Goode."

[3] Reese to Attorney General, Apr. 25, 1903, ff 5280–03, Dept. of Justice, NA, RG 60. See also Reese to Attorney General, June 10, 1903, ibid.

like an exposé of big-city corruption, read like Progressive era muck-raking, Southern style.

The Alabama peonage cases of 1903 came to light when a young attorney named Erastus J. Parsons attempted to free a black laborer imprisoned in Shelby County. A native of Coosa County whose grandfather had been governor of Alabama, Parsons instituted habeas corpus proceedings to free his client from a fraudulent prosecution. Rack Parsons, as he was known, had suddenly realized that in Goodwater, a small town in Coosa County, the system of local justice had broken down. The officials there evaded his writ, so he appealed to District Attorney Reese, who assured him that he would investigate the alleged violations of civil rights.[4]

The practices gained general public attention as Judge Thomas G. Jones presided over a federal grand jury in Birmingham. Jones maintained friendly contact with Booker T. Washington and perhaps responded to the distress of black laborers more enthusiastically because of his paternalistic humanitarianism.[5] Through Reese, Jones learned of the complaints in Shelby and Coosa counties, and he urged Attorney General Philander C. Knox to send a detective to "camp for a while in that territory." He then outlined how the peonage system operated. "The plan is to accuse the negro of some petty offense, and then require him, in order to escape conviction, to enter into an agreement to pay his accusers so much money, and sign a contract, under the terms of which his bondsmen can hire him out until he pays a certain sum." The Negro, he added, "is made to believe he is a convict, and treated as such."[6]

The Justice Department responded to Jones's call. On April 2, 1903,

[4] Richard B. Kelly to Theodore Roosevelt, Mar. 6, 1905; Charles C. Whitson to Roosevelt, May 26, 1905; Reese to Parsons, Jan. 27, Apr. 11, 1903; typescript, "The Slave Traffic Today," Appointment and Credentials Files, ibid.

[5] See Jones to Washington, June 10, Oct. 2, 1901, Washington Papers, Manuscript Division, Library of Congress, Washington, D.C., Box 201. Hereafter cited as Washington Papers. Washington to Roosevelt, Oct. 2, 1901, Appointment and Credentials Files, Dept. of Justice, NA, RG 60. Washington wrote in part: "I do not believe that in all the South you could select a better man through whom to emphasize your idea of the character of a man to hold office than you can do through ex-Gov. Jones," in his recommendation for Jones's appointment to the federal bench.

[6] Jones to Philander C. Knox, Mar. 21, 1903, ff 5280–03, Dept. of Justice, NA, RG 60.

the Attorney General instructed the U.S. attorneys in Birmingham and Montgomery to investigate the complaints of peonage in their districts. A week later Thomas R. Roulhac, whose background and influential contacts resembled Jones's, reported that the grand jury sitting in Birmingham with Jones presiding had found indictments for peonage against nine persons.[7] By June President Theodore Roosevelt showed interest in the peonage cases and asked Attorney General Knox for a report. Knox summed up the activity of the Justice Department and promised "vigorous and uncompromising prosecutions."[8]

By mid-June, 1903, investigations and grand jury testimony in Montgomery brought the peonage practices in Coosa and Tallapoosa counties into clear focus. Reese, who encouraged press coverage and emerged as the hero of the cases, explained the system used in mid-Alabama, adding documentation to what Jones had earlier explained. Negroes, he wrote to the Attorney General, were carried before justices of the peace on "the most baseless charges." The justices of the peace, usually in the pay of the planters, then conducted a trial or just went through the motions but invariably found the victim guilty and assessed a fine that the black was unable to pay. Then one of the "slave dealers steps up, pretends to be the friend of the negro, and has a short conference with him telling him he will pay him out if he will sign a contract to work for him on his farm, to which the negro readily agrees rather than go to the mines." The black was then "placed into a condition of involuntary servitude, he is locked up at nights in a cell, worked under guards during the day from 3 o'clock in the morning until 7 or 8 o'clock at night, whipped in a most cruel manner, is insufficiently fed and poorly clad." The black man faced a dilemma; he could go to the mines as a convict-lease prisoner or go to virtually the same fate by allowing a planter to pay his fine.

[7] Attorney General to Reese, Apr. 2, 1903; Attorney General to Thomas R. Roulhac, Apr. 2, 1903, Instruction Book 176, pp. 1, 3; Roulhac to Attorney General, Apr. 9, 1903, ibid.

[8] Attorney General to Roosevelt, June 8, 1903, Executive and Congressional Letter Book 64, p. 341, ibid. Roosevelt continued his interest in peonage, writing in 1904 that he was "appalled at some of the revelations as to peonage in Mississippi" (Roosevelt to Lyman Abbott, Aug. 8, 1904, Theodore Roosevelt Papers, Manuscript Division, Library of Congress, Washington, D.C., Series 2, Box 2. Hereafter cited as Theodore Roosevelt Papers. Note courtesy of James B. Lane).

Though this was bad enough, Reese illustrated how the condition could become endless. "When the time of a good working negro is nearing an end," he explained, "he is rearrested upon some trumped up charge and again carried before some bribed justice and resentenced to an additional time." The peon was helpless; the planter allowed no contact with the outside world and censored all letters. "If they run away the dogs are placed upon their track," Reese explained, "and they are invariably retaken and subjected to more cruel treatment."

The system of recurring arrests depended upon the cooperation of four groups of conspirators. The first of these were the owners of the plantations, sawmills, or mines. John W. Pace, J. F. Turner, and the Cosby family were the most prominent of the wealthy landowners. The constables who rounded up the victims constituted the second group; Robert N. Franklin headed the list. The third group consisted of the justices of the peace. Reese listed James M. Kennedy (who worked for Pace) and W. D. Cosby in this category. In the fourth group he cited numerous overseers and guards on the plantations. On June 15, when Reese wrote his informative letter, the grand jury in Montgomery had already returned eighty indictments against men in the two counties.[9]

The grand jurors, unfamiliar with the peonage law, continually asked Judge Jones to explain points to them, and on June 16 Jones, whose research into peonage showed a profound grasp of state labor laws and legal precedent, delivered his elaborate charge to the jury. He reached back into the history of peonage in Mexico and brought it forward to his time. Countering some Alabamians' claim that custom should rule, Jones stated that the "good custom and habit of a locality . . . cannot be pleaded to shield an offender." Contracts between parties were valid, Jones argued, as long as they were voluntary, but "it certainly becomes involuntary the moment the person desires to withdraw, and then is coerced to remain and perform service against his will." He also pointed out that the peonage statute did not cover simple imprisonment, "assault and battery," or other such offenses that did not involve holding a man for debt.[10]

Jones then outlined the many practices that did constitute peonage.

[9] Reese to Attorney General, June 15, 1903, ff 5280–03, ibid.
[10] *Peonage Cases*, 123 F. 678–81 (M.D. Ala. 1903).

Most of his examples included contract violations. First, Jones ruled, an employer could not hold a laborer by force to perform a contract.[11] Then he struck at one of the most popular methods used in Coosa and Tallapoosa counties, charging the jury that an employer who falsely accused a man of a crime and told him that in order to escape conviction he must enter into a contract had violated the peonage law. Both the judge and the employer who took the peon could be held for violating the law, he warned. He then instructed the jury that a properly convicted defendant, who entered into a contract with his employer assuming court costs and fines, could be worked—but only up to the terms of the contract signed in court. Jones warned the jurors not to confuse the informal practice of "confessing judgment" with signing a contract by written approval of the court, for the former practice did not entitle the employer to hold the defendant against his will.[12] Under the law the jury should convict a magistrate who knowingly fines innocent victims in order to provide employers with labor. After pointing out more technicalities, Jones labeled a 1901 Alabama contract-labor law unconstitutional. The statute in question punished a laborer if he broke a contract with one employer and then signed a contract with a second party without first informing his former employer. "One of the most valuable liberties of man is to work where he pleases, and to quit one employment and go to another, subject of course to civil liability for breach of contract obligations," he ruled. Jones branded this contract law "a vicious species of class legislation" and argued that it was "designed solely in the interest of the employer or landlord."[13] If Jones believed that men would change their behavior if they only knew the path of right conduct, his charge was a model, for it sternly sifted the wheat from the chaff.

Having Jones's explanation before it, the grand jury continued to hand down indictments. Every few days from April through June a marshal would trek to Coosa or Tallapoosa County and take in one of the alleged peon-masters, justices of the peace, constables, or overseers. In mid-July, when the grand jury released its final report, it had found

[11] Ibid., p. 682.
[12] See *U.S.* v. *Reynolds*, 235 U.S. 133.
[13] *Peonage Cases*, 123 F. 682–88. For an unfavorable critique of Jones's charge, see "The Peonage Cases," *Harvard Law Review* 17 (Dec. 1903), 121–22.

ninety-nine true bills involving eighteen offenders.[14] To dampen the interest of the Northern press, the *Montgomery Advertiser* expressed relief that the grand jury found peonage "in but two counties and involving only eighteen persons." The *Advertiser* claimed that this was a "triumphant refutation" of the distortions in "certain newspapers."[15] If there is slavery, the *Advertiser* seemed to say, look at the small amount of it, not at the fact that it exists forty years after it was abolished.

What bothered the editors of the *Montgomery Advertiser* and surely upset Southern politicians was the vociferous Northern attack on Southern injustice to blacks. The *New York Evening Post*, for example, pointed out that the peonage indictments were "instructive if unwitting confessions that the question of justice to the negro is and must be national." The *Nation*, indignant at what it considered a revival of antebellum slavery, complained that at least chattel slaves were "fed and housed and clothed, after a fashion; but these new Alabama slaves are sometimes worked naked and barely kept from starvation." On June 6 *Outlook* gave an account of one charge against constable Robert Franklin and denounced him for "being a party to a revolting system of enslaving helpless negro laborers." A week later the same journal condemned planter John W. Pace, constables, and marshals for running "an inhuman form of slave catching and slaveholding." While castigating the culprits, the Northern press praised the Southern men who were involved in cleaning up these practices, singling out Judge Jones for special praise.[16] Yet the old demon was there; would not those few Southerners who battled peonage need Northern support? The vision of neo-abolitionists descending into the South and meddling in local affairs undoubtedly conjured up a grandfather's tale of the old South or a father's frightening story of Reconstruction; indeed, such meddling could challenge the white South's violently won right to control blacks. The alternative was to press through with the cases, minimizing the extent of peonage.

While the *New York Evening Post* had its own correspondent pres-

[14] *Montgomery Advertiser*, July 18, 1903, p. 7.

[15] Ibid., p. 4.

[16] *New York Evening Post*, June 2, 1903, p. 6; "The Nation and the Negro," *Nation* 76 (June 4, 1903), 448; "Illegal Forced Labor in Alabama," *Outlook* 74 (June 6, 1903), 301–2; "Peonage in the South," *Outlook* 74 (June 13, 1903), 391. See also *New York Evening Post*, June 12, 1903, p. 7.

ent in Montgomery, *Outlook* requested information of Booker T. Washington. When the peonage cases came to the attention of *Outlook* editor Lyman Abbott, he informed Washington that if the reports he had received were true, the situation deserved "vigorous condemnation." Informing Washington that *Outlook*, which had serialized Washington's autobiography, *Up from Slavery*, had "spoken the best word we can for the South," Abbott declared that he was in a "better position to condemn injustice." Assuring Washington that his name would not be mentioned, Abbott asked the black educator to send "facts in this matter for our editorial use." Later a member of the *Outlook* staff thanked Washington for his information, adding that the material "practically gave us our second editorial on this subject."[17]

No doubt Washington also encouraged vigorous coverage of the peonage cases by the *Evening Post*. On June 16, 1903, Washington wrote to Oswald Garrison Villard, reminding him of the competent work that Judge Jones was doing, and he told Villard that they all owed Jones "a great debt of gratitude for what is being done in regard to exposing the peonage system in Alabama." Even educator Edgar Gardner Murphy, who wrote two letters defending the white Southerners while condemning peonage, informed Washington of his stand on the matter.[18] As was his wont, Washington carefully straddled the sectional fence.

After much investigation and press coverage, John W. Pace emerged as the arch-villain in the Alabama peonage cases. No novelist, except perhaps Harriet Beecher Stowe, could have constructed a figure as nefarious as Pace. Weighing 275 pounds and standing six feet tall, he walked the land dressed in "a homespun shirt without a collar and a broad-brimmed black hat."[19] The *Evening Post* correspondent described him as "a grave, animal-like person, with two feet almost eaten off with disease, with fingers which are expected to drop away within a year, and to whom life itself is declared by law counsel to be a matter of no

[17] Lyman Abbott to Washington, May 28, 1903, Box 248; Charles B. Spahr to Washington, June 23, 1903, Washington Papers, Box 270.

[18] Washington to Villard, June 16, 1903, Box 249; Murphy to Washington, [June 16?] 1903, ibid., Box 267. For Murphy's letters, see *Montgomery Advertiser*, June 19, 1903, p. 9; *New York Evening Post*, July 20, 1903, p. 7. For editorial comment, see *New York Evening Post*, July 20, 1903, p. 6. See also Hugh C. Bailey, *Edgar Gardner Murphy: Gentle Progressive* (Coral Gables, 1968), pp. 121–24.

[19] *Montgomery Advertiser*, May 30, 1903, p. 1.

more than four years." The *Evening Post* correspondent could not help adding that Pace was "quite like the slave-whipping characters of 'Uncle Tom's Cabin.' "[20] Pace obtained his power from his position as contractor for convict labor in Tallapoosa County, a position he had held for twenty years despite complaints against him dating back to 1886.[21] "Having always some legal convicts on his plantation," the *Evening Post* reporter explained, "he found it easy, with magistrates and constables under obligations to him, to mix among them a lot of black men and women guilty of nothing and accused of nothing."[22]

Pace's deeds led the grand jury to indict him on some thirty-six counts of either peonage or conspiracy to deprive Negroes of their rights by placing them in peonage.[23] Constables with blacks in tow invariably checked with Pace to ascertain if he needed extra labor; if not, the constables would consult other landowners of Tallapoosa County. By this method Pace kept a large labor force of valid convict-lease prisoners and also the victims that local constables brought in for minor infractions, men supposedly on bond. Pace made no distinction between those on bond and the genuine prisoners, as he placed them all under the gun.[24]

Pace's system encompassed all the laborers on his domain, keeping them in peonage by accusing them of some infraction as their term of imprisonment ended. On Pace's plantation James M. Kennedy served as justice of the peace. In one case, five or six Negroes came before Kennedy for "harboring a runaway." The Cosbys, a family of large landowners, notified Pace that they wanted several of the blacks, for they were good workers. Pace told Kennedy to keep the cases off the docket

[20] *New York Evening Post*, June 25, 1903, p. 7.

[21] *Montgomery Advertiser*, Dec. 17, 1903, p. 2; *New York Evening Post*, July 8, 1903, p. 7. See also Booker T. Washington's observations of a Tallapoosa County convict farm in 1886, a testimony to the enduring nature of the system, in Washington to *Southern Workman*, Feb. 18, 1886, in *Southern Workman* 15 (Apr. 1886), 47.

[22] *New York Evening Post*, July 8, 1903, p. 7.

[23] Parsons to Attorney General, June 4, 1906, ff 5280–03, Dept. of Justice, NA, RG 60. The indictments were drawn under the then-current U.S. *Code*, secs. 5526 and 5508. For an example of the kinds of contracts that Pace drew up, see the numerous contracts in *Peonage Cases*, 123 F. 671, FRC, Georgia.

[24] Affidavit of John W. Pace, May 11, 1903, *Peonage Cases*, 123 F. 671, FRC, Georgia.

but to go through the formality of a trial. After the mock proceeding Pace and the Cosbys led the unsuspecting blacks to think that they had been through a legitimate trial and had drawn fines and costs. Pretending friendship, Pace and the Cosbys allowed the laborers to sign contracts. They were then divided and put under guard on the respective farms. If there were laborers on the Cosby farm that Pace wanted, W. D. Cosby opened his justice of the peace court, and similar proceedings took place. "In other words," Kennedy revealed, "it was sort of understood, that I was to try the men that Cosby wanted, and Cosby was to try the men that Pace wanted."[25] The *Evening Post* correspondent wrote on June 29 that upon contemplation of the plantation owners in that area one "comes to think of them as half feudal in a mediaeval way, and half Western after the lurid fashion of 'nickel library' romances." An editorial from the same newspaper the next day concluded that the "trouble with the back counties of Alabama is not so much bad laws as bad men."[26]

With the first Pace case ready for trial and the Northern press in attendance, the stage was set for the South to either prove it could handle the labor problems involving black laborers or fall under the condemnation of the neo-abolitionists. As court convened on June 22, Judge Jones first read the peonage law to the jury, instructed them of their duty, and finally ruled out concealed weapons in the courtroom. The trials began quietly enough. Wily old John W. Pace pled guilty to eleven counts of peonage after Judge Jones overruled demurrers. Pace, however, secured a writ of error, hoping to appeal his case at a later time. Jones sentenced him to five years for each of the eleven counts, the sentences to run concurrently.[27] By pleading guilty, Pace prevented the entire story of his role from becoming public and, as central as he was to the Tallapoosa County peonage conspiracy, inexplicably faded into the background. The *Evening Post* justly praised the "completeness of the proof which the Federal prosecuting officers had amassed." Pace "has been a sort of combination of feudal baron and wholesale slavedriver in the county which was the scene of his operations." The *Evening Post* also praised Jones, "himself a Southerner," and predicted

[25] Grand jury testimony of James M. Kennedy, May 28, 1903, ibid. See also complaints in ibid.

[26] *New York Evening Post*, June 29, 1903, p. 1; June 30, 1903, p. 6.

[27] *Montgomery Advertiser*, June 23, 1903, p. 7; June 25, 1903, p. 5.

that the "moral value" of Pace's conviction would "count tremendously."[28] The anxious Southerners had won the first round.

The court continued to work its way through the ninety-nine indictments. George D. Cosby and his nephew Barancas accounted for forty-five of the indictments. The Cosbys had tried to arrange a deal with Judge Jones that they would only receive a fine, but Jones balked. Finally, they decided to plead guilty and chance a jail sentence. The *Montgomery Advertiser* vividly portrayed the scene: "The two Cosbys, uncle and nephew, their bright eyes downcast, and their fine well-shaped heads bowed, stood at the bar and pleaded guilty to the charges preferred by the Government." Judge Jones reprimanded them for their offenses against black laborers and added that the two defendants had "prostituted the authority of God and of this State in the administration of justice." Each of the men received a sentence of a year and a day in the Atlanta penitentiary. It was too much for twenty-three-year-old Barancas Cosby; he wept as Jones delivered the sentence.[29]

As the cases revolving around John W. Pace and the Cosby family illuminated peonage in Tallapoosa County, a case involving Glenny Helms exposed the corruption in Coosa County and the role of the deputies who delivered peons to Tallapoosa County landowners. On April 25, 1902, eighteen-year-old Glenny Helms and two friends were passing through Goodwater in Coosa County on their way to Columbus, Georgia. Night marshal John G. Dunbar arrested the blacks for vagrancy; the next morning he took them before the mayor, who fined them $6.60 each, a fine they could not pay. Dunbar then took them to the neighborhood in Tallapoosa County where John W. Pace and J. Fletcher Turner, a forty-six-year-old farmer and sawmill owner, resided. Pace declined to take them but suggested that Turner might be interested. Finding Turner near a store, Dunbar asked $50.00 for the three victims. Turner balked, saying that he did not want those "cigarette dudes," and they settled for $40.00. Dunbar then went back to Goodwater and paid the mayor $19.80 and pocketed the profit.[30]

[28] *New York Evening Post*, June 25, 1903, p. 6.
[29] Warren Reese, Jr., to Attorney General, June 30, 1903, ff 5280–03, Dept. of Justice, NA, RG 60; *Montgomery Advertiser*, June 23, 1903, p. 1. See also ibid., June 11, 1903, p. 3.
[30] *Montgomery Advertiser*, June 9, 1903, p. 1. See also testimony of Fletcher Turner, May 12, 1903, *Peonage Cases*, 123 F. 671, FRC, Georgia.

Once on the Turner farm, Helms and his two friends were worked under guard and received occasional beatings. Dunbar told Turner that the sentence for the blacks was four and one-half months. Before the term of service expired, Helms attempted to escape, but the guards caught him and took him back. Helms somehow got word to his father that Turner was holding him, and his father sent L. E. White, a retired retail merchant from Columbus, Georgia, to free his son. White reported that the blacks were working at a sawmill and were practically naked. Turner said that Helms and his companions could leave if White would pay him $50. White declined and left but later returned and paid $46 for the three laborers. Turner got the best of the bargain, for he got the labor of three blacks for four months and received six dollars more than he had originally paid.[31]

Unlike Pace and the Cosbys, sawmill owner Fletcher Turner decided to stand trial for his alleged offenses. The first indictment concerned the case of Glenny Helms. On July 7 Helms took the stand and told his story. "His demeanor was that of bravado rather than of fright," reported the *Advertiser*, "and he was at all times self-possessed and self-conscious." The next day, night marshal John G. Dunbar, the officer who sold Helms to Turner, took the witness stand and confessed the entire story. After Dunbar finished his account of selling the blacks to Turner, the defense lawyer asked, "Is it not a fact, Mr. Dunbar, that you saw an opportunity to put some money down in your jeans?" "Well, yes," the night marshal replied, embarrassed, "if you want to put it that way."[32]

Turner's lawyers argued that the three blacks volunteered to hire out to Turner instead of serving a jail sentence. To bolster the case against the black laborers, several character witnesses (including Thomas Heflin, then secretary of state of Alabama) praised Turner's good character. In the end, however, the defense rested upon the fact that Turner was white. "Are you going to brand Fletch Turner as a convict," Turner's lawyer asked the jury in closing, "on such testimony from three negroes and one sorry white man?"[33]

Judge Thomas G. Jones, anxious to secure a guilty verdict in this

31 *Montgomery Advertiser*, July 8, p. 5; July 9, 1903, p. 1. See also statement of L. E. White, May, 1903, *Peonage Cases*, 123 F. 671, FRC, Georgia.
32 *Montgomery Advertiser*, July 8, 1903, p. 5; July 9, 1903, p. 1.
33 Ibid., July 10, 1903, p. 7.

first peonage case to come to trial, reminded the jurors of the fact that blacks were more than the semi-citizens that the defense had charged. He also asked the jury to ignore the inevitable allusions to the Civil War by both sides. Then Jones outlined the case for the jury, stressing that the facts of the case showed that Turner had broken the peonage law. "The question between us and God and our consciences is can we rise above our prejudices, if we have them, so far that we as white men are able and willing to do a negro justice."[34] When the jurors later returned to get a clarification of the contract law, Jones in effect instructed the jury to return a guilty verdict. "There cannot be any voluntary contract in the eye of the law made in this country by which a man surrenders his liberty and his person to the dominion of another to secure an obligation," Jones warned, "if in consequence of that obligation and claim the man is forced to do labor against his will to pay that debt or obligation. The law steps in, and says to people who attempt it, You shall not do it."[35]

After debating the merits of the case for several days, the jury on July 13 failed to agree on a verdict, standing seven to five for conviction. Then Jones reprimanded the jury, arguing that it "has divided and declined to enforce the laws for no other reason than the base one that the defendant was a white man and the victim of the law he violated is a negro boy."[36] Judge Jones expressed disappointment at the hung jury, for he had undoubtedly counted on a guilty verdict to prove that black men could secure justice in a Southern court—that, once men knew the law, they would see their errors.[37] Jones had seriously underestimated both racial prejudice and the custom of exploiting black labor.

While Jones probably hoped that a guilty verdict would blunt criticism by the Northern press, the attack came from another direction. On July 18 thirty-four-year-old Thomas Heflin, a rising champion of the rural masses, spoke to a picnic crowd of some 2,000 Sons of the Confederacy at Luverne, Alabama. The vitriolic Heflin branded as lies the attacks of the Northern press, and then, showing how seriously Jones had miscalculated local sentiment, he turned on Jones, a symbol of the

[34] Ibid., July 11, 1903, p. 7.
[35] "Peonage: A Significant Mistrial," *Outlook* 74 (July 25, 1903), 733.
[36] *Montgomery Advertiser*, July 14, 1903, p. 1; "Peonage: A Significant Mistrial," p. 733. See also, "The Case of Turner Ended," *Outlook* 74 (Aug. 1, 1903), 772–73.
[37] *New York Evening Post*, July 15, 1903, p. 6.

planter class. Jones's charge to the jury, said Heflin, was "wholly un-called for and out of place and it tended in my judgment to intimidate rather than enlighten, to trespass on the domain of the jury, and to usurp its function." Warming to his subject and his audience, Heflin said that some of the jurors had fought in the Civil War and did not need any judge to tell them about their duties. He continued his at-tack throughout the summer, but the *Montgomery Advertiser* defended Jones, calling Helflin's attack a political sally against a defenseless judge who could not speak for himself.[38]

Heflin had hardly gotten his attack launched when Turner pled guilty on July 20. His lawyer explained that Turner was technically guilty of peonage, though the sawmill owner did not understand the law when he broke it. The cruelty charges, the lawyer argued, were unfounded. Jones then fined Turner $1,000—the lightest sentence allowed under the law.[39]

The *New York Evening Post*, in the abolitionist tradition, took the occasion to give some moral preachments. Hitting the South in its most sensitive spot, the editorial charged that the peonage cases "illustrate very clearly the need of outside criticism, if the South is to be held up to its duty towards the negro race." The South's insistence on being "let alone during slavery days was as familiar a theme as the price of cotton." Had the North not intervened, the editorial charged, the South "would have been economically and morally ruined ere this." The way to end the criticism of the South, it pontificated, was "by the triumph of justice within her borders."[40] With their consciences salved, the neo-abolitionists, as had their forebears, quickly retreated back North after winning a symbolic victory, and the Alabamians were left alone with their peonage problems. Though neo-abolitionist sermons did not set well with Southerners, rhetoric digested better than actual meddling.

[38] *Montgomery Advertiser*, July 19, 1903, p. 10; July 21, p. 4; Aug. 6, p. 4; Aug. 7, 1903, p. 4.
[39] Reese to Attorney General (telegram), July 20, 1903, ff 5280–03, Dept. of Justice, NA, RG 60; *Montgomery Advertiser*, July 21, 1903, p. 1. The cruelty charges stemmed from grand jury testimony. Allen Turner allegedly beat a black woman to death while she was working out her fine. See testimony of John Davis, James M. Kennedy, A. E. Shealey, and Pat Hill, May 28, 1903; Ephram Pope, June 6, 1903; Dr. George W. Vine, June 12, 1903; *Peonage Cases*, 123 F. 671, FRC, Georgia.
[40] *New York Evening Post*, July 24, 1903, p. 6.

One other case reached the jury in the series of cases tried in Montgomery in the summer of 1903. Again the principals were from the Coosa-Tallapoosa area. Robert Franklin, dubbed "the kidnapping constable," took some blacks from a notary public and sold them to John W. Pace. The notary, W. H. Cous of Clay County, swore that he did try several blacks for "false pretense" in order to recover money forwarded to them for transportation. After the grand jury indicted Franklin, a lawyer who worked for the lumber company instructed Cous to change the docket. He did so, but he failed to destroy the old docket and produced it on the witness stand. Pat Hill, a native of Roanoke, Virginia, told of being informed by a labor agent of sawmill work in Hollins, Alabama. The Sample Lumber Company would pay transportation, board, lodging, and $1 a day wages. Arriving in Hollins, Hill was put to work grading a railroad, compelled to buy his own meals, and given a shanty with no bed. He fled but was stopped in Goodwater and carried back to Hollins, fined $5 for leaving, and then carried to Pace's farm by Franklin. There he signed a contract to work for seven months. Hill stated that he was whipped and kept under guard.[41]

In contrast to the *Turner* case, the jury on July 25 found Franklin guilty. Judge Jones fined Franklin $1,000. Elated at the guilty verdict, the *Montgomery Advertiser* sanguinely predicted that "we have witnessed the passing of peonage in Alabama." The *Advertiser* seized the guilty verdict and stated that Alabama "stands today without a stain upon her escutcheon in this matter."[42] Now both Northern and Southern consciences were cleansed. On July 27 District Attorney Reese boasted that the government had "convicted every man that we put on trial, either by pleas of guilt or by a verdict of guilty."[43]

After the Franklin verdict, Justice Department attorneys attempted to further destroy peonage throughout the state, though state officials claimed that the worst was over. But while Thomas Heflin attacked

[41] "Peonage in the South," *Outlook* 74 (June 13, 1903), 391; *Montgomery Advertiser*, July 22, 1903, p. 3. See also July 23, p. 7; July 24, p. 8; July 25, 1903, p. 7, ibid. Another justice of the peace testified before the grand jury on June 6 that "on March 20th my store was destroyed. My docket was destroyed in the fire" (testimony of A. J. Jenkins, *Peonage Cases*, 123 F. 671, FRC, Georgia).

[42] *Montgomery Advertiser*, July 26, 1903, pp. 4–5. See also "Southern Sentiment Concerning Peonage," *Outlook* 74 (Aug. 1, 1903), 772.

[43] Reese to Attorney General, July 27, 1903, ff 5280–03, Dept. of Justice, NA, RG 60.

Jones for reminding Civil War veterans of their duty, the U.S. attorney at Mobile informed the attorney general on August 4 that there were an estimated fifty more cases of peonage in Monroe and Wilcox counties.[44] Even as Heflin continued to go "about the state like a roaring lion" conjuring up Civil War memories, and Governor William D. Jelks whistled New South and minimized the amount of peonage, a report from Coffee County announced that Bob English, a white man, had been held in peonage.[45] Southern politicians had conditioned their constituents to respond to the myths of the Old South, the lost cause, the New South, and white supremacy. Peonage, an embarrassing reality, was too similar to slavery to ever become a political issue, so politicians took the easier road and denied that it existed, thereby preserving the myth.

Yet the *English* case, arising in south Alabama's Coffee County, illustrated not only the extent of peonage throughout the state but also that a poor man, whatever his color, could become a victim. Noah J. Prestwood had threatened Bob English with jail unless he signed a contract to work out $50 to pay for a small fire which he had allegedly set in Prestwood's orchard. On August 30 the *Advertiser* attempted to explain that the case was unique, emphasizing that the trouble happened in an isolated part of the country and that Prestwood operated a store, farm, and turpentine still, giving him economic control over the area. The *Advertiser* also reported that English could not write, that he had eleven children, and that the members of his family were "strangers to a square meal." Ironically, the story continued, the constable in Coffee County who drew up English's contract could not sign his name or read or write. "How he manages to execute papers is not known, unless the justices he serves, or some one else, make the returns for him; yet he was elected by the voters of his beat."[46] The old elements of isolation, ignorance, and vulnerability had combined, and Bob English slipped into peonage. As surely as English's desperate circumstances proved typical of peons, the outcome of the case typified peonage prosecutions. A

44 M. D. Wickersham to Attorney General, Aug. 4, 1903, ibid.
45 E. P. McAdams to John E. Wilkie, Aug. 28, 1903, ibid.; *Montgomery Advertiser*, Aug. 29, p. 7; Sept. 2, 1903, p. 3.
46 *Montgomery Advertiser*, Aug. 29, p. 7; Aug. 30, 1903, p. 14.

grand jury indicted Prestwood on January 16, 1904, but the case was nol-prossed on July 28, 1906.[47] Justice Department officials left no evidence as to why they dropped the case.

Peonage in Alabama thus stretched far beyond the borders of Coosa and Tallapoosa counties. The center of the system, according to a June, 1903, report from Reese, existed in the heart of the black belt in Lowndes County, just south of Montgomery. "This county, it is claimed, is honeycombed with slavery," Reese related. Lowndes County Sheriff J. W. Dixon and his friends had a reputation for being ruthless and reputedly "killed several men." "These Dixons are men of the highest political and financial influence not only in Lowndes county but in the State of Alabama," Reese explained. "They are large planters and control a great deal of labor." Reese gave a typical story of the methods of Sheriff Dixon and his allies. Dixon paid the fine of Dillard Freeman, a black laborer, and then Freeman signed a contract. Theoretically free on bail, Freeman insisted that Dixon allow him to visit his sick brother at his mother's house several miles down the road. Dixon refused the request several times, and finally Freeman walked off one day to see his ailing brother. While Freeman was visiting his family, Will Dixon and Bob May appeared and "beat the boy in the presence of his mother unmercifully with a pistol until he was bloody." After this Dixon put a rope around Freeman's neck and part carried, part dragged, and part beat him back to the farm. There Dixon whipped the laborer until he grew weary and gave the gin belt to another man who whipped him "nigh unto death." Then Dixon chained him to a bed, and two days later, despite the condition of his back, put him in the fields.[48]

When Dillard Freeman appeared to testify before the grand jury in Montgomery, Bob Dixon met him in the hallway of the courthouse and "he said if I wanted to live I had better tell what he told me," Freeman remembered. Not content with intimidating Freeman, five Dixon brothers visited one of the Lowndes County blacks on the grand jury at midnight and demanded to know what was going on in Montgomery. The Dixons reminded the juror that he had to live in Lowndes County "and

---

[47] Statement of all peonage cases since May 1, 1902, by J. W. Dimmick, clerk, U.S. District Court, Middle District, Ala., file 50-1-0, Dept. of Justice, NA, RG 60.
[48] Reese to Attorney General, June 15, 1903, ff 5280-03, ibid.

if he did not stand up for his own people he knew what to expect." Reese explained that Lowndes County Negroes "are practically compelled to prejudice their souls because they fear their lives."[49] At first such intimidation caused Dillard Freeman to deny that he had been beaten or held against his will. Later, promised federal protection, he told the entire story. Nevertheless, the Dixons escaped indictment.[50]

The violence and threats in Lowndes County also thwarted Justice Department investigations. In February, 1904, federal examiner Stanley Finch toured Alabama and discovered that one of the Alabamians whom Reese had recommended as an investigator had "been spending a considerable portion of his time at Troy, Alabama, his private residence, charging the Government with his meals and lodging." The same was true of Deputy Marshal J. W. Barnes, Finch observed. The reason, he concluded, was that the tough men from Dallas and Lowndes counties sent out word that it would be unhealthy for investigators to go there. The hotbed of peonage remained inviolate.[51] Later, one of Reese's most able assistants unwittingly (according to his testimony) held two positions under the Justice Department. Though the confusion may have been as much bureaucratic inefficiency as an attempt to get more pay, the Justice Department dismissed him.[52]

Finch, who toured the South, reported in 1903 that peonage "is a very extensive practice throughout this 'black belt,' and that it is by no means confined to a few isolated communities. Reese, of course, agreed with Finch and referred to "hundreds of other cases" and "hundreds of these people in this district who are held in abject slavery." And the caseload confirming these descriptions continued to mount. Reese reported in the fall of 1903 that four Coffee County men were to be taken before a U.S. commissioner for peonage. Later the men were

[49] Testimony of Dillard Freeman, June 6, 1903, *Peonage Cases*, 123 F. 671, FRC, Georgia; Reese to Attorney General, June 15, 1903, ff 5280–03, Dept. of Justice, NA, RG 60.

[50] Testimony of Freeman, June 6, 1903, *Peonage Cases*, 123 F. 671, FRC, Georgia; Russell to Attorney General (memo), n.d. [1907?], ff 5280–03–3, Dept. of Justice, NA, RG 60.

[51] Stanley Finch to Attorney General, Feb. 18, 1904, ff 5280–03, Dept. of Justice, NA, RG 60.

[52] See Attorney General to all concerned, Nov. 21, 1905; Julius Sternfield to Attorney General, Nov. 22, 1905; Acting Attorney General to Sternfield, Nov. 29, 1905; Roosevelt to Attorney General, Feb. 18, 1906, ff 5280–03, ibid.

held on bonds of $500 each.[53] From Birmingham, U.S. Attorney Thomas A. Roulhac wrote at about the same time that "peonage is about done here," but he noted that there was a case from Marion County, "a most flagrant one of holding both white and black to involuntary servitude, accompanied with extreme harshness and severity." The *New York Times* on September 27 reported four cases occurring in Lamar County. Even three men from Coosa County, where the evil was supposedly quashed, made the sad trip to Montgomery to make bond.[54] Several other cases emerged before the federal court convened in Montgomery in January, 1904.

Contrasted with the electric atmosphere in Montgomery in the summer of 1903, the January session of federal court was dull. As Robert W. Franklin and R. M. Pruett of Goodwater pled guilty and received the minimum $1,000 fine (which Jones suspended), "the sentencing was of the same outward appearance as the sentencing of a moonshiner." Though several other men were indicted for peonage, the issue failed to receive the attention that it had six months earlier.[55] Peonage trials had thus become institutionalized like bootlegging. Men would break such laws, and the community understood.

Judge Jones, in keeping with his philosophy of exposing evil and then allowing men's consciences to be their guides, gave out very lenient sentences and fines to all the men convicted in the peonage cases. As of February, 1904, two persons had been jailed for thirty days each, two served three months, and three others paid fines totaling $500.[56] Though fines and sentences were levied in profusion, Jones's mercy was also abundant, as he often suspended the sentences and modified the fines.

In keeping with his lenient attitude toward the convicted men, Jones recommended a pardon for the Cosbys. Jones explained to his friend Booker T. Washington that his motivation for recommending this

[53] Finch to Frank Strong, June 23, 1903; Reese to Attorney General, June 15, Sept. 5, 1903, ff 5280–03, ibid.; *Montgomery Advertiser*, Sept. 12, 1903, p. 8.
[54] Roulhac to Attorney General, Sept. 12, 1903, ff 5280–03, Dept. of Justice, NA, RG 60; *New York Times*, Sept. 27, 1903, p. 3; *Montgomery Advertiser*, Oct. 7, 1903, p. 5.
[55] *Montgomery Advertiser*, Jan. 7, p. 7; Jan. 19, 1904, p. 12.
[56] Finch to Attorney General, Feb. 18, 1904, ff 5280–03, Dept. of Justice, NA, RG 60.

pardon went beyond simply extending mercy to them. "The object of all good men now," he wrote, revealing his paternalistic-progressive thinking, "is to lessen the friction between the races & to put the blacks especially on as high a plane as possible. Would or would it not confound those who are filled with low hates," Jones inquired of his black friend, "if the representatives of the negro race, should publicly take the ground that it had no desire, now that the system was broken up, for vengeance, or to subject the families of the men who are now in prison, to the suffering that they inflicted on others." Jones admitted that he had not thought the matter through completely and, carefully pointing out to Washington that the letter was "for your eye only," asked him for his advice. Later Jones informed Washington that he had forwarded the recommendation for pardon and was pleased that so many blacks had joined in backing it. "I would be glad," Jones urged on September 10, 1903, "if you would write the president, though not *as upon suggested by me*, on the subject."[57]

On September 16, 1903, President Roosevelt pardoned the Cosbys. The *Montgomery Advertiser* reported that the men had suffered enough. "The law has been thoroughly vindicated," it argued with premature optimism, "and the evil against which it was directed, in these communities, has been completely crushed." The *Advertiser* stressed that the supposedly wealthy Cosbys were relatively poor and had large families that were plagued with sickness. Later a visitor to President Roosevelt reported that the pardons came "wholly on the advice of Judge Jones."[58]

The fate of John W. Pace furnished the final irony of the case. On August 9, 1903, even while the cases against him were pending appeal, a grand jury in Tallapoosa County reported that Pace had earlier prevented a woman from testifying before the grand jury. "We do not hesitate to say," the county grand jury continued, "that it is our opinion that John W. Pace and his convict farm are more responsible by far than all others in our county, for the abuse of ignorant and helpless people, which is a crime known as peonage in the Federal Court." Neither the rumors of mistreatment of convicts nor the conviction

[57] Jones to Washington, Aug. 17, 1903, Box 262; Sept. 10, 1903, Washington Papers, Box 261. Italics in original.

[58] *Montgomery Advertiser*, Sept. 17, p. 5; Nov. 4, 1903, p. 5.

for peonage prevented the county commissioners of Tallapoosa County from awarding Pace his yearly contract for convicts. The *Montgomery Advertiser* on December 17, 1903, protested against allowing Pace to continue his convict farm and urged Governor William D. Jelks to find some remedy for "this unseemly act."[59]

Besides continuing business as usual in Tallapoosa County, Pace managed to delay his case in the courts. On June 18, 1904, a year after his conviction, the attorney general queried Reese about the *Pace* case; he had heard nothing since Pace went free on $5,000 bail.[60] A year later the Circuit Court of Appeals in New Orleans affirmed the judgment of the lower court, agreeing that the five-year sentence should stand. But Reese informed the attorney general that, because of Pace's age and "owing to the sloughing of his feet from frostbite in his youth," execution of the sentence would "amount to practically capital punishment." Pace had not gone to jail because his pardon was pending, though he should actually have begun serving his sentence before the pardoning process began, the attorney general ruled. Yet he remained free on bail until he received his pardon in April, 1906.[61] John W. Pace, unscathed by the entire episode, managed to escape imprisonment and fine and continued to carry on his convict system in Tallapoosa County. Custom counted immeasurably in the backcountry, and Pace had used cunning in breaking the lances of both the Justice Department and Jones.

A few years later, Charles W. Russell, assistant attorney general and expert on peonage, summarized the Alabama peonage cases of 1903. Judge Thomas G. Jones, he wrote, "created the impression that peonage was all over in the middle district of Alabama, and that the prosecutions were abandoned in the belief that a sufficient lesson had been learned and that no more peonage would occur." Russell then caustically reviewed the net results: four persons had served a combination of five months in jail and others had paid aggregate fines of $500. At the time that Russell wrote his review, he was in the midst of another case in Alabama concerning immigrants held in peonage. With a tone of finality and frustration Russell declared that Jones's policy of "pardoning every

[59] Ibid., Aug. 9, p. 1; Dec. 17, 1903, p. 2.

[60] Attorney General to Reese, June 18, 1904, ff 5280–03, Dept. of Justice, NA, RG 60.

[61] Reese to Attorney General, Dec. 2, 1905; Attorney General to Reese, Dec. 8, 1905; Parsons to Attorney General, June 4, 1906, ibid.

one on a general promise of good behavior, was a failure."[62] Jones, as well as other well-intentioned knights of justice in the Progressive era, made a fatal flaw in his reasoning: he believed that public exposure and disgrace alone would perfect human nature. But local custom and racism, anchored in ignorance, poverty, and apathy, demanded more than an experiment in leniency before it would yield.

[62] Charles W. Russell to Attorney General, n.d. [1907?], ff 5280–03, ibid.

CHAPTER IV

The Alonzo Bailey Case

Booker T. Washington and Alonzo Bailey never met, yet their lives interacted in dramatic fashion. Though they were both black, they were as unlike in their conditions as the prince and the pauper. Washington, an educator and politician, lived in the ethereal realm of presidents, millionaires, journalists, and "best" Southern whites. Bailey, a peon and agricultural worker, existed in the "other America" at the bottom of the social order. He lived the life of a toad under the harrow. As Washington personified the heights that a Negro could achieve, Bailey plumbed the black man's depths of misery. Yet Washington's compassion for Bailey—not as an individual, but as a long-sought symbol of injustice—led him into a secret effort to test the Alabama contract-labor law that had brought Bailey from freedom into peonage. The *Bailey* case not only revealed peonage, as lifting a rotten log exposes the crawling life underneath, but also illuminated the secret life of Booker T. Washington. The Tuskegeean's life bent to the wind, accommodating to the oppression of the era's social weather, but the *Bailey* case signified that in at least one instance Washington made his unique contribution to civil rights.

Following the exposé that made Alabama the peonage capital of the nation in 1903, official reports of peonage in Alabama diminished. Complaints, however, indicated that the institution persisted. The seclusion of the plantations, collusion between local law officers and planters, and the violence that visited those who threatened the peonage system shielded the institution from view. After the brief 1903 neo-abolitionist crusade in Alabama many of the critics of Southern labor practices retired to the North to attack the ills besetting cities. Yet throughout the

South there remained a form of legal peonage. Though much peonage existed outside the law and even in defiance of law, largely invisible, nearly all Southern states passed restrictive contract-labor laws. These laws clearly revealed Southern attitudes toward the problem of black labor. The Southern employer's request for a binding contract, first expressed during the years of Reconstruction and constantly reiterated, eventually became reality.

The labor law that ensnared Bailey was but one of many ways that a laborer could fall into peonage. "The tendency of the legislative enactments of this State since the Reconstruction period," observed U.S. Attorney Erastus J. Parsons, "has been uniformly, to weave about the ignorant laborer, and especially the blacks, a system of laws intended to keep him absolutely dependent upon the will of the employer and the land owner."[1] The enactment of the laws coincided with the other proscriptive laws of the 1890s regarding the civil and political rights of blacks. The law that sent Bailey to jail, similar to laws in other Southern states, had originated in 1885 and had been called a "false pretenses" law. It read that if a laborer signed a contract, obtained an advance in money intending fraud, and then left his job without repaying the money, he should be punished "as if he had stolen it."[2] Prosecution under the law rested on the intent of the laborer. Unless he intended to defraud the employer when he signed the contract, he could not be convicted of a criminal offense but could only be sued in a civil action for breach of contract. In the 1890s the Alabama Supreme Court insisted that intent to defraud had to be proven. As illustrated by a series of cases won by laborers, this was no easy task.[3]

[1] Erastus J. Parsons to Charles J. Bonaparte, Mar. 7, 1908, file 50–162–5, Dept. of Justice, NA, RG 60.
[2] Alabama *Code*, 1886, Sec. 3812. (This measure followed Sec. 3811, "False Pretenses.") "Same under contract for performance of act of service. Any person, who, with intent to injure or defraud his employer, enters into a contract in writing for the performance of any act or service, and thereby obtains money or other personal property from such employer, and, with like intent, and without just cause, and without refunding such money, or paying for such property, refuses to perform such act or service, must, on conviction, be punished as if he had stolen it."
[3] In *Ex Parte Riley*, 94 Ala. 82, for example, Enoch Riley signed a contract binding his son Ben to work out a $60 advance. Ben left without working the contracted ten months, and T. J. Counters, who lent the money, prosecuted Enoch

The defeat of the Federal Elections Bill of 1890, Booker T. Washington's Atlanta speech in 1895, and the *Plessy* v. *Ferguson* separate-but-equal decision in 1896 were omens of coming interdictions. When the Southern states finished their anti-black legislation early in the twentieth century, the black man's burden weighed him down with second-class restrictions. The vote, first-class travel, good jobs, and justice were all denied to most Southern blacks.

Consistent with the oppressive trend, the Alabama legislature amended the contract-labor law in 1903, plugging the loophole that allowed a laborer to escape conviction. This action was typical of the trend in other Southern states, for the legislatures of Georgia (1903) and Florida (1907) passed almost identical laws. The laborer's taking the money and failing either to pay it back or work it out, the new Alabama restriction read, "shall be prima facie evidence of the intent to injure or defraud his employer."[4] As a result of the amendment, the prosecution did not have the burden of proving the motive of the laborer. Taking the money and not paying it back served as evidence of fraudulent intent, making conviction easier. In 1907 the Alabama legislature spelled out the punishment for violating the law. The laborer would be fined "double the damage suffered by the injured party, but not more than $300.00."[5] An Alabama rule of evidence absolutely prohibited testimony from a laborer indicted under this law, making conviction under the contract-labor law almost certain.[6] "This simply means," explained Booker T. Washington, "that any white man, who cares to charge that a Colored man has promised to work for him and has not done so, or who has gotten money from him and not paid it back, can have the Colored man sent to the chain gang." Peonage disturbed the Tuskegeean, and it probably caused him more personal concern than disfranchisement and segregation. His optimistic formula for success that combined obsequiousness and hard work would never work if peonage persisted. Though

---

Riley under the law. The Alabama Supreme Court held that there was no evidence introduced to show that Riley had fraud in mind when he signed the contract. For other cases bearing on the law, see *Copeland* v. *State*, 97 Ala. 30; *Thompson* v. *State*, 97 Ala. 78; *Jackson* v. *State*, 106 Ala. 136; *Dorsey* v. *State*, 111 Ala. 40.

[4] Georgia *Laws* 1903, pp. 90–91; Florida *Laws* 1907, c. 5678; Alabama *Laws* 1903, pp. 345–46. The latter law was passed on Oct. 1, 1903.

[5] Alabama *Laws* 1907, pp. 636–37. See also Alabama *Code*, 1907, Sec. 6845.

[6] Brief for Plaintiff (by Edward Watts), p. 7, *Bailey* v. *Alabama*, 211 U.S. 452.

he had previously expressed passing interest in court battles concerning the Jim Crow car, he energetically fought against debt slavery.[7]

The contract-labor law disturbed not only Booker T. Washington but also whites both in Alabama and in the North. William H. Thomas, city court judge in Montgomery since 1901, had watched with misgivings the operation of the law. Even before Washington committed himself to fighting the law, Thomas had attempted to strike it down in his court. In a 1905 case involving the law in question, he instructed the jury that the 1903 amendment regarding prima facie evidence was unconstitutional. The Alabama Supreme Court upheld the measure, however, arguing that the legislature had the right to establish what was prima facie evidence so long as it did not make such evidence conclusive.[8] Thomas complained to Washington on January 17, 1907, that had the case been appealed to the U.S. Supreme Court it would have been reversed. What spurred Thomas's letter was another case that came before the Alabama Supreme Court involving the same law. He hoped that Washington would help secure financial support for an appeal, but the black educator failed to push the case.[9]

Thomas continued to look for a test case, however. On April 14, 1908, Alonzo Bailey, a black agricultural worker, petitioned for a writ of habeas corpus in Thomas's court, charging that the contract-labor law was unconstitutional. Bailey had been jailed eight days earlier and would have perhaps gone to the chain gang had not his wife appealed to Edward S. Watts, a young Montgomery attorney.[10] Bailey's predicament typified the plight of many black agricultural workers in the South. H. C. Borden, manager of the Riverside Company, complained that Bailey signed a contract in his presence on December 26, 1907, binding him to work as a farm laborer for a year at the Scotts Bend

[7] Washington to Oswald Garrison Villard, Sept. 7, 1908, Washington Papers, Box 42; August Meier, *Negro Thought in America, 1880–1915: Racial Ideologies in the Age of Booker T. Washington* (Ann Arbor, 1963), pp. 110–14.

[8] *State* v. *Thomas*, 144 Ala. 77; Thomas to Washington, Jan. 17, 1907, Washington Papers, Box 7.

[9] Thomas to Washington, Jan. 17, 1907, Washington Papers, Box 7. The case that Thomas heard was *State* v. *Vann*, 43 So. 357. In this case the Alabama Supreme Court, pointing out the earlier case, ruled that the law did not establish imprisonment for debt; the laborer "cannot be convicted without fraudulent intent, whether he does or does not repay the money."

[10] *Bailey* v. *State*, 158 Ala. 22; Ray Stannard Baker, "A Pawn in the Struggle for Freedom," *American Magazine* 72 (Sept. 1911), 609.

Place in Montgomery County. As usual in such cases, Bailey secured an advance on his wages. The $15.00 advance was to be repaid on the basis of $1.25 per month from Bailey's $12.00 monthly salary. He worked a month and three or four days and then quit.[11] The act of leaving the farm without repaying the money, according to the contract-labor law, was prima facie evidence of intent to defraud the Riverside Company; and the Alabama rules of evidence prohibited him from explaining his reason for leaving. Judge Thomas, feeling bound by the earlier rulings of the Alabama Supreme Court, denied the petition for habeas corpus. Watts appealed.[12]

With the case underway, a group of interested white citizens in Montgomery began a secret collaboration to raise money and win influential friends to the cause. Having substantial influence with federal officials and with the Northern press which could pave the way for a successful appeal, Booker T. Washington at nearby Tuskegee served as coordinator of the group. By aiding in the battle to defeat peonage, he was perhaps secretly attempting to atone for what his public accommodation had encouraged. Even before the Alabama Supreme Court ruled on the case, Washington—carefully keeping his support of the case secret—sent Ernest T. Attwell, the business agent at Tuskegee Institute, to talk with Judge Thomas. Attwell reported on June 24 that "the court official in Montgomery" thought that the case had a good chance of reaching the U.S. Supreme Court if enough money could be raised for expenses. He estimated the cost of appeal at $200 to $300, and he urged Washington to hurry and raise the money, for the state supreme court would hear the case in a few days. "He is very anxious," Attwell warned Washington, "that you not be known in the transaction, and that his connection with it be kept secret."[13] When working on civil rights issues during this era of repression, both Washington and

[11] Transcript of Record, p. 4, *Bailey* v. *Alabama*, 211 U.S. 452. See also unidentified brief, *State* v. *Bailey*, file 21790, Appealed Casefiles of the Department of Justice, NA, RG 267.

[12] Baker, "A Pawn in the Struggle for Freedom," p. 609. One interesting question that never came out in the courts was whether or not Bailey received his pay for his first month's work. If so, he had paid $1.25 on his debt, for it was to be automatically taken out of his pay. If not, it appears that Bailey had nearly worked off the advance.

[13] Washington to Thomas, June 16, 1908, Washington Papers, Box 383; Attwell to Emmett J. Scott, July 6, 1908, ibid., Box 583.

his white collaborators found it imperative to keep their identities secret.

Not surprisingly, the Alabama Supreme Court upheld the constitutionality of the law for the third time, reiterating that its purpose was "to punish fraudulent practices, not the mere failure to pay a debt."[14] Bailey's lawyer Edward Watts again appealed the case, this time to the U.S. Supreme Court.

Washington then began energetically assembling support for the case. Fred Ball, another Montgomery attorney and former law partner of Thomas, joined Watts in Bailey's defense. Federal District Judge Thomas G. Jones also took an active interest. Hoping to gain Northern financial and press support, Washington furnished Judge Thomas with a list of his prominent friends. This was not the first time he had called on them. Thomas later wrote that he had contacted men in New York and was hopeful of support.[15] Washington asked Oswald Garrison Villard, his close friend and editor of the *New York Evening Post*, "to assist in the matter." The black educator explained the case to neo-abolitionist Villard, adding that his own pocketbook "has been drawn upon in so many directions, that I can do nothing at present." Villard replied that he could not help financially either, for he had been "squeezed dry." He offered support, however, in the columns of the *New York Evening Post*. "You see," he confided to Washington, "this is precisely the kind of a case for which I want my endowed 'Committee for the Advancement of the Negro Race.'" "Sooner or later," he prophesied, "we must get that committee going."[16] A year later he helped found the National Association for the Advancement of Colored People, but, despite the persistence of peonage following the *Bailey* case, that crusading organization only briefly and unsuccessfully dealt with peonage. Villard's decision to help organize a Northern association marked a shift in approach from individual to institutional action; Washington's effort to help Bailey was his last secret gambit into civil rights and probably the last major civil rights case backed by a lone black leader.

Meanwhile, Thomas G. Jones confidentially wrote to President Theodore Roosevelt that the *Bailey* case was in good hands and praised the

<hr />

14 *Bailey* v. *State*, 158 Ala. 18.

15 Thomas to Washington, n.d. [1908]; Washington to Thomas, Aug. 5, 1908, Washington Papers, Box 383.

16 Washington to Villard, Sept. 7, 1908; Villard to Washington, Sept. 10, 1908, ibid., Box 42. See also Villard to Washington, Jan. 27, 1908, ibid.

efforts of Watts and Ball. Jones wanted the young lawyers to get all the credit for the case, he said, though he made clear to the President that he had helped write the briefs. Simultaneously, Jones wrote an official letter to the President explaining that "if this statute, with the *presumption* of leaving and fact which it authorizes from the mere fact of *quitting the service*, is upheld, we will at last have a constitutional system of peonage."[17]

Booker T. Washington, anxious for a successful appeal, feared that the young duo of Watts and Ball might lack the experience to win the case before the U.S. Supreme Court. Washington asked Thomas if perhaps a lawyer of national reputation might give the case a better chance. Thomas replied that such an arrangement would be "satisfactory."[18] Washington then appealed directly to Attorney General Charles J. Bonaparte. He informed the Attorney General of the efforts of the "philanthropic white men of this state" but asked "if it will be possible for the Attorney General's office to interest itself in some way so that the matter may be thoroughly probed." Bonaparte, whose efforts to crush peonage were primarily aimed at immigrants, replied that the "Bailey case had already been brought to the attention of the Department by the President, and I have instructed a competent Attorney to review it carefully and to give me a memorandum as to appropriate procedure on the part of this Department." Jones's earlier appeal had brought support from President Roosevelt. Washington passed the good news along to Thomas.[19]

The secret collaboration continued as time drew near for the case to be heard before the Supreme Court. Thomas remained in close contact with Booker T. Washington, who forwarded briefs and messages to Bonaparte.[20] Later Thomas praised the efforts of Fred Ball, informing the attorney general directly that the case would not have been "able to proceed further than the Alabama Supreme Court" had Ball not

[17] Jones to Roosevelt, confidential, Oct. 2, 1908; Jones to Roosevelt, Oct, 2, 1908; ff 143691, Dept. of Justice, NA, RG 60. Italics in original.

[18] Washington to Thomas, Oct. 1, 1908; Thomas to Washington, n.d. [1908], Washington Papers, Box 363.

[19] Washington to Bonaparte, Oct. 20, 1908; Bonaparte to Washington, Oct. 23, 1908, Box 365; Washington to Thomas, Oct. 23, 1908, ibid., Box 383.

[20] Thomas to Washington, Nov. 3, 1908, ibid., Box 383; Washington to Bonaparte, Nov. 3, 1908; Bonaparte to Washington, Nov. 5, 1908, ff 143691, Dept. of Justice, NA, RG 60.

pushed it. The mutual praise among Bailey's secret white backers was understandable; they knew that when federal judgeships or other jobs opened, the government would first reward its friends.[21]

Despite the careful preparation, the Supreme Court on December 21, 1909, decided that "the trouble with the whole case is that it is brought here prematurely by an attempt to take a short cut." The decision, read by Justice Oliver Wendell Holmes, sidestepped the constitutional issue, arguing that a jury trial might have brought out evidence that Bailey had fraudulent intent when he entered the contract with the Riverside Company. The Supreme Court sent the case back to Alabama for jury trial.[22] As in the *Clyatt* case, the *Bailey* case brought forth a dissent from Justice John Marshall Harlan. After reviewing the history of the case, he wrote that if "that statute is repugnant to the Constitution and laws of the United States it is void, and the accused is deprived of his liberty in violation of Federal law." Joined in the dissent by William R. Day, he disagreed with the majority, arguing that the direct appeal through the habeas corpus petition did not deny the Supreme Court jurisdiction in the case.[23]

There was nothing to do but begin all over again. In February, 1909, the collaborators attempted to raise $600 for a new test of the law. The white Alabamians raised $200 while Ray Stannard Baker, a leading muckraker and author of *Following the Color-Line*, headed the fundraising campaign in the North. Baker secured $150 from William J. Schieffelin, a close friend of Booker T. Washington's and descendant of abolitionists. Editor Lawrence Abbott gave $100, and Baker contributed the remaining $150 himself.[24] Abbott, however, expected something in return. He asked Thomas to inform him of "the present status of the case" and to give him "a little information as to the support of the contract labor law, honest and dishonest in Alabama and neighboring southern States." Abbott promised to use the information in his *Outlook*

21 Thomas to Bonaparte, Nov. 5, 1908, ff 143691, Dept. of Justice, NA, RG 60. See also Washington to Bonaparte, Nov. 10, 1908; Bonaparte to Thomas, Nov. 11, 1908; Bonaparte to Washington, Nov. 12, 1908, ibid. For a hint of the political overtones, see Washington to Thomas, Feb. 19, 1909, Washington Papers, Box 900.

22 *Bailey* v. *Alabama*, 211 U.S. 455.

23 Ibid., p. 457. See *Clyatt* v. *United States*, 197 U. S. 222.

24 Schieffelin to Baker, Feb. 2, 1909; Baker to Lawrence Abbott, Feb. 3, 1909; Abbott to Baker, Feb. 5, 1909, Ray Stannard Baker Papers, Manuscript Division, Library of Congress, Washington, D.C., Series 2, Box 92.

magazine "without the slightest reference to your name." The fund-raising campaign remained so secret that even lawyer Fred Ball did not know the source of the money.[25]

Thus, a year after the original push for the *Bailey* case began, the backers of the defendant found themselves in the same exhausting position of preparing briefs and gathering support. President William H. Taft had replaced Theodore Roosevelt; thus the Justice Department had to be wooed again. Fred Ball wrote to Attorney General George W. Wickersham on June 18, 1909, and reminded him that former Attorney General Bonaparte had been helpful in the *Bailey* case. Because the case had been sent back for trial, Ball informed Wickersham of the new developments in the case. It had been tried again in the city court, Ball informed him, and appealed to the Alabama Supreme Court, where it was affirmed. Ball hoped to have a writ of error prepared soon and appeal the case again to the U.S. Supreme Court. Wickersham told Ball that he would be glad to hear more on the case.[26]

Local conditions had changed also. Erastus J. Parsons, a young lawyer who had exposed the peonage system in Tallapoosa County in 1903, had taken over as district attorney in Montgomery, and he had not been sounded out on the *Bailey* case. Thomas warned Booker T. Washington that Parsons might attempt to get credit for the case at the expense of Fred Ball and Edward Watts. On the other hand, Thomas suspected treachery and speculated that Parsons had told Alabama state officials of the U.S. attorney general's interest in the case, causing the state officials to be more careful in their preparation. Washington seemed unperturbed about Parsons and replied, "It certainly is a fine thing to have men in Alabama who stick to a case of this kind in the way that is now being done for the single reason that they want to see justice done."[27]

Unlike the first appeal to the Supreme Court, the second appeal became involved in numerous delays. Bailey himself disappeared, for like

[25] Abbott to Thomas, Feb. 5, 1909; Thomas to Baker, Feb. 13, 1909, ibid. See also Thomas to Washington, n.d. [Jan. 1909]; Washington to Thomas, Jan. 3, 1909, Washington Papers, Box 900.

[26] Ball to Attorney General, June 18, 1909; Attorney General to Ball, June 30, 1909, ff 143691, Dept. of Justice, NA, RG 60. The case was *Bailey* v. *State*, 161 Ala. 75.

[27] Thomas to Washington, n.d. [July 1909]; Washington to Thomas, July 3, 1909, Washington Papers, Box 399.

Dred Scott a half century before, he was only a cipher. The *Bailey* case, like other peonage cases before it, seemed to lose energy as time passed.[28] As preparation went forward again to present a tight case before the high court, Judge Thomas felt the sting of his activism, for in early 1910 he lost his elective seat on the Montgomery city court.[29] Lamenting to Washington, he blamed his opponents for the "liquor and labor contract stories they circulated." He asked Washington if he could do something, perhaps help Fred Ball to get the vacant district attorney's post, for "it might ultimately mean help for me getting on my feet again." Meanwhile, Thomas continued his support of the *Bailey* case.[30]

As the fall of 1910 approached, Fred Ball and Edward Watts began a contest to decide who would argue the case before the Supreme Court. Both had done much to get the case before the Court, though Thomas G. Jones affirmed to Attorney General Wickersham that Ball had "furnished the sinews of war for the briefs." Both men could have appeared, had not the Justice Department decided to submit a brief and oral argument amicus curiae. Thomas thought that Ball should represent Bailey, since Watts was "a very bright but very young man." Judge Jones also backed Ball but noted that Watts, who secured the case originally, "naturally wished to make one of the oral arguments himself." Ball gallantly but reluctantly yielded to Watts.[31] It was no small thing for a young lawyer from Montgomery to appear before the Supreme Court.

Eventually seven briefs were submitted to the Supreme Court as it

---

[28] *Clyatt* v. *United States*, 197 U.S. 207, for example, continued from 1901 to 1905. The Alabama cases of 1903 began as a dramatic exposé of slavery, but interest in peonage quickly diminished.

[29] Ball to Assistant Attorney General, Jan. 31, 1910; Assistant Attorney General to Ball, Feb. 5, 1910; Assistant Attorney General to Ball, May 2, 1910, ff 143691, Dept. of Justice, NA, RG 60.

[30] Thomas to Washington, n.d. [noted by Emmett J. Scott, Washington's secretary, Mar. 4, 1910], Box 596; Thomas to Washington, n.d. [noted Dec. 1, 1910], Box 399; Thomas to Washington, n.d. [noted Sept. 1910], Washington Papers, Box 413; Thomas to Wickersham, Sept. 17, 1910, ff 143691, Dept. of Justice, NA, RG 60.

[31] Jones to Wickersham, confidential, Oct. 11, 1910; Thomas to Wickersham, Oct. 2, 1910, ff 143691, Dept. of Justice, NA, RG 60. See also Ball to Attorney General, Sept. 22, 1910; Ball to Assistant Attorney General, Oct. 6, 1910; Assistant Attorney General to Ball, Oct. 10, 1910, ibid.

heard the case on October 20 and 21, 1910.[32] Alabama Attorney General Alexander M. Garber and his assistant Thomas W. Martin presented the Alabama case. They defended the law, arguing that the Alabama Supreme Court had "consistently held that the purpose of the statute was to punish fraudulent practices and not the mere failure to pay a debt." The Alabama officials went on to claim that the law did not offend the Fourteenth Amendment or due process, citing numerous cases to support their argument. Obviously hoping to return to Alabama with part of their law intact, they argued that the fraud provision of the statute and the restriction on testimony were separate laws.[33]

The five briefs submitted in defense of Bailey were thorough but repetitious. As Jones had observed, Fred Ball's brief supplied the "sinews of war." "The real object of the statute," Ball wrote, was "... to enable the employer to keep the employee in involuntary servitude by the overhanging menace of prosecution which he knows must be successful on account of the artificial presumption or rule of evidence making the quitting prima facie evidence of the crime, which is practically conclusive because the defendant cannot testify in his own behalf as to his unexpressed intent." The rule of evidence, he noted, "denies to plaintiff-in-error his right to trial by jury because it arbitrarily overcomes the presumption of his innocence and gives him no fair opportunity to rebut the prima facie evidence of his guilt."[34] Ball added that the law was vague, denied the equal protection of the laws, and led to involuntary servitude.[35]

Having argued the case, the Bailey supporters sat back to await the decision of the Supreme Court. Reflecting upon the vast amount of work that it took to present the case, Thomas sent Washington a set of the briefs that the lawyers had used. "I am surprised at the immense amount of work involved in this case," Washington replied, "and I am

[32] U.S. Supreme Court Records and Briefs, No. 300, Vol. 219, *Bailey* v. *Alabama*, 219 U.S. 219.

[33] *Bailey* v. *Alabama*, 219 U.S. 219.

[34] Brief for Plaintiff (by Fred Ball), pp. 20, 42, *Bailey* v. *Alabama*, 219 U.S. 219. Original quotations were in italics.

[35] Ibid., pp. 32–42. See also Supplemental Brief for Plaintiff (by Fred Ball); Brief for Plaintiff (by Edward Watts); Brief for the Attorney General as Amicus Curiae; Supplemental Brief for the Attorney General as Amicus Curiae, *Bailey* v. *Alabama*, 219 U.S. 219.

sure that all of us are deeply grateful to you and your friends for the tremendous amount of unselfish and generous service you have put into it." Washington promised to send the briefs to "some friends," perhaps a vague reference to someone who could give Thomas a job. Thomas, who more than anyone kept the momentum of the case going, related to Washington that he was still on a $750 bond for the first Bailey appeal and $250 for the latter. "I hope we will win & not take the risk of procedure by the State," he concluded.[36]

On January 3, 1911, Justice Charles Evans Hughes delivered the opinion in *Bailey* v. *Alabama*. He reviewed the process of the lower courts as it had progressed. The decision tore through the superfluous issues of Bailey's color raised by Bailey's defenders and the prosecution's charge that the case was sectional in nature.[37] The case rested upon the question of fraud. Yet, the decision pointed out, there was "not a particle of evidence of any circumstance indicating that he made the contract or received the money with any intent to injure or defraud his employer." He had even shown good faith, for he had worked for over a month.[38] "In the absence, however, of evidence from which such inferences may be drawn," Hughes wrote, "the jury are not justified in indulging in mere unsupported conjectures, speculations, or suspicions as to intentions which were not disclosed by any visible or tangible act, expression or circumstances."[39] Because he could not testify, Bailey was "stripped by the statute of the presumption of innocence, and exposed to conviction for fraud upon evidence only of breach of contract and failure to pay." Countering the claim by the Alabama Supreme Court that the jury would ascertain the facts of the case and find a verdict warranted by those facts, Hughes stated that in this case no such evidence was introduced to show fraudulent intent.[40]

Hughes, agreeing with the defense, summed up what the Court saw as the "natural operation" of the law. "The state may impose involuntary servitude as a punishment for crime," he wrote, "but it may not compel

---

[36] Thomas to Washington, Nov. 2, 1910; Washington to Thomas, Nov. 11, 1910; Thomas to Washington, n.d. [noted by Scott on Nov. 14, 1910], Washington Papers, Box 913.

[37] *Bailey* v. *Alabama*, 219 U.S. 231.

[38] Ibid., p. 236.

[39] Ibid., p. 233.

[40] Ibid., p. 236.

one man to labor for another in payment of a debt, by punishing him as a criminal if he does not perform the service or pay the debt." He then hit at the circumvention of the law ruling that what "the state may not do directly it may not do indirectly." Finally, Hughes noted that the law served as an "instrument of compulsion peculiarly effective as against the poor and the ignorant, its most likely victims." Ignoring the questions raised about the due-process provisions of the Fourteenth Amendment, Hughes declared the Alabama contract-labor law unconstitutional solely on the basis of its violating the peonage statute passed under the provisions of the Thirteenth Amendment.[41]

Justices Oliver Wendell Holmes and Horace H. Lurton dissented. Holmes, showing a tender regard for both sectionalism and the rights of employers, wrote the dissent, claiming that had New York passed a similar law it would have been found constitutional and that the prima facie rule was not conclusive. He argued that states could pass laws that motivated the laborer to practice right conduct. He also argued that the jury would ascertain enough facts to dismiss the case if there were no fraudulent intent. In essence, Holmes argued that a state did have the right to pass a contract law such as the one his colleagues struck down; such a law, he concluded, did not violate the Thirteenth Amendment.[42]

Elated at the "great victory," Booker T. Washington thanked Attorney General Wickersham, adding a word of praise for the unemployed Thomas. Then he began urging his friends in the Northern press to publicize the matter. William Hayes Ward, editor of the *In-*

[41] Ibid., pp. 244–45.

[42] Ibid., pp. 245–50. Holmes's conclusion read: "To sum up, I think that obtaining money by fraud may be made a crime as well as murder or theft; that a false representation, expressed or implied, at the time of making a contract of labor, that one intends to perform it, and thereby obtaining an advance, may be declared a case of fraudulently obtaining money as well as any other; that if made a crime it may be punished like any other crime; and that an unjustified departure from the promised service without repayment may be declared a sufficient case to go to the jury for their judgment; all without in any way infringing on the 13th Amendment or the statutes of the United States." For a critique of Holmes's dissent, see "Constitutional Law—Violation of the Thirteenth Amendment," *University of Pennsylvania Law Review* 60 (Feb. 1912), 336–38. For a brief sketch of the *Bailey* case, see Waite, "The Negro in the Supreme Court," pp. 264–66. See also "Labor Contract and the Thirteenth Amendment," *Harvard Law Review* 24 (Mar. 1911), 391–93; "Criminal Enforcement of Contracts for Labor as 'Involuntary Servitude,'" *Columbia Law Review* 11 (Apr. 1911), 363–65.

dependent, thanked Washington for reminding him of the importance of the case and volunteered to print an article on peonage in the Gulf states if Washington or someone who knew the conditions could furnish some facts. Washington complied.[43] He then wrote to Walter Hines Page, editor of *World's Work*, enclosing the briefs of the *Bailey* case and promising to send an article later.[44]

Many of the men involved in the case were upset that William Thomas had invested so much and lost his job as a result. Thomas remained in contact with Washington, telling him of several articles on the *Bailey* case. Washington replied that the editorial in the *Independent* "you may be interested to learn was prepared here."[45] Washington continued to express concern over Thomas's ill fortune. He informed Lyman Abbott of Thomas's defeat in the judgeship election and asked if "the clerkship in Judge Thomas G. Jones court is to be vacant soon." Thomas, Washington wrote, "has the idea that Colonel Roosevelt could see his way clear to drop Judge Jones a letter in his interest that would result in his being appointed to this clerkship." Thomas took it upon himself to write Roosevelt, obliquely mentioning that he had been "the judge who first declared the statute bad, and tried the case, and was recently defeated on this, among other arguments."[46] After practicing law privately for several years, Thomas won a seat on the Alabama Supreme Court in 1915.

Most white Alabamians did not share the elation of Washington's band of supporters. Such a decision could be expected from the U.S. Supreme Court, lamented Southern whites; they predicted trouble with black labor as a result. One writer for the *Montgomery Advertiser* made much of Oliver Wendell Holmes's dissent and agreed that had New York passed the same law, it would have stood.[47] H. C. Borden,

---

[43] Washington to Wickersham, Jan. 7, 1911, ff 143691, Dept. of Justice, NA, RG 60; Washington to Ward, Jan. 6, 1911; Ward to Washington, Jan. 13, 1911; Washington to Ward, Jan. 18, 1911, Washington Papers, Box 445. See also "The Last Traces of Peonage," *Independent* 70 (Jan. 26, 1911), 213–14.

[44] Washington to Page, Feb. 9, 1911, Washington Papers, Box 53. See also "The Case of Alonzo Bailey," *Outlook* 97 (Jan. 21, 1911), 101–4.

[45] Thomas to Washington, Feb. 9, 1911; Washington to Thomas, Feb. 13, 1911, Washington Papers, Box 443.

[46] Washington to Abbott, Jan. 16, 1911, ibid., Box 6; Thomas to Roosevelt, Jan. 20, 1911, Theodore Roosevelt Papers, Series 1, Box 155.

[47] C. S. Partridge, "Labor Contract Law Defended," *Montgomery Advertiser*, Jan. 11, 1911, pp. 1–2.

who first bound Alonzo Bailey to the contract, predicted that the Negro laborer would be the "real sufferer." If the system of advances disappeared, he predicted, "I expect to see acute conditions in some sections of the State as a result of the far reaching decision of the Supreme Court." The *Advertiser* also incorrectly reported that because of the *Bailey* decision a Negro could "sign a contract to perform a service, receive his money and immediately leave that service, without the employer having any recourse of law, however fraudulent the intent might be when the laborer signed the contract."[48] Employers could sue employees in a civil action if they broke a contract, but collecting damages from impoverished workers would be difficult. Such a dilemma no doubt led to the enactment of the contract-labor law in the first place.

Despite the grim predictions of Southern whites and though Thomas had lost his seat on the bench, the compact group that had pushed the case had won a substantial victory. In the face of opposition from the Alabama Supreme Court and with no sympathy from the governor of Alabama or the large landowners of the state, they had managed to raise money, secure legal talent, win publicity from the Northern press, and take the case to the Supreme Court twice. The group must have had a good private laugh when William Hayes Ward editorialized in the *Independent* of January 26, 1911: "As far as can be learned, no negro or Northern man took a hand in the fight."[49] Part of the tragedy of this case, and of the South generally, however, was that Booker T. Washington kept his identity in civil rights activities secret. Even Washington's most severe critics did not learn of the secret role that the great accommodator played. Indeed, the secrecy of the entire group suggested that they all enjoyed playing Washington's complicated game of deception. Perhaps cooperating with and helping black men led both Southern and Northern whites to take on some of the invisibility of their black friends.

Despite the *Bailey* decision, peonage continued, not only in Alabama but throughout the South. Yet in Alabama the laws that sanctioned the practice were gone. Though the Alabama legislature passed a contract-labor law in 1911 only months after the *Bailey* decision, it carefully

[48] Ibid., Jan. 4, 1911, pp. 1, 4.
[49] "The Last Traces of Peonage," p. 214.

avoided violating the ruling of the Supreme Court.[50] Three years later, in *U.S.* v. *Reynolds*, the Supreme Court held unconstitutional an Alabama law that allowed an employer to take a man from jail after paying his fine and work him as a prisoner. The case arose not from any outside group or even from Booker T. Washington, but from local Justice Department attorneys who objected to the oppressive practice.[51] By 1914, then, the statutes of Alabama had been purged of the legal basis for peonage. While Alabama complaints of peonage dropped off abruptly and other states revised their contract laws, complaints continued to pour in to the Justice Department from neighboring Georgia and Florida. The difference was that there the contract-labor laws continued on the books for another thirty years. The Supreme Court struck down Georgia's contract-labor law in 1942, and that of Florida in 1944.[52]

The results of the *Bailey* case were not spectacular, but they were nevertheless significant. Future court battles regarding civil rights often came from large, organized efforts. Despite the persistence of peonage and even spectacular exposés in the 1920s and 1940s, however, neither the Justice Department nor a civil rights or labor group finished what Bailey's supporters began in 1911. Peonage continued to the 1940s and beyond, and the legal basis for the practice endured thirty years after the precedent-setting *Bailey* case had been decided. When Justice Robert Jackson handed down the decision that crushed the Florida contract-labor law in 1944, he quoted the 1867 federal statute prohibiting peonage and then stated: "Congress thus raised both a shield and a sword against forced labor because of debt."[53] But for many agricultural workers less fortunate than Alonzo Bailey, the federal weapons had proved impotent.

[50] Alabama *Laws*, 1911, pp. 93–94.

[51] *United States* v. *Reynolds*, 235 U.S. 133. See pp. 26–28, above.

[52] *Taylor* v. *Georgia*, 315 U.S. 25; *Pollock* v. *Williams*, 322 U.S. 4. See *State* v. *Armstead*, 103 Miss. 790 (1913), and *State* v. *Oliva*, 144 La. 51 (1918). Though South Carolina had its labor contract held unconstitutional by both a federal ruling (*Ex parte Drayton*, 153 F. 986 [1907]) and a state ruling (*Ex parte Hollman*, 79 S.C. 9 [1908]), the *Taylor* v. *U.S.* (244 F. 321 [1917]) decision again made the law constitutional. The efforts of U.S. Attorney Francis H. Weston to appeal the case raise the question of the Wilson Administration's interest in peonage, as Solicitor General John W. Davis informed Weston that a technicality forbade appeal. See Weston to Attorney General, Aug. 11, 1917; Davis to Weston, Aug. 25, 1917; Weston to Davis, Sept. 1, 1917; Davis to Weston, Sept. 7, 1917, file 50–372, Dept. of Justice, NA, RG 60.

[53] *Pollock* v. *Williams*, 322 U.S. 8.

Ray Stannard Baker, who had raised money for the *Bailey* case, did not predict that peonage had been crushed by the favorable ruling. In a 1911 review of the case in *American Magazine*, Baker printed a picture of Bailey standing hat in hand, dressed in his work clothes. "Look well at the dull black face," Baker wrote, "and you will see there the unmistakable marks of ignorance, inertia, irresponsibility." He described Bailey as a "pawn" and compared him with Dred Scott, noting that Bailey was "a sort of symbol in this new struggle for freedom." Baker concluded prophetically that as long as "so many negroes are densely ignorant and poverty stricken, and while so many white men are short-sighted enough to take advantage of this ignorance and poverty, so long will forms of slavery prevail."[54]

[54] Baker, "A Pawn in the Struggle for Freedom," pp. 608, 610.

CHAPTER V

The Land Where It Never Snows

Until 1906 most peonage cases had involved black Americans, but immigrants who traveled to the sunny South in search of the American dream quickly discovered that they were just as vulnerable. Schemes to lure immigrant labor into the South were not new, but in 1906 Southern employers stepped up their efforts to find a supplementary labor supply.[1] Employers secured their immigrants primarily from New York labor agents, who improvised a variation on the unlawful European contract-labor scheme. Taking $3.00 a head from Southern firms, the agents packed the unsuspecting laborers into guarded trains or ships and forwarded them south, often to desolate turpentine stills or isolated railroad camps.[2]

Poverty-stricken, usually speaking only their native tongue, easily exploited, and looking for the golden dream of American wealth, they furnished the backbone for much of American industrialization as they were herded into factories and fell victim to ghetto conditions and discrimination. Lured to the South ("the land where it never snows") by promises of high wages and good accommodations, many of the immigrants undoubtedly had grave apprehensions when they saw their

[1] See Rowland T. Berthoff, "Southern Attitudes toward Immigration, 1865–1914," *Journal of Southern History* 17 (Aug. 1951), 328–60; "Southern Peonage and Immigration," *Nation* 85 (Dec. 19, 1907), 557; Alfred H. Stone, "The Italian Cotton Grower: The Negro's Problem," *South Atlantic Quarterly* 4 (Jan. 1905), 42–47.

[2] For such a bargain regarding immigrant labor, see S. S. Schwartz to Atlanta & St. Andrews Ry Co., n.d.; Atlanta & St. Andrews Bay Railway Company to J. C. Horton, Apr. 17, 1906, file 50–162–8, Dept. of Justice, NA, RG 60. See also evidence in the case *United States* v. *Sabbia, Triay and Others*, unreported case, copy in Box 083, ibid. Hereafter cited as *U.S.* v. *Sabbia*. See also Louis S. Posner to Mary Grace Quackenbos, Dec. 7, 1907, file 50–162–5, ibid.

desolate surroundings and were completely disillusioned when they put in their first day of backbreaking work. But all these misfortunes did not approach the supreme disappointment of discovering that their bosses had charged more for transportation and had paid less wages than their contract called for, or that in their first week on the job they owed the commissary more than their first week's paycheck. And so they collapsed into the familiar pattern of debt as the boss demanded that they pay their charges before leaving their jobs; they became peons.

The major investigation of immigrant peonage began not in the South but in New York. Mary Grace Quackenbos, an attorney for "The People's Law Firm," appealed to the attorney general on July 24, 1906. Enclosing several complaints from immigrants with her letter, she urged the Justice Department to stop a peonage trial in Florida because she knew of several potential witnesses who had escaped to New York. Not satisfied with the action of the Justice Department, Quackenbos on August 1 appealed directly to President Theodore Roosevelt. "I represent the poor of the lower East Side and in an endeavor to trace certain men and boys who have not been heard of for months and who are apparently lost, I am intending to go to Florida this week," she announced.[3] A wealthy woman in her own right, Quackenbos had thrown her substantial energy into aiding the poor following her divorce several years earlier. By October, 1906, her investigations both in New York and in Florida had made her so valuable to the Justice Department that she secured an appointment as a special assistant U.S. attorney, the first woman to hold such a position. "She is an enthusiast & intelligent," wrote Assistant Attorney General Charles Wells Russell.[4]

Russell, born in 1856 in Wheeling, headed Justice Department investigations of peonage. A graduate of Georgetown University, he began his federal career in 1886 as a clerk in the Bureau of French Spoliation Claims, and from 1902 to 1905 he was special assistant to the attorney general in charge of insular and territorial affairs. In 1905

[3] Quackenbos to Attorney General, July 24, 1906; Quackenbos to Theodore Roosevelt, Aug. 1, 1906, file 50–162–1, ibid.

[4] Quackenbos to Attorney General, Nov. 2, 1906; Acting Attorney General to Henry L. Stimson, Nov. 14, 1906, file 50–162–1, ibid.; Stimson to Henry M. Hoyt, Oct. 27, 1906; *New York American*, May 13, 1908, clipping in Appointment and Credentials Files; Russell to W. H. Moody, Oct. 23, 1906, file 50–162–1, ibid.

Russell became assistant attorney general, having in the meantime gained wide experience in his private and government law practices.[5] When the Justice Department became interested in combating immigrant peonage in 1906, the attorney threw his experience and ability into the fight.[6] Though some of the investigators and attorneys found her too energetic for their tastes, Russell recognized Mary Grace Quackenbos's ability to win the confidence of the poor, an indispensable aid in securing affidavits from peons. Accompanied by interpreters, the duo plunged into the peonage camps of the South to free the peons and to bring the employers and labor agents to trial.

F. J. O'Hara, the peon-master who had first attracted Quackenbos's attention, superintended a sawmill at Buffalo Bluff and a naval stores operation at Maytown, both in northeast Florida. The work in either place required endurance, even had there been no compulsion. The felling and hauling of trees to the mill, the danger of working near the buzzing saw, and the weight of freshly cut lumber all demanded men who could stand heavy physical labor. Notching trees and collecting the gum in a turpentine camp also required endurance and strength.

A vivid picture of immigrant peonage emerged from the affidavits gathered by attorneys Quackenbos and Russell, as the woods seemed to ring with threats of death, random brutality, beatings, exploitation, and anti-Semitism. For example, twenty-four-year-old Hyman Kahn, a native of Russia, complained that once he had been ill and unable to work. O'Hara and Kirt Sanders, an ex-sailor foreman who bore an American shield-of-arms tattoo on his breast and a skull-and-crossbones

[5] Charles W. Russell, oath of office, Appointment and Credentials Files, ibid.; *Register of the Department of Justice*, 16th ed. (Washington, 1906), pp. 13, 213; Attorney General to Russell, Feb. 25, 1902, Appointment Book 5, p. 172, Dept. of Justice, NA, RG 60.

[6] *Register of the Department of Justice*, 23rd ed. (Washington, 1915), p. 230. In 1909 Russell was appointed U.S. envoy extraordinary and minister plenipotentiary to Persia. There he aided U.S. efforts to maintain Persia's sovereignty as European powers threatened to dismember the country. Returning to the United States in 1914, he apparently retired from government service and then edited *The Memoirs of Colonel John S. Mosby* (1917). His interest in Mosby no doubt came from his marriages, for in 1879 he married Lucy Floyd Mosby, sister of Colonel Mosby, and after her death he married her sister Lelia James Mosby. He published several volumes of poetry, collected in *Poems* (1921). He died in 1927 in Washington (*Dictionary of American Biography*, s.v. "Russell, Charles Wells").

tattoo on his arm, came to him in his tent. "You G—D—Jew, you must come to work!" they said. Then they beat him.[7] Jake Leonard stated that he was at work when Sanders hit him with a stick. "Why did you hit me?" Leonard asked. "You damn Jew, I'll kill you," Sanders threatened. German-born Heinrich Yonge noted that the overseers were harsh on all the men. "I saw Sanders hit the Germans too, but he hit the Jews more," he reported.[8]

According to immigrant Benjamin Wilenski, O'Hara even charged the workers $.15 for a drink of water. When the men took a water break, they were not only charged for water, Wilenski said, but also were docked an hour of time. At the end of the week the immigrant sadly revealed that he received $6.30 in wages but owed the commissary $7.[9]

In Jacksonville on December 10, 1906, O'Hara and his overseers stood trial for conspiracy to commit peonage. The indictment charged a long list of abuses and threats. The jury heard the evidence over fourteen days, and in seventeen minutes on Christmas Eve it returned a verdict of not guilty.[10] Failing in this conspiracy case, Charles W. Russell, who had prepared the cases, put O'Hara alone on trial for peonage on January 2, 1907. The testimony continued for twenty-two days as more than fifty witnesses took the stand to relate the conditions. It took the jury only twelve minutes to return a not-guilty verdict. Russell blamed his defeat on the Florida press and the sympathy of the people there with peonage practices.[11]

While Russell and Quackenbos were gathering evidence to prosecute O'Hara, another case emerged from the turpentine district along the

[7] Affidavit of Hyman Kahn, n.d., file 50–162–8, Dept. of Justice, NA, RG 60. For a description of Sanders, see A. J. Hoyt to Attorney General, Dec. 28, 1906, file 50–162–2, ibid.

[8] Affidavit of Jake Leonard, Aug. 13, 1906; Heinrich Yonge, Aug. 13, 1906, ibid.

[9] Affidavit of Benjamin Wilenski, n.d., ibid. See also the revealing affidavits of Sam Fink, Oct. 10, 1906; Bennie Rubenstein, Aug. 13, 1906; Bennie Graubart, Aug. 20, 1906; Edward Shock, Oct. 10, 1906, ibid.

[10] Russell to Attorney General, Jan. 27, 1907, file 50–162–2, Dept. of Justice, NA, RG 60; *Florida Times-Union*, Dec. 25, 1906, p. 2. For a copy of the indictments, see Charles W. Russell, *Report on Peonage* (Washington, 1908), pp. 36–38.

[11] Russell, *Report on Peonage*, pp. 8–12; Russell to Attorney General, Dec. 27, 1906, file 50–162; Russell to Attorney General, Jan. 27, 1907, file 50–162–2, Dept. of Justice, NA, RG 60; *Florida Times-Union*, Jan. 25, 1907, p. 12. For the complete testimony in the case, see testimony in *United States* v. *O'Hara*, copy in Box 084, Dept. of Justice, NA, RG 60.

Florida-Alabama border. The tale related by Mike Trudics, a Hungarian immigrant, must have been fairly representative of the blighted hopes of many immigrants. His father had gone to America when Mike was seven, promising to send for the family in a year; he died in America, unable to find a job. After serving as an apprentice and experiencing many hardships in Hungary, Mike followed his father to America in 1906. For a while he seemed to be doing well, but then the factory in which he worked burned, and Mike soon found himself unable to pay his rent.[12] Penniless and desperate, Trudics met Rudolf Lanninger, a man who had been on the same ship with him. Lanninger told him that there were plentiful jobs in the South and both went to a labor agency to inquire. "You will work in a sawmill," the labor agents told them, "and you will get $1.50 a day and your food." They were to pay back the railroad fee of $18 at $3 a month; even that would be struck off their bill if they stayed a certain number of months, the agents promised.

These promises lighted the imaginations of the two Hungarians, and they eagerly shipped out on a boat to Savannah and then boarded a train destined for Lockhart, Alabama.[13] Both on the ship and on the train ride, Tom Maginnis, a "ruffian" Irishman, caused trouble, playing jokes on the men and even carving a square on the forehead of one of the laborers. The bravado continued when the group reached Lockhart on July 18, and Maginnis informed foreman Robert Gallagher that he would not sleep "in there with that d—d bunch of polacks." At that point Gallagher, "a stout little man with a revolver sticking out of his hip pocket," intervened. "You are going to sleep right in there," Gallagher snapped at him. "You're not here to run the camp." Maginnis then pulled "his little old dinky dirby down over his eyes" and called Gallagher a son of a bitch.[14] Gallagher kicked Maginnis; when the Irishman attempted to kick Gallagher back, the foreman whipped out his pistol and told Maginnis to get down on his knees. Then, with Maginnis cowed, Gallagher fired several shots alongside the subdued Irishman

[12] Mike Trudics (as told to Alexander Irvine), "The Life Story of a Hungarian Peon," *Independent* 63 (Sept. 5, 1907), 557–61.

[13] Ibid., p. 561.

[14] Testimony of William Tolbott, pp. 331–32, *United States* v. *W. S. Harlan, et al.*, Circuit Court of U.S., Northern District of Florida, copy in Box 086, Dept. of Justice, NA, RG 60. Hereafter cited as testimony in *U.S.* v. *Harlan*; "Charge of Peonage against Jackson Lumber Co.," *Southern Lumberman* 49 (Aug. 10, 1906), 24.

and told him to be a good boy. All the immigrants, Mike Trudics remembered, quickly heard stories of Gallagher's wrath.[15]

The Jackson Lumber Company, where the immigrants were herded, was a large lumbering and turpentine operation on the Alabama-Florida border. The valuable tract of timber attracted the attention of Milton H. Smith, president of the Louisville and Nashville Railroad Company. In 1902 a group of investors from Iowa, Arkansas, and Maryland joined Smith and purchased the land. The Louisville and Nashville Railroad pushed its tracks twenty-two miles farther into the wilderness, and at the end of the spur emerged Lockhart, Alabama.[16]

Trudics, isolated in the wilderness, discovered that the labor agents had misinformed him. Instead of working at the sawmill, he went down the tracks seven miles to the logging operation. "The work in the woods sawing logs was hot, too hot and too heavy for me," he grieved. He complained to Gallagher that his contract called for sawmill work and also $1.50 a day instead of $1. The foreman "paid no attention, but just looked at me as if I were crazy." The stark tragedy of his situation was dizzying; he was "out in a wild place, helpless and at the mercy of men who laughed at contracts and out of whose hip pockets bulged revolvers."[17]

At the first opportunity Trudics fled. At first he stumbled about aimlessly, not knowing where he was going. About noon a buggy with a vanguard of hounds approached carrying Gallagher, a Hungarian interpreter named Sandor, and the camp veterinarian Dr. Walter E. Grace. As the woman across the road described the confrontation, the surprised Trudics began "running backwards throwing up his hands and they went to whipping him." Dr. Grace seized Trudics with one hand, holding a revolver in the other; Gallagher beat Trudics "right smart severe," the woman remembered. She was so terrified that she ran back into her house. Then with his back bleeding, Trudics related, "they drove me like a steer at the point of a revolver along the road toward Lockhart."

[15] See testimony of John Smith, pp. 204–5, 331–32, *U.S. v. Harlan*, Box 086, Dept. of Justice, NA, RG 60; Trudics, "Life Story," p. 562. For Gallagher's account of the affray, see "Charges of Peonage against Jackson Lumber Co.," p. 24. Gallagher, after emerging from his indictment by the grand jury, claimed that only a fistfight took place.

[16] Milton H. Smith to George W. Wickersham, Apr. 20, 1909, file 50–162–7, Dept. of Justice, NA, RG 60.

[17] Trudics, "Life Story," p. 562.

Gallagher beat him again when Trudics reminded him of his contract, and then that night "armed guards kept watch over the laborers in the box cars."[18]

Trudics's case typified the system used by the Jackson Lumber Company to keep the labor they obtained from New York. "Hardly a day passed after that," Trudics noted, "without some one being run down by the bosses or the bloodhounds and returned and whipped." Indeed, neighbors acknowledged the fact that the dogs kept behind the manager's house were used to track men. "The hounds," related a citizen of the area, "were tolerably large size dogs and the cur was a tolerably small sized dog." With the transportation debt hanging over their heads, with an occasional beating by the bosses, and with the dogs nearby to remind them of the futility of escape, the laborers at the Jackson Lumber Company found themselves unable to leave; they had become a servile labor force. "In the woods," Trudics summed up, "they can do anything they please, and no one can see them but God."[19]

Mike Trudics's harrowing tale, substantiated by numerous witnesses, led to the indictment of William S. Harlan, Robert Gallagher, C. C. Hilton, S. E. Huggins, and Walter E. Grace. The government especially wanted to convict Harlan, manager of the Jackson Lumber Company. A native of Iowa, Harlan became manager at Lockhart in May, 1902, as the enterprise began, and his superiors thought that he had done an outstanding job.[20] The government charged that Harlan had conspired with two of his foremen, S. E. Huggins and C. C. Hilton, to operate a peonage system. The victim of the conspiracy was Rudolf Lanninger, Mike Trudics's shipmate and fellow Hungarian. Gallagher and Grace stood trial separately.[21]

The overt act of returning Lanninger to a condition of peonage occurred when he fled with two other men and was apprehended by

[18] Testimony of Mrs. Paul, p. 281, *U.S.* v. *Harlan*, Box 086, Dept. of Justice, NA, RG 60; Trudics, "Life Story," p. 563. See also testimony of Trulich Mahaley (Mike Trudics), p. 270, *U.S.* v. *Harlan*, Box 086, Dept. of Justice, NA, RG 60.

[19] Trudics, "Life Story," p. 563; Testimony of Julius Rhodes, p. 63, *U.S.* v. *Harlan*, Box 086, Dept. of Justice, NA, RG 60. See also testimony of H. M. Stokes, p. 50; G. W. Hudson, pp. 55–56; Alexander Norman, p. 288, ibid.

[20] Smith to Wickersham, Apr. 20, 1909, file 50–162–7, Dept. of Justice, NA, RG 60. See also Alpheus H. Harlan, comp., *History and Genealogy of the Harlan Family* (Baltimore, 1914), pp. 833–34.

[21] See indictments prefacing testimony in *U.S.* v. *Harlan*, p. 26, Box 086, Dept. of Justice, NA, RG 60.

Hilton and a local sheriff. Lanninger's two companions escaped, but Lanninger halted when Hilton "took out his revolver and presented it to them." Hilton then took the refugee to the village of Crestview, Florida, called Lockhart for S. E. Huggins to pick up Lanninger, and proceeded to get drunk.[22]

When the trial began on November 14, 1906, sawmill men filled the courtroom. The *Southern Lumberman*, an industry periodical, noted the anxiety of the employers and observed that "upon the result of these trials will depend to some extent the future controlling of labor in the forests as well as the mills." It was an admission that the turpentine industry thrived on peonage. The defense attempted to prove that there was no whipping and introduced witnesses who saw no violence. Emil Lesser, head of the German Immigration Society for Alabama, testified that he had visited the camp after the story broke and concluded that if there had been peonage at the lumber company "every trace of it had been removed before I came."[23]

The prosecution, however, countered the defense testimony with numerous examples of violence and peonage. The government introduced evidence that Hilton was not the mild-mannered man that the defense suggested. One laborer, speaking through an interpreter, reported that he stayed away from work one day because he was sick, and Hilton entered the bedroom and "was going to shoot him if he was not going to work."[24]

S. E. Huggins emerged as the man who traveled for the company. Besides picking up Lanninger in Crestview (Huggins stated that he was just standing at the depot when Hilton casually said, "Here is a man that wants to go back with you"), Huggins took another trip when the investigations revealed conditions of peonage in the Lockhart camp. He and a Negro accomplice took two of the laborers who were witnesses to the beatings on a forced train-ride to Georgia. When in court the lawyers asked him why he took them away, Huggins replied, "I don't suppose they was giving satisfaction and then there was some trouble

[22] Testimony of Rudolf Lanninger, p. 26; C. C. Hilton, pp. 493–508; S. E. Huggins, p. 510, *U.S.* v. *Harlan*, ibid.

[23] "Peonage Charge against Jackson Lumber Company Now Being Heard," *Southern Lumberman* 50 (Nov. 25, 1906), 30; Testimony of Emil Lesser, p. 444, *U.S.* v. *Harlan*, Box 086, Dept. of Justice, NA, RG 60.

[24] Testimony of Joseph Borgstran, p. 104, *U.S.* v. *Harlan*, Box 086, Dept. of Justice, NA, RG 60.

around there; might eventually brought up more trouble by them staying there." Arthur Buckley, one of the men spirited away, clarified the reason for the trip. Buckley testified that when Huggins thought he was asleep, Huggins told his Negro friend that "as long as we get away from the Government we are all right."[25]

William S. Harlan, manager of the Jackson Lumber Company, naturally denied that peonage existed at the lumber camp. Yet the testimony revealed that Harlan held men to labor who were indebted to the company. J. C. Satterwhite, an office employee of the company, testified that a deputy sheriff informed the company by telegram, "Two foreigners here from your camp. Shall I stop them." Harlan, he said, directed him to send the reply, "Hold them." The manager of another company in the area testified that Harlan once told him that he had "one of my men out there, and if I would pay fifty or fifty-four dollars that I could have him." A justice of the peace from nearby Florala, Alabama, swore that Harlan once drew up a warrant for a laborer for "obtaining goods and money under false pretenses." This charge was not enough to hold the man, but before the laborer got out of the office Harlan had another warrant drawn for abandoning "the service of the Jackson Lumber Company without paying back said passageway money and other advances."[26]

The jury returned a guilty verdict on November 23, 1906, and a month later the judge sentenced Harlan and his underlings. Harlan received a sentence of eighteen months in jail and a $5,000 fine, Gallagher fifteen months and $1,000, and the others thirteen months and $1,000. The *Southern Lumberman* complained that the sentences, especially imprisonment, were "a great surprise to lumbermen, and the general impression is that it was entirely too severe and not warranted by the facts." Charles W. Russell knew that the fight to get the men behind bars had only begun, for he wrote the attorney general on November

[25] Testimony of Huggins, p. 513; Buckley, p. 192, ibid. See also testimony of Herman Osmenski, pp. 305–6, ibid.; William Nanse to Grace Winterton (Grace Quackenbos), Aug. 18, 1906, file 50–162–3, ibid. Attorney Quackenbos sometimes used her maiden name while investigating in the South.
[26] "Charge of Peonage against Jackson Lumber Co.," p. 23; Testimony of J. C. Satterwhite, p. 85; J. H. Givens, p. 114; James Johnson, pp. 213–15, *U.S.* v. *Harlan*, Box 086, Dept. of Justice, NA, RG 60. See also affidavit of Mary Grace Quackenbos, n.d., file 50–162–8, ibid.

24 that many prominent and powerful Alabamians supported Harlan. The government could expect a long fight through appeals.[27]

Two years passed before the Circuit Court of Appeals affirmed the lower court decision (February 24, 1909), and the U.S. Supreme Court refused to review the lower court decision (May 3, 1909). It appeared certain that Harlan's lawyers had exhausted the legal appeals until R. Pope Reese, a U.S. attorney, reported on September 5, 1909, that something was afoot in Alabama. Reese learned that Harlan's lawyers were attempting to have habeas corpus proceedings begun as soon as the men were put in custody of the government; the lawyers wanted the defendants to be taken into custody in Alabama, where they had more influence with the judges. He then revealed misgivings about the Alabama federal judges. "I believe that each and all of these Judges are high-minded, honorable and conscientious officers of the Government," Reese continued, but if there were to be habeas corpus hearings the government would stand a better chance in Florida.[28]

A week later Reese further informed the attorney general that "the defendants are acting in open defiance to the lawful process of this Court and the mandate of the Circuit court of Appeals." Outraged at these "puerile moves," Reese suggested that "it might be well for the Department to call the matter to the attention of the President that he might be given the opportunity to revoke the commutation of sentence of imprisonment upon Harlan, Huggins and Hilton." On August 26, 1909, President William H. Taft had agreed to commute the sentences of the three men—but only after they "are surrendered to accept the action of the court." Attorney General George W. Wickersham agreed with Reese on September 17 and told the solicitor general to bring the case to the President's attention.[29]

Despite Reese's warning and despite the fact that the men returned

[27] Russell to Attorney General, Nov. 15, 1906; Russell to Attorney General, Nov. 24, 1906, file 50–162, Dept. of Justice, NA, RG 60; "Heavy Penalty Imposed in Peonage Cases," *Southern Lumberman* 51 (Dec. 25, 1906), 65; Russell, *Report on Peonage*, pp. 8–12.
[28] Reese to Attorney General, Sept. 5, 1909, file 50–162–7, Dept. of Justice, NA, RG 60.
[29] Reese to Attorney General, Sept. 11, 1909; Frank Cole (private secretary) to O. J. Field (Chief Clerk, Dept. of Justice), Aug. 26, 1909, ibid.; Wickersham to Lloyd W. Bowers, Sept. 17, 1909, file 50–162–8, ibid.

to Pensacola, Harlan's lawyers presented a writ of habeas corpus to the court. For four days the attorneys introduced statements and arguments supporting their respective positions. The defense lawyers claimed that the grand jury which indicted the men had not met in a legal court, that no evidence had been introduced in the grand-jury hearings that constituted peonage, that imprisonment for hard labor instead of simple imprisonment went beyond the law, and that the President had commuted the sentences to six months. Judge Thomas G. Jones, presiding over yet another peonage trial, ruled against the Harlan group on the first two points. The government had already moved to amend the sentence to imprisonment, Jones replied, for the sentence of imprisonment at hard labor "was illegal." On the fourth point the Judge noted that there was "no evidence that sentences have ever been commuted." He did, however, allow the men to remain on bail until they had exhausted their appeals on the habeas corpus proceedings.[30]

A year later (November 28, 1910), the U.S. Supreme Court ruled in favor of the prosecution.[31] Finding their legal appeals finally at an end, Harlan's Alabama friends attempted to use their political influence to secure a pardon. Realizing that their earlier effort to get a pardon for Harlan had miscarried, the white Alabamians tried a new approach: they appealed to the most influential Republican in Alabama, Booker T. Washington.

At the same time that Washington and his group of collaborators in the *Bailey* case were anxiously awaiting the Supreme Court verdict in that peonage case, Harlan's friends imposed on him for a letter in behalf of Harlan. Emmett J. Scott, Washington's trusted private secretary, warned Washington that Attorney General Wickersham "very strongly interposed in this peonage case, and is, in the main, responsible for the conviction of these men." Scott warned his chief not to commit himself too far. Washington had other problems, however, and told Scott to tell Charles W. Hare, a local Tuskegee white man, that it "would be very dangerous just now when I am under fire from certain parties in my

---

[30] Reese to Attorney General, Nov. 5, 1909; *Pensacola Journal*, Nov. 4, 1909, clipping in ibid. See also Reese to Attorney General, Nov. 5, 1909, ibid. For an explanation of what happened to the commutations, see Attorney General to Jones, June 14, 1910, ibid.

[31] Assistant Attorney General to Reese, Nov. 28, 1910, ibid.

own race to interfere in this matter." Washington sounded uncharacter-
istically indignant as he concluded his message to Scott, "I must consider
the feeling of my race as well as that of others."[32] Washington felt the
strain of his complicated life as a public accommodator-politician and
private civil rights advocate.

Ominously, one day after the Bailey decision, Washington agreed to
write a letter in behalf of Harlan. Admitting that he did not know the
facts of the case, Washington wrote that "there are few men anywhere
in the South who have stood higher than Mr. Harlan or have done more
for the development of the South than is true of Mr. Harlan. Sixty-five
per cent of the people employed at his mill plant are colored, and without exception they tell me that he has treated them with the greatest
degree of kindness." The appeal had a touch of paradox as Washington
wrote of how well Harlan provided for the needs of blacks at Lockhart
when the case involved white immigrants. A fine would suffice in this
case, the Tuskegeean pled, for Harlan "has already been severely punished in his feelings and reputation." Washington argued that by Harlan's entering the penitentiary for a week, "his reputation and usefulness
in that community are blasted for all time."[33] Yet the appeal of Washington and the efforts of Harlan's Alabama friends were not enough, for
at last Harlan did go to jail.[34] President Taft replied in no uncertain
terms to the men who urged Harlan's pardon. "Fines are not effective
against men of wealth," he wrote. "Imprisonment is necessary." To
allow a man justly convicted to go free "would be to break down the
authority of the law with those of power and influence, and would
tempt on their part further breaches." But most important, President

---

[32] Washington to Charles W. Hare, Dec. 6, 1910, Box 906; Scott to Washington,
Dec. 7, 1910, Box 596; Washington to Scott, Dec. 8, 1910; Scott to Hare, Dec. 9,
1910; Washington to Scott, Dec. 8, 1910, Washington Papers, Box 906.

[33] Reuben F. Kolb (telegram) to Washington, Dec. 31, 1910; Kolb to Washington, Jan. 2, 1911; Washington to Kolb, Jan. 4, 1911, Box 427; Washington to William
H. Taft, Jan. 6, 1911, ibid., Box 7.

[34] Four months later Washington changed his appeal and urged Taft to excuse
the fine of $5,000 that Harlan had to pay. "His financial condition had been mis-
represented I am convinced," Washington pled, adding that the case had cost Harlan his entire fortune. "I would be the last to justify peonage," he concluded, but
he did want to spare Harlan this financial burden. (Washington to Charles D. Hillis
[Secretary to the President], May, 1911, ibid., Box 424. See also William W.
Flournoy to Wickersham, Feb. 8, 1911, file 50–162–8, Dept. of Justice, NA, RG 60.)

Taft concluded, "It would give real ground for the contention so often heard that it is only the poor criminals who are really punished."[35] Though Harlan served only four of his imposed eighteen months, there was something novel about a wealthy peon-master behind bars.

Immigrant Mike Trudics, sleeping in a jail cell with a local tramp while awaiting the Harlan trial, learned some conventional wisdom about the South. "Do they flog men everywhere in this country?" he asked. "No, just down here in the South where they used to flog niggers," the tramp replied. After the ordeal was over, Trudics concluded that "there was law in America, but its benefits to the poor were accidental."[36]

Perhaps in Mike Trudics's case justice was accidental, but there were, at least in the cases of Italian immigrants, avenues of redress. In May, 1906, before immigrant peonage had attracted wide attention, U.S. Attorney A. E. Holton of Winston-Salem received a complaint from Giovanni Sottile, Italian consular agent in Charleston, South Carolina, that some 1,500 Italians were held in peonage. Sottile demanded immediate action and met Holton at the Marion, North Carolina, jail, where nine Italians were held for conspiracy to kill a superintendent of the South and Western Railroad Company. Holton quickly got to the facts of the incident. A group of Italians, evidently underfed and unpaid, had attempted to convey this complaint to the superintendent. "The Italian was insisting upon his being paid," Holton explained, "with a sign pointed to his mouth, then to his stomach and marked upon the ground with his feet to indicate a grave." Lacking an interpreter, the Italian hoped to convey that unless he ate he would need to be buried. The superintendent misinterpreted the drama, thinking that unless the Italians were paid the superintendent would need to be buried. Believing that a mutiny was brewing, the superintendent gathered a posse complete with a deputy sheriff and invaded the tents of the Italians; two Italians died in the

35 Quoted in "The Case of W. S. Harlan," *Outlook* 97 (Jan. 21, 1911), 87. For a complete account of the President's ruling on the case, see *Harlan* v. *United States*, 184 F. 702; "In re. application for the pardon of W. S. Harlan," n.d. [Jan. 1911], William H. Taft Papers, Manuscript Division, Library of Congress, Washington, D.C., Series 6, Box 400. See also numerous letters recommending Harlan's pardon in ibid.
36 Trudics, "Life Story," p. 563.

fracas. In August, 1906, due largely to Italian diplomatic pressure, the South and Western Railroad Company settled out of court for $7,500 in damages to the families of the murdered men.[37]

If this case was typical, Italian immigrants received more aid from their government than did other immigrants or even native Americans who remained in peonage.[38] One New York native, writing from the Marion jail, complained that he had been flogged and marched eighteen miles to Marion for attempting to escape from the South and Western Railroad camp. He stated that the conditions in the jail were "unsurpassed even in the days of Andersonville and Libby." The Italian government had secured the release of the Italians, he reminded the Justice Department. "Are we in a free country to be treated like criminals when we have not even transgressed?" Evidently the settlement with the Italians had forced the railroad company to extract even more labor from its other peons. However, by June, 1907, Assistant Attorney General Russell reported that the prosecutions for peonage in North Carolina were progressing nicely. He had special praise for U.S. Attorney A. E. Holton. But there were many other complaints from immigrants, including some two dozen appended to the *Attorney General's Annual Report* of 1907.[39]

No other case brought out the intricate combinations that led to immigrant peonage as clearly as the cases involving the extension of the Florida East Coast Railroad into the keys. The lures of the New York labor agents, the locked trains that pulled into the depot in Miami, the guarded trip to the isolated keys, the whitewash investigations, and the

[37] Holton to Attorney General, June 6, 1906, file 50–324; Holton to Attorney General, Aug. 28, 1906, file 50–343, Dept. of Justice, NA, RG 60. See also G. Sottile to Holton, Apr. 30, 1906; Speranza to Conte A. R. Massiglia, May 25, 1906; Speranza, "Relazione. Sull 'inchiesta pei fatti della Carolina Company nel North Carolian," untranslated typescript, Gino C. Speranza Papers, Manuscript Division, New York Public Library, Apr.–Dec., 1907, folder.

[38] An earlier case that gained public attention in March, 1903, involved twenty-three Italian immigrants from New York who ended up in the mountains of West Virginia. There they were held in peonage and threatened with guns. See Gino C. Speranza, "Forced Labor in West Virginia," *Outlook* 74 (June 13, 1903), 407–10. See also *Special Message of Governor Dawson Concerning Cases of Peonage and Labor Conditions* (Charleston, W. Va., 1907).

[39] William Burke to Dept. of Justice, Oct. 22, 1906; Russell to Attorney General, June 14, 1907, file 50–342, Dept. of Justice, NA, RG 60; *Annual Report of the Attorney General*, 1907, 2 vols. (Washington, 1908), I: Appendix.

reluctance of the courts to find the conspirators guilty all pointed out the extreme difficulty of prosecuting wealthy peonage offenders. The affidavits that attorneys Quackenbos and Russell collected revealed a massive collaboration to secure forced labor. The New York labor agents, the local law-enforcement officers and judges in Florida, and the foremen on the keys all aided in supplying peon labor to construct Henry M. Flagler's railroad.

In 1904 Flagler decided to extend his Florida East Coast Railroad to Key West. Then seventy-four, the retired Standard Oil millionaire was not deterred by the incredible engineering feats required to stretch rails across swamps, jungles, and open water. After several firms had refused to tackle the mammoth project, J. C. Meredith, an engineer who had worked on the Panama Canal, accepted the task. Meredith, who stated that "no man had any business being connected with this work who couldn't stand grief," discovered that engineering problems were but a fraction of his troubles. Before Flagler rode his private car down the line in 1913 just prior to his death, Meredith had seen three hurricanes, had experienced logistical problems feeding his laborers, and had been accused of holding men in slavery.[40]

Meredith secured his workers from New York, as had F. J. O'Hara and William S. Harlan. In November, 1906, Harry Hermanson, a nineteen-year-old Brooklyn resident, signed a contract in the offices of labor agent Francesco Sabbia. When his train reached the dock in Miami, the gate slammed shut behind it. Next morning a boat pulled up to the dock; after some resistance, the men boarded and went out to the keys to begin work. Hungry and exhausted, Hermanson ended up on Matecumbe Island—but he got no food, and the foreman pointed out some rocks for his bed. The next day a boat ferried the men to a sunken island. Seeing no ground, they refused to leave the boat until the foreman shouted, "Jump overboard or I will blow your brains out." Hermanson remained at the camp for five weeks, becoming progressively sicker. Boats provided the only avenue of escape, but the company refused to allow the men to leave until they had worked out their transportation and commissary bills. Hermanson somehow got word to his mother, who sent him some money which the foreman confiscated. The

[40] Kathryn Trimmer Abbey Hanna, *Florida. Land of Change* (Chapel Hill, 1948), pp. 371–72.

bosses finally allowed him to leave, and in December, 1906, he returned to New York with his mother.[41]

Affidavits revealed an incredible series of brutalities. E. T. Clyatt, an ex-foreman on the keys who later became a federal special agent, admitted that "the men were obliged to sleep on the bare rocks; that the mosquitoes were poisonous and many men became ill because of the insects and fever and lack of decent food." Foremen warned fishermen who occasionally strayed near the keys that they would "shoot any fisherman who steals our men." A woman who kept a private eating-place on Key Largo told of one case when a laborer died because he remained sick in his tent and starved. "To my personal knowledge, Mr. Ball, a foreman, did on several occasions shoot men and break their arms," she lamented, "and I had to care for them and dress their wounds." In October, 1906, a hurricane struck the keys and a houseboat broke loose and drifted to sea, killing some eighty men. Jake Anderson, who worked on Key Largo for eight months, revealed that he was "shot through the arm by the foreman and did not receive any attention from the company after I was shot but was cared for and fed by one Mr. Dell and brought back to Miami." He had to carry water to the other workmen for two days before the boat arrived to take him back.[42] Another man reported that one day when he was sick a "big, powerful man pressed a pistol to my forehead and said 'Go to work, you bum; if you do not I will shoot you.' " Several reports included instances when men fell overboard and no one attempted to rescue them.[43]

Eventually, though, some of the men did escape from the keys and return to Miami, seeking a way back north. Samuel Rosen reported that he spent three weeks on Matecumba Island and did not receive any pay. Somehow escaping to Miami, he called on superintendent of construction J. C. Meredith, who accused him of failing to pay his transportation and hauled him before a judge who gave him the option of "going back to the Keys or going to jail for ten days." He chose the latter, served the time, and started north. He traveled forty miles to Palm Beach, was

[41] Affidavit of Harry Hermanson, n.d., file 50–162–4, Dept. of Justice, NA, RG 60. See also affidavit of Joseph Sharpe, Mar. 12, 1907, ibid.
[42] Affidavit of E. T. Clyatt, n.d.; Sophie English, n.d.; Thomas Wilson, n.d.; Jake Anderson, n.d.; ibid.
[43] Affidavit of George Morris, n.d.; Winifield Ronald, n.d.; George Morris, n.d., ibid.

rearrested, returned to Miami, again chose the jail sentence, and then had to pay Meredith for his transportation a second time before he left Miami.[44]

Joseph Halpin, another Brooklynite, told of being paid twice, once $.90 and another time $.40. Many of the peons wanted to leave Key West, he said, but lacked the $3.50 transportation to Miami. After leaving the keys, Halpin worked his way from vagrancy arrest to vagrancy arrest through Florida and Georgia until he finally caught a freight train to New York. Another immigrant who made the train ride from New York to Miami stayed on the train and missed the boat for the keys. "I was arrested for vagrancy and the Judge gave me the alternative of working at building roads at Snake Creek in the chain gang, or going to the island of Key Largo," he stated. "I was sent to the island where I worked for two months."[45]

As early as March, 1906, the Department of Commerce and Labor sent an agent to the keys to investigate peonage complaints. The agent, accompanied by Florida East Coast representative Edward J. Triay, stopped at thirteen camps along the keys and found that sometimes men were held for transportation, though it was not official company policy. There were no guns, according to the agent's report. Most of the men, he concluded, had wanted to visit Florida in the winter and had quickly left their work to seek a vacation. This report sharply contrasted with the statement made by one of the workers. The boss, he remembered, herded them into a dining room, and they told the agent "that we were treated like dogs, and that the food was not fit to eat." They also complained that they "were kept there for debt and could not get away." The agent promised the workmen that he would report the conditions, but his misleading report did not appear until 1907, a year later, when Secretary of Commerce Oscar S. Straus sent it to Attorney General Charles J. Bonaparte.[46]

Florida looked like a massive slave-labor camp when the federal government began its investigation, yet some investigators seemed blind to

---

[44] Affidavit of Samuel Rosen, n.d., ibid.
[45] Affidavit of Joseph Halpin, n.d.; John Reiss, n.d., ibid. For an excellent account of peonage on the keys, see two undated affidavits of E. T. Clyatt, ibid.
[46] "Report of Mr. McNeill, Commissioner of Labor," enclosure in Oscar Straus to Bonaparte, Feb. 12, 1907, file 50–162–2; affidavit of Percy White, n.d., file 50–162–4, ibid.

what actually happened on the keys. One agent, for example, reported to Russell that there was no peonage on the keys. He reached his conclusion while living in a Miami hotel, interviewing men who had returned from the keys. They complained of hard work, he noted, but did not reveal any peonage.[47] The agent never went to the keys, where he would surely have found many men being held against their wills.

Responding to the peonage complaints, the Florida East Coast Railroad amassed its own 199-page "Report on Labor Conditions on the Florida East Coast Railway Extension" and presented it to the government. While the generalizations and conclusions of the report denied that peonage existed on the keys, the text of the report contained many instances of peonage. "We would not let a man go on the boat if he was in debt to the camp," one foreman related. He continued that though "we sometimes threatened to club a man who was in debt and would not work to pay it, we never did club anybody." Another foreman stated that the bosses never carried guns. The report utilized the statements of the foremen and not the statements of the men who were supposedly held in peonage. Answering the charges of wholesale arrests in Miami, the report stated that the men were thirsty for whiskey when they landed in Miami and were "inclined to over-indulge."[48]

The Florida East Coast Railroad's investigation of itself gave a detailed and unintentionally damning description of the sleeping quarters on the keys. The railroad supplied the men with "a slat-bunk, which is made of planed pine slats, 3 or 4 inches wide, nailed together with battens, the whole measuring about 3 ft by 6½ feet." The company also furnished wood for legs, it continued, but the men did not bother to put them on "but rest their bunks only on the coral surface or prop them up with rocks or sticks of wood." The company did not sell mattresses for the wood bunks because the "company officers hold that mattresses are objectionable on account of breeding vermin." But there were plenty of palmetto leaves available, the report pointed out, ignoring the fact that palmetto leaves might also breed vermin. Despite some foremen's revelations and admissions that they held men for debt, the report concluded: "All reports which may have been circulated to the

---

[47] O. E. Wright to Russell, Nov. 5, 1906, Box 083, ibid.
[48] "Report on Labor Conditions on the Florida East Coast Railway Extension," ca. Feb. 12, 1907, p. 36, Box 084, ibid.

effect that the men have been guarded by bosses with guns, or that they have been kept in a condition of 'white slavery', may be dismissed as entirely unfounded."[49] With the exception of the complaints gathered by attorneys Russell and Quackenbos, the investigations of peonage on the Florida keys were either poorly done or purposely misleading.

As enough evidence gradually accumulated to show some basis for the rumors of peonage in Florida, business and civic leaders there sought to brunt the peonage charges that swept the country. On February 20, 1907, a meeting of the Florida State Board of Trade asked for an investigation—not of peonage, but of the "greatest menace to increased immigration to this state, namely, the unceasing agitation of the peonage question." Adept at muddling the central issue of peonage by attacking the federal government, the key speaker attacked Russell for taking F. J. O'Hara before a jury twice and labeled the prosecution as harassment. The kingpin on the Board of Trade, reported U.S. attorney J. M. Cheney, was S. A. Rawls, the head of the convict-lease system in Florida. "He is one of the moving spirits in the political 'ring' that controls the Democratic politics of Florida," Cheney wrote, "and the influence from that ring extends into the turpentine and lumber interests on account of the necessity for labor and its scarcity." Cheney was pessimistic about the coming peonage trials, reporting that the powerful interests in Florida were "organized and unscrupulous" and would "strive to influence juries" even if they had to "follow the jurymen into the box."[50]

Several days after the Board of Trade launched its public relations obfuscation campaign, Wisconsin Congressman John J. Jenkins, chairman of the Committee on the Judiciary, demanded that Attorney General Bonaparte account for the expenses of attorneys Russell and Quackenbos. Bonaparte, defending his energetic employees and returning the argument to the issue of peonage, first reminded Jenkins that the conditions in Florida were "repugnant to the enlightened opinion of modern times in all civilized countries." He explained that attorney Quackenbos had acted from "philanthropic motives" and had received no other pay than that which "she is obliged to pay a competent person for taking her place in the office she has established." Russell had been designated by

49 Ibid., pp. 44, 65–66.
50 *Florida Times-Union*, Feb. 21, 1907, clipping in file 50–162–2; Cheney to Attorney General, Feb. 21, 1907, ibid.

the former attorney general to "exercise a general supervision over prosecution for peonage." As to the expenses, Bonaparte explained, it would be impossible to separate the investigations for peonage from the other investigations done simultaneously.[51]

A month later Floridians were again outraged as Richard Barry's muckraking article, "Slavery in the South To-Day," appeared in the March, 1907, *Cosmopolitan Magazine*. The preface proved almost as damaging as the text. "The Standard Oil Clique, H. M. Flagler's Florida East Coast Railway Co., the turpentine trust, the lumber trust, and other trusts have put in force a system of peonage which is actual slavery," it charged, "and it is done under the legal sanction of state laws—not by direct laws, but by subterfuges and circumventions which nevertheless attain the end in view." Barry, using material gathered by a clerk in the U.S. Circuit Court in Pensacola, gave accounts of the *Harlan* case, the conditions on the keys, the role of the political interests in Florida, and the North Carolina cases.[52] The sensational exposé carried photographs of man-tracking dogs, fleeing peons, and several posed pictures of local law-enforcement officials. Outraged, the Florida legislature acted quickly to defend its honor, condemning not only Barry but passing a resolution condemning publisher William Randolph Hearst for allowing versions of the "infamous, false, and libelous article referred to" to be carried in his newspapers.[53]

A month later the Florida House debated a contract-labor law almost identical to Alabama's. Representative R. Pope Reese of Escambia County, who later worked on the *Harlan* case, led the fight to defeat the bill, pointing out that the actual purpose of the law "is to authorize the collection of a debt by criminal process—to justify imprisonment for debt in violation of both the Constitution of Florida and the United States." The majority of the legislature, however, argued that the measure would be beneficial even if unconstitutional, and it became law.[54]

[51] John J. Jenkins to Bonaparte, Feb. 26, 1907; Bonaparte to Jenkins, Feb. 27, 1907, ibid.

[52] Richard Barry, "Slavery in the South To-Day," *Cosmopolitan Magazine* 42 (Mar. 1907), 482. See F. W. Marsh to Barry, n.d.; Barry to Marsh, Dec. 28, 1906, FRC, Georgia.

[53] Florida *House Journal*, 11th sess., Apr. 1907, pp. 5–6.

[54] Florida *Laws*, 1907, c. 5678. See also Florida *House Journal*, 11th sess., Apr. 1907, pp. 421–22; 949–50; *Tallahassee Morning Sun*, May 7, 1907, clipping in file 50–162–4; Quackenbos to Bonaparte, May 18, 1907, file 50–162–4, Dept. of Justice, NA, RG 60.

By early 1908 Richard Barry, Charles W. Russell, and Mary Grace Quackenbos were under fire from irate Southerners who blamed them for Florida's bad publicity. The secretary of the Tampa Chamber of Commerce complained to Secretary of State Elihu Root on January 28, 1908, that most of the peonage stories were untrue. He singled out Barry and Quackenbos for special criticism. "We are already preventing peonage," he wrote two years after the rash of cases broke out, "but, unfortunately, we have not been able to offset the misguided work of the Department of Justice or of the slanderers who have brought upon us so much undeserved censure." A month later Florida Congressman Frank Clark of Polk County demanded that the attorney general forward him all the peonage reports submitted by attorneys Quackenbos and Russell.[55]

In an effort to shift the focus of peonage and reclaim their virtuous image, Southern congressmen introduced a bill calling for the Immigration Commission to investigate peonage throughout the United States. The debate over the merits of an investigation soon became a direct thrust at the Justice Department. Three Southern congressmen attacked former Attorney General Bonaparte, Russell, and Quackenbos. Congressman Clark launched the most bitter tirade. He labeled Bonaparte as a "transplanted bud of alleged French nobility" who "instead of looking after the law business of the United States Government, began a crusade in certain States to regulate sociological conditions." Clark explained that parliamentary rules "prohibit my characterizing this man," but he went on to liken Russell, a Southerner, to "a dirty bird that fouls its own nest." Clark defended F. J. O'Hara and was outraged that Russell tried him twice for peonage. O'Hara was a "gentleman of high standing the latchet of whose shoes this assistant attorney general is not worthy to loosen." The Floridian concluded that all accusations that the Florida East Coast Railroad practiced peonage were "absolutely, and I believe willfully, untrue."[56]

Two Mississippi congressmen, Benjamin G. Humphreys and John Sharp Williams, joined in the attack. Williams complained that adverse

55 C. Fred Thompson to Root, Jan. 28, 1908; Clark to Attorney General, Feb. 24, 1908, file 50–162–5, Dept. of Justice, NA, RG 60.

56 U.S., Congress, House, *Congressional Record*, 60th Cong., 1st sess., 1908, 42, pt. 3: 2750.

publicity had decreased emigration into Mississippi. Humphreys, reminding the House that the Southerner's respect for womanhood "is taken into their being with their mother's milk," said Quackenbos had taken advantage of all the courtesies extended by a gracious people. In her visit to his state, he charged, she had perpetrated "an outrage on the State of Mississippi." He then reviewed her investigation of Sunnyside plantation in Arkansas, a so-called utopian experiment owned by two prominent Mississippians. Quoting letters from Albert Bushnell Hart, a noted historian, and Leroy Percy, ex-governor of Mississippi and stockholder in Sunnyside, Humphreys argued that Sunnyside was a model farm community where there was no peonage.[57] After the smoke cleared following the debate, Congress passed the bill authorizing an Immigration Commission examination of peonage among immigrants throughout the United States. Nothing had been mentioned about black victims of peonage.

As the Immigration Commission began its investigation, Quackenbos continued her quest for the successful prosecution of Francesco Sabbia, the notorious labor agent so often mentioned by the men who worked on the keys. On March 27, 1907, after the failure of the *O'Hara* case, a grand jury in New York had indicted Sabbia, Florida East Coast Railroad agent Edward J. Triay, and two other men under the 1866 slave-kidnapping law. No reason emerged for indicting the men for slavery instead of peonage. Sabbia and the other men pled not guilty, and a long and involved appeal began.[58]

Florida East Coast representatives immediately attempted to obtain the names of witnesses, and apparently the cloak-and-dagger effort

[57] Ibid., pp. 2746–50. See also Clark to Attorney General, Feb. 24, 1908, file 50–162–5, Dept. of Justice, NA, RG 60. "Thus far," Quackenbos wrote from Pine Bluff, Arkansas, "I have found a system of bondage existing uniformly where Italians are employed. The so-called 'colonists' are in reality, slaves, and are treated worse than the negroes." Quackenbos to Attorney General, July 20, 1907, Box 084, ibid. For other material relating to Quackenbos's investigation and Italian immigrant farmers, see Quackenbos to Russell, Sept. 27, 1907, Box 083; Quackenbos to Attorney General, July 20, 1907; Quackenbos to Russell, Oct. 8, 1907, Box 084, Dept. of Justice, NA, RG 60; Robert L. Brandfon, "The End of Immigration to the Cotton Fields," *Journal of American History* 50 (Mar. 1964), 591–611; Alfred H. Stone, *Studies in the American Race Problem* (New York, 1908), pp. 87–89; Stone, "The Italian Cotton Grower: The Negro's Problem," *South Atlantic Quarterly* 4 (Jan. 1905), 42–47.

[58] See copy of docket in Circuit Court of New York, file 50–162–8, Dept. of Justice, NA, RG 60.

proved successful.[59] U.S. Attorney Henry L. Stimson in New York later advised the attorney general that he had serious doubts about the government's chances in the *Sabbia* case. The indictment had been found under the vague slavery statute, he warned, and he doubted that the government could prove what the indictment charged. Stimson also complained that "the attitude of Mrs. Quackenbos is giving me considerable difficulty and concern." After praising her investigative ability, Stimson labeled "her judgment as a lawyer on both the facts and the law entirely untrustworthy." Stimson also outlined the enormous task of "dealing with an unscrupulous enemy." He reminded the attorney general that "certain of the agents of the Florida East Coast Railway attempted to bribe one of my investigators to steal a list of our witnesses."[60]

Mary Grace Quackenbos's enthusiasm for immigrants led her to propose in May, 1907, that the federal government handle the movement of immigrant labor throughout the states. Such a labor bureau, she suggested, should "be organized for the supervision of all immigrants and laborers sent from one state to another, the purpose of such a Bureau to be the protection of the immigrant against all forms of fraud practices; such as labor agencies, colonization societies, leagues, etc." Four months later she reminded Russell of her suggestion and was pleased that Russell had recommended much the same thing to Congress earlier. She hoped that their mutual support of the measure would bring "a realization of the true state of affairs in the South and bring about a speedy relief with assured and permanent protection."[61]

The longer the *Sabbia* case went untried, the more unlikely appeared the chances for success. On January 19, 1908, Quackenbos reported that the witnesses were scattered all over the country. Moreover, the U.S. attorney assigned to prepare the case had been involved in the earlier bribery incident. Stimson dismissed these complaints and stated that he had more cases than he could then handle because he was in-

---

[59] See affidavits of Julius J. Kron, Mar. 31, Apr. 1, 2, 3, 1907; Quackenbos to Bonaparte, Apr. 29, 1907, file 50–162–8; Quackenbos to Attorney General, June 24, July 9, 1908, file 50–162–6, ibid.

[60] Stimson to Attorney General, Apr. 22, 1907, file 50–162–3, ibid.

[61] Quackenbos to Attorney General, May 7, 1907, file 50–162–4; Quackenbos to Russell, Sept. 23, 1907, file 50–162–5, ibid. See also Mary Grace Quackenbos, *A Question for the House of Governors* (New York, 1909), copy in New York Public Library.

vestigating "the national banks." Because of the pressing business of his office, Stimson wrote that he was "a little embarrassed to know what to do with Mrs. Quackenbos until I know what your ultimate decision as to these cases is."[62] In the summer of 1908 railroad agents attempted to tamper with the witnesses, offering them money to sign statements that cleared the Florida East Coast Railroad of any responsibility for peonage. Quackenbos informed the attorney general that the U.S. attorney's office was filled with people who were in sympathy with the railroad. The only bright spot appeared when Sabbia lost his license as an employment agent.[63]

Finally, on November 10, 1908, the trial began. For six days Assistant Attorney General Russell experienced continual frustration. The defense attorneys admitted that their clients were guilty of peonage. By having them admit guilt of peonage, the lawyers argued that the men were thereby not guilty of slavery as charged in the indictment. The defense lawyers also used the same argument that Samuel M. Clyatt's lawyers had used: because slavery had been outlawed in the United States, there could be no slavery in Florida. Russell then argued that slavery, peonage, and involuntary servitude were all legally related, even synonymous. Judge Charles M. Hough, however, agreed with the defense lawyers.[64] This initial ruling on definitions set the pattern for the entire trial, as it seemed that Judge Hough and chief defense attorney John B. Stanchfield, hired by the Florida East Coast Railroad for Edward J. Triay, reinforced each other's thoughts. Whenever Russell would get a witness to the point of revealing slavery, Stanchfield would leap to his feet and object.

Russell argued that the conditions on the keys enslaved men, for they were forced to remain on the keys after they had paid their transportation and were thus slaves and no longer peons. Judge Hough ruled that it was peonage. Even if Russell proved peonage, Hough ruled that it

---

[62] Quackenbos to Attorney General, Jan. 19, 1908; Stimson to Attorney General, Jan. 20, 1908, file 50–162–5, Dept. of Justice, NA, RG 60.

[63] Quackenbos to Attorney General, June 24, July 1, 9, 30, 1908, file 50–162–6, ibid.

[64] *U.S. v. Sabbia*, pp. 42–45, Box 083, ibid. See Fred G. Folsom, Jr., "A Slave Trade Law in a Contemporary Setting," *Cornell Law Quarterly* 29 (Nov. 1943), 208–10.

would be "peonage and not slavery, and *if you prove that up to the hilt, I will dismiss the indictment*."[65] Russell's witnesses never got to the testimony that would show slavery, as the defense lawyers continually objected and were sustained by the judge.[66] At one point, when a witness stated that some Greeks once held up the departure of a ship while they were locked behind the Florida East Coast dock gates in Miami, the judge ruled that this showed slavery but proved no conspiracy among the defendants. Then Russell attempted to question the witnesses and bring out the fact that several of the defendants were present at the scene, but the judge refused to allow the testimony. "If we cannot show one of the defendants *in the midst of these scenes* as giving him knowledge of what was going on," Russell complained, "I don't see how we can show anything."[67]

As the trial continued, Hough's rulings became more farcical. Having used an interpreter earlier in the trial and needing to hear some of the testimony from non-English speaking immigrants, Russell again requested an interpreter. The judge refused. Seeing that he needed more witnesses, Russell informed the judge that some men were on the way from Florida, but Hough refused to continue the proceedings a day to hear them.[68] "I want to hear any more evidence you have got *and it must be produced now*," he ruled. Finally, on November 18 Hough killed the case. "This evidence shows, if it tends to show anything, knowledge of a condition of peonage," he concluded, "that is, the holding of men to servitude until such time as they shall have worked out debts which they had created." Such evidence, he charged the jury, was useless under the indictment, and he instructed the jury to dismiss the case.[69] As had been the difficulty in the *Clyatt* case, the *Sabbia* case failed, at least in part, because of the indictment. Had the indictment been drawn for peonage, however, it appears likely that the defense lawyers would have admitted slavery to evade the peonage charge. What did appear vividly was the obstinacy of Stimson, the bribery of the witnesses, the confidential government evidence that the defense managed to secure, the

[65] *U.S.* v. *Sabbia*, pp. 63–69, Box 083, Dept. of Justice, NA, RG 60. Italics in original.
[66] See ibid., pp. 83, 86, 96, 116, 122, 129.
[67] Ibid., pp. 160–61. Italics in original.
[68] Ibid., pp. 176, 202.
[69] Ibid., pp. 210, 234. Italics in original.

judge's rulings, and the smooth courtroom performance of Stanchfield; these factors combined to wreck the case so carefully prepared by attorneys Quackenbos and Russell. Though the Justice Department had many more failures than successes in its work with immigrant peons, this brand of exploitation obviously declined by 1910, leaving the black men of the South to bear the burden of peonage.

As if to give the frustrating story of immigrant peonage its official burial, the Immigration Commission in 1911 published its forty-two-volume report. Seven pages of the report concerned peonage. Some peonage had existed in the Southern states in 1906 and 1907, it read, "but these were only sporadic instances and the Commission found no general system of peonage anywhere." The report clearly attempted to remove the stigma that peonage existed only in the South. Legal peonage, it continued, had existed in every state of the union with the exceptions of Oklahoma and Connecticut, but prosecution had ended the practice altogether. No peonage had been found in the construction of the Florida East Coast Railroad, though when the first immigrants arrived, "there was some coercion of this sorry labor." This statement, of course, contradicted what even the railroad lawyers had admitted in the Sabbia trial in 1908. "The cases of beating and brutal treatment," the report read with unintended *double entendre*, "have been exceptional."[70] The most complete system of peonage, according to the report, existed in the Maine logging woods.[71] The Southern congressmen who had managed to sidetrack a specifically Southern investigation and get the investigation not only in an immigration context but also buried in a voluminous report could not have been more pleased.

The Immigration Commission's report on peonage contrasted sharply with the reports from Russell's team of investigators. Veteran investigator A. J. Hoyt wrote from Florida in August, 1906, that "from the

[70] Senate Documents, "Report on Peonage," *Abstracts of Reports of the Immigration Commission*, 42 vols., 61st Cong., 3rd sess., 1910–11, no. 747, II:444–46.

[71] Ibid., II:447. See report of peonage in Maine by John Clifton Elder, a twenty-one-page typescript in file 50–34–0, Dept. of Justice, NA, RG 60. In a personal letter to Congressman William S. Bennet of New York, Elder suggested that peonage should be vigorously prosecuted. His revealing letter contrasted with the Immigration Commission's brief report. "It is my opinion that the investigation of the Commission should be followed up by some practical work," Elder urged (Elder to Bennet, Mar. 28, 1910, ibid.). Bennet passed Elder's letter to the Justice Department, but apparently nothing came of Elder's recommendations nor did the report on peonage reflect Elder's concern.

investigation which I have made thus far in this State, I find that peonage exists everywhere." Russell on February 4, 1907, informed Attorney General Bonaparte that he had "found peonage involving thousands of workmen, especially foreigners fooled or trapped into the keys."[72] But Russell could not overcome the public relations efforts of the Southern ruling class. The concept of a New South, a war-torn area that emerged from its ashes sprouting smokestacks, spindles, and railroads, maximized tangible symbols, not the exploited laborers who slaved much as men had a century before. As they had responded to pre–Civil War abolitionists, Southerners admitted no wrong and attacked their critics as outsiders, meddlers, turncoats, themes that attracted much popular support.

The inadequacy of the peonage statute was also frustrating to government attorneys. The Justice Department could not act in cases of enslavement, because the key to prosecuting under the peonage law was the indebtedness of the laborer. The 1866 slave-kidnapping law had been passed to stop traffic in blacks from the Southern states to Latin America and was not consistently applicable to domestic slavery. In 1907 one baffled U.S. attorney wrote from Virginia that "unless Congress gives us some legislation that forbids slavery or involuntary servitude we will not be able to reach the great majority of cases arising in the camps of contractors." Russell also complained that the federal government was often handicapped by the narrowness of the peonage statute. In 1911 the *Annual Report of the Attorney General* called on Congress to pass additional legislation making slavery illegal—to no avail.[73]

Though thousands of immigrants fell prey to peonage, immigrant peonage apparently lasted only several years and was not typical of the practice. Blacks bore the major burden of Southern peonage, but no thorough investigation of peonage ever revealed even an approximate estimate of black peons. A. J. Hoyt's 1907 estimate that in the three states of Georgia, Alabama, and Mississippi "investigations will prove that 33 1/3 per cent of the planters operating from five to one-hundred

[72] Hoyt to Attorney General, Aug. 28, 1906; Russell to Bonaparte, Feb. 4, 1907, file 50–162–1, Dept. of Justice, NA, RG 60.
[73] Thomas L. Moore to Attorney General, Feb. 14, 1907, file 50–412; Russell to Mr. Wolfe, Feb. 7, 1907, Box 083, ibid.; *Annual Report of the Attorney General*, 1911 (Washington, 1912), p. 27.

plows, are holding their negro employees to a condition of peonage" remained the sole generalization.[74] Four years later, after immigrant peonage had declined, investigations and successful court cases had failed to crack the wall of Southern custom regarding black labor. After talking to citizens in Hawkinsville, Georgia, in 1911 a U.S. attorney revealed that "the public sentiment in regard to the peonage laws is in a most deplorable condition, many people not hesitating to say that negroes will be compelled to work out labor contracts even if a few of them have to be lynched in order to terrorize the remaining ones into complying with these iniquitous contracts." The *Annual Report of the Attorney General* in 1911 agreed, concluding that despite the prosecution carried out for ten years, "in some of the Southern States this practice appears to be still quite extensively carried on."[75]

[74] Hoyt to Attorney General, Feb. 4, 1907, file 50–162–1, Dept. of Justice, NA, RG 60.
[75] Alexander Akerman to Attorney General, Aug. 24, 1911, file 50–211, ibid.; *Annual Report of the Attorney General*, 1911 (Washington, 1912), p. 26.

CHAPTER VI

The Savage Ideal

On February 18, 1921, federal agents George W. Brown and A. J. Wismer investigated the 2,000 acre plantation of John S. Williams in Jasper County, Georgia. Finding the owner away that Friday afternoon, they talked to several of his black workers before he arrived twenty minutes later. They were especially interested in questioning twenty-seven-year-old Clyde Manning, Williams's black foreman. They took Manning out behind a barn and asked him if he and Williams had once caught a black laborer named Gus Chapman who had fled from the plantation. Manning denied it.[1] Williams, a fifty-four-year-old man who one observer said was a "giant in stature," returned to discover that the agents were investigating a complaint that he held men in peonage.[2] The planter quickly offered to show the agents anything on the plantation; then he asked about the peonage law. Agent Wismer recalled that they told him if "he paid a nigger out of the stockade, paid his fine, and kept him working on his plantation . . . he would be guilty of peonage, since he worked the nigger against his will." Williams expressed amazement and declared that "I and most all of the farmers in this county must be guilty of peonage." The agents then asked Williams, as they had Manning, whether he had caught and returned Gus Chapman to his farm; the planter admitted that he had, claiming that Chapman had assaulted Manning's wife and that they thought of prosecuting him.

[1] Testimony of George W. Brown, p. 11, trial transcript, *Georgia* v. *John S. Williams*, Newton Superior Court, March term 1921. (Hereafter cited as *Georgia* v. *Williams*, Newton Superior Court.)

[2] *New York Call*, Mar. 29, 1921, clipping in National Association for the Advancement of Colored People Papers, Manuscript Division, Library of Congress, Washington, D.C., Box C 357. (Hereafter cited as NAACP Papers.)

Brown then turned to Manning, "You lied to us about that." Williams then escorted the agents to his sons' two farms five miles away, allowing the agents to talk with any of the hands. Before the agents left, Williams asked if the agents had found conditions that would lead to prosecution. Getting no specific commitment, he assured the departing agents that though he might technically be guilty of peonage he would never break the law again.[3] After the agents departed, Williams turned to his black foreman Clyde Manning and said, "Clyde, we have got to do away with these negroes, or they are going up to Atlanta and break me and my boys's necks."[4]

Less than a month later a small white boy named Cash spied the "foot of a human body on the surface of the stream" near Allen's Bridge in Newton County. He immediately went for help, and before nightfall on March 13 two Negro bodies had been brought up from the Yellow River. The coroner ruled that the men had been murdered and postulated that they had been bound and weighted and thrown from the bridge alive. The large crowd that had gathered at Allen's Bridge on that March Sunday speculated about the identity of the slain men. Neighboring Jasper County, they surmised, would be the place to look for the murderer; unlike Newton County, it experienced much racial turmoil.[5] County pride and a conscionable group of local officers combined to launch one of the South's most unusual murder cases.

The murder trail eventually led from Allen's Bridge to the Williams plantation in Jasper County. The tale that unfolded in the weeks after the arrest of Clyde Manning and John S. Williams revealed not only a grotesque and unusual murder case but also a vivid picture of peonage. The events leading up to the murders questioned the thoroughness of peonage investigations, as well as the effectiveness of the chain of command from the agents to the district attorneys to the officials in the Justice Department in Washington.

The story began while John S. Williams's four oldest sons were fight-

---

[3] Testimony of A. J. Wismer, p. 19; Brown, pp. 4, 9–11, *Georgia* v. *Williams*, Newton Superior Court; *New York Tribune*, Apr. 8, 1921, clipping in NAACP Papers, Box C 387.

[4] *Manning* v. *Georgia*, 153 Ga. 190; testimony of Manning, p. 50, trial transcript, *Georgia* v. *Clyde Manning*, Newton Superior Court, July term 1922. (Hereafter cited as *Georgia* v. *Manning*, Newton Superior Court.) This is the transcript of Manning's second trial after a successful appeal to the Georgia Supreme Court.

[5] *Augusta Chronicle*, Mar. 14, 1921, p. 2.

ing in World War I, and their father began to accumulate black laborers for his plantation. To secure labor Williams (or, later, one of his sons) would travel to Atlanta or to Macon or to some nearby jail, pay the fine of a black who had run afoul of the law, and take the victim back to Jasper County. Indebted to Williams for their bond, the peons worked not only until they paid back their bonds but for as long as Williams could hold them; they moved from peonage to slavery. Once the victim reached the Williams farm, he went through a seasoning process. "When we got down there that night he told me to go in there and stay with the other boys," explained one laborer, "and when I went in there I just laid down on the floor, I didn't have any cover and I begun to work the next day, they took me out to work on new ground and I got a whipping that Saturday."[6]

To prevent escape Williams gave two trusted black men, Clyde Manning and Claude Freeman, authority over the "stockade" (or jail) Negroes. Freeman remembered that Williams gave them both pistols. "He said if any of the hands got away or tried to get away, or did anything to me to kill them, and he said if I let any one get away I would know what was coming then to me." Manning remembered that his "boss job begun after the Armistice was signed and his boys come home and he got some of these stockade boys, he told me he was looking to me to see after them." Manning claimed that he did not relish his job but having observed Williams for thirteen years "I was there long enough to find out you had to go ahead and do what he said." While Manning managed the peons on the Williams home place, Freeman helped Huland, Marvin, and Leroy Williams on farms five miles away. The year that Huland Williams returned from the navy, Claude Freeman remembered, they began locking up the stockade Negroes. The house on Huland Williams's farm had a hall running through it; Williams stayed on one side of the hall and the blacks on the other. "They had a cleat across there and they had it fastened on the outside of the door and they had a hole through and a big wire run through the hole and there was a bolt in the door, and a hook on the outside, so they couldn't get out," Clyde Freeman recalled. As many as eighteen prison-

[6] Testimony of Gus Chapman, pp. 131, 133; Frank Dozier, p. 134, *Georgia* v. *Manning*, Newton Superior Court. Though the system of bailing out prisoners had been declared unconstitutional in *United States* v. *Reynolds*, 235 U.S. 133 (1914), the custom prevailed throughout Georgia and the South in the 1920s.

ers were there at one time. Later the stockade Negroes lived in a shack while Leroy and Marvin Williams joined their brother Huland; the white Williamses and the black Freemans lived in the same house. Clyde Manning resided in a similar duplex dwelling five miles away near John S. Williams's house.[7]

To enforce discipline on the Williams plantations, the overseers often administered beatings. The brutality went even beyond keeping the stockade men in line; the Williams family also beat the free blacks who lived on the place. Clyde Freeman's wife Emma stated that she had been whipped "a heap of times" so severely that "the whelps come." She had seen and experienced much cruelty in her twenty-six years and revealed that Huland Williams had hit her with his pistol; she bore the scar years later. Twenty-seven-year-old Lessie May Whitlow, who cooked for the hands, revealed that the peons were whipped at least once a week. Huland, she said, once got mad at her when she did not have the evening meal ready on time and "whipped me and then hit me over the head with a pistol." She, too, bore the mark for years. Nearly all the hands who worked at the Williams plantation remembered the savage beatings, often for trivial or imagined offenses.[8]

Though John S. Williams and his sons warned the men that they would catch and kill them if they tried to escape, several of the peons attempted to run away. Sixteen-year-old Frank Dozier, who had been arrested for vagrancy for sitting down at the Macon depot, successfully escaped. He reached Covington, some twenty miles away, but Huland Williams spotted him and chased him with the bloodhound. The chief of police in Covington remembered that two of the Williams boys once asked him for permission to go into the Negro section of town to pursue some fugitives. He refused to grant them permission but admitted that he heard their dog barking "as though he was running something" (probably Frank Dozier) a little later. Dozier fled up a creek "and lay in the water all night, under the bridge." Gus Chapman, whose successful escape and complaint led the special agents to the Williams

[7] Testimony of Claude Freeman, pp. 89–90; Emma Freeman, p. 120, *Georgia v. Manning*, Newton Superior Court. Testimony of Manning, pp. 33–34, 55, *Georgia v. Williams*, Newton Superior Court.
[8] Testimony of Emma Freeman, p. 115; Lessie May Whitlow, pp. 124, 126, *Georgia v. Manning*, Newton Superior Court. See also testimony of Wismer, p. 56; Clyde Freeman, pp. 64, 70; Frank Dozier, pp. 134–35, ibid. Huland Williams "whipped me just because he was mad," said Lessie May Whitlow, in ibid., p. 126.

plantations, had once failed to get away. He had run for miles but finally surrendered; then "Mr. Williams took me back and took me down in the wagon shelter and made me pull down my clothes and said he would kill me, but as I was a kind of an old son of a bitch he would let me go that time but if I ever did it again he would sure kill me, but would let me go this time. He whipped me with a buggy trace."[9]

Despite the warnings, beatings, and bloodhound, the black peons continued to trouble the Williams family. When threats and beatings failed, the atmosphere of the farm became more macabre, more unreal. James Strickland recalled that the Williams men carried pistols about and often shot at the peons when their work did not suit the overseers. They "didn't just shoot to scare me because one time they shot at me and the bullet went through my hat and knocked my hat off. He shot at me to make me hurry across the field, to make me trot, I was not going fast enough, he hollered at me to go faster and then shot at me." Another time John S. Williams "snapped his pistol" at a worker named Jake "three times and it didn't fire because it didn't have nothing in it."[10] The Williams family knew how to keep men insecure, afraid, and ready to perform any task at a trot. And unlike slaves, these peons had no monetary value; they could be replaced at the nearest jail.

When the black foremen, the pistols, the beatings, and the bloodhounds could not keep the peons cowed, the Williamses resorted to murder. According to a statement of an old man who had once worked on the Williams place, three laborers had been killed as early as 1911.[11] The killings were random, bizarre, without predictability or reason. In 1919, as near as is determinable, Long John Singleton "went to the goat pasture and never come back." Rumor around the plantation said that Marvin Williams shot Singleton. Claude Freeman remembered that he did not see the body until over a week after the killing. "One day, me and Mr. Marvin and Barber was pulling corn, and the buzzards was flying around, and Mr. Marvin went on and come back up there and he said, when I asked him what was the matter, he said John Singleton

[9] Testimony of B. B. Bohannon, pp. 106–7; Frank Dozier, p. 136; Gus Chapman, p. 131, ibid. Claude Freeman stated that Williams had several dogs, that he "run niggers with them." Testimony of Freeman, p. 95, ibid.
[10] Testimony of James Strickland, pp. 137–38, ibid.
[11] *New York Times*, Apr. 15, 1921, clipping in NAACP Papers, Box C 387.

had come to the top." Then Marvin went to the house, got some "ropes and wire and then they went back down there [to the pond] and took the body out there and put some rock to it and sunk it again."[12]

In the spring of 1920 Leroy Williams shot Iron Jaw, a stockade Negro. They were building a hog lot, Clyde Freeman remembered. "They whipped him claimed he was not working, he was rolling some wire, he was not rolling the wire straight and they whipped him." When Iron Jaw said he would rather be dead than be treated that way, "Mr. Leroy pulled out his pistol and shot him." During the same year Nathaniel Wade, nicknamed Blackstrap, was killed for running away. Rumor had it that one of the other hands on the farm had killed him at the orders of Huland Williams.[13] Will Napeer died at hog-killing time in the winter of 1920–21, shot by Huland Williams. Claude Freeman said that Huland and Will "was away behind the little house and I heard a shot and he then called us to come down there; we went down there and picked him up, he was laying up behind the little house there." Three doctors (including one of Williams's sons) tended the wounded man, but he died that night of a gunshot wound in the abdomen. The doctors failed either to inquire how the shooting occurred or to report it to the authorities. What a white man did to his black laborers was his own business.[14] Three of John Williams's sons, according to accounts of the black laborers on the plantation, had committed murder.

By the spring of 1921, the Williams plantations had become places of fear and dread. The Williams family took men from the jails of the area, held, chased, beat, and sometimes murdered them. Exactly where peonage stopped and slavery began remained unclear. Williams stated that he took the men from the jails and worked them, but he never said how much he paid them or how long he kept them. Though he claimed that he worked them only until they had paid their fines, some only owed $5, and there remains no record of his allowing a man to leave.

[12] Testimony of Lessie May Whitlow, p. 124; Claude Freeman, p. 85, *Georgia* v. *Manning*, Newton Superior Court. See also testimony of Emma Freeman, pp. 110–11, ibid.

[13] Testimony of Clyde Freeman, pp. 61–63; Claude Freeman, p. 88; Emma Freeman, pp. 111–12; Lessie May Whitlow, pp. 125–26, ibid.

[14] Testimony of Dr. T. E. Hardeman, pp. 93–94; Claude Freeman, p. 86, ibid. See also testimony of Clyde Freeman, pp. 59–60; Emma Freeman, p. 111; Lessie May Whitlow, p. 123, ibid.

Charlie Chisholm, for example, had been on the place for three or four years after Huland Williams had paid his bond.[15] All the Negroes who survived the Williams plantations agreed that they were afraid to leave or to disobey the Williamses, and that they lived in fear of their lives.

The terrorism practiced on the Williams plantations took place within several miles of houses and a store. Strangely, either the neighbors were unaware of the atrocities, or they were intimidated by the savage reputation of the family. The Williamses seemed secure in their stronghold until two black men escaped. Gus Chapman, who had been threatened with death if he ran away again, took his chance on Thanksgiving, 1920, and fled. He complained to the Justice Department that he had been held in peonage and that several laborers had been murdered on the Williams plantation. James Strickland escaped on Labor Day, 1920; he also complained to the Justice Department.[16]

The complaints of these two men led special agents Brown and Wismer to the Williams farm in February, 1921. Williams probably suspected that more than peonage had been reported, but he also surmised that his brand of terror would keep the blacks quiet about the killings and the peonage. Only one peon gave information to the agents, yet Williams thought that he had reason to fear prosecution. Sometime during the week after the agents visited the plantation, Williams evidently had a serious talk with his sons about their chances before a federal court. About February 24 or 25, Huland, Marvin, and Leroy Williams left for some unannounced destination.[17] If any charges emerged, the old man decided he would face them alone. After his sons left, Williams talked to Manning, his trusted black foreman. "Clyde, we are going to do away with these boys and I want you to help." Manning, who knew of the other killings, said he did not want to do that. "Well, by God,

[15] Statement of John S. Williams, p. 76, *Georgia* v. *Williams*, Newton Superior Court. He admitted that "I am like most farmers that I know, that at times I have bonded out and paid fines for niggers with actual agreement that they would stay there till their fines were paid, or till he was relieved from his bond, which in many instances I have rehired them after that and paid them wages just like I would any other nigger I would hire going through the country and which I thought I had a perfect right to do." See also testimony of Clyde Manning, p. 24, ibid.

[16] Testimony of Claude Freeman, pp. 103–4; Chapman, p. 132; Wismer, pp. 50–51; Strickland, p. 138, *Georgia* v. *Manning*, Newton Superior Court.

[17] Testimony of Manning, p. 49; statement of John S. Williams, p. 81; *Georgia* v. *Williams*, Newton Superior Court; statement of Manning, p. 139, *Georgia* v. *Manning*, Newton Superior Court.

Fred Cubberly. A Florida attorney who used an 1867 federal peonage statute to inaugurate the battle against peonage. Compliments of Helen Cubberly Ellerbe, Gainesville, Florida.

Emory Speer. A Georgia judge who spoke for the common man. From " 'Peonage' as Now Exposed," *The American Monthly Review of Reviews* 28 (Aug. 1903), 137.

John W. Pace. An Alabama peon-master who could have come from the pages of *Uncle Tom's Cabin*. From *Montgomery Advertiser*, June 23, 1907, p. 7; courtesy of the Alabama Department of Archives and History.

Thomas Goode Jones. A governor of Alabama who later became a legal expert on peonage. From "'Peonage' as Now Exposed," *The American Monthly Review of Reviews* 28 (Aug. 1903), 137.

William H. Thomas. A Montgomery city
court judge who saw in an Alabama contract labor law a form of peonage. From
Ray Stannard Baker, "A Pawn in the
Struggle for Freedom," *American Magazine* 72 (Sept. 1011), 610.

Booker T. Washington. The calm ex-
terior masked a complicated soul. Courtesy of Booker T. Washington Photo
Collection, Library of Congress.

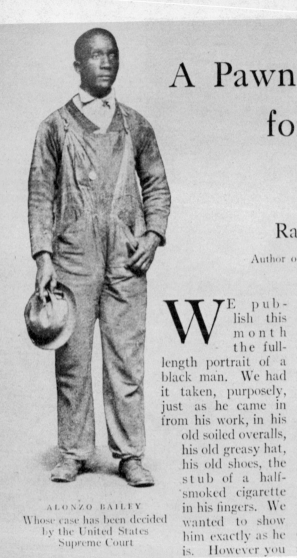

ALONZO BAILEY
Whose case has been decided
by the United States
Supreme Court

A Pawn

for

Ray

WE pub-
lish this
month
the full-
length portrait of a
black man. We had
it taken, purposely,
just as he came in
from his work, in his
old soiled overalls,
his old greasy hat,
his old shoes, the
stub of a half-
smoked cigarette
in his fingers. We
wanted to show
him exactly as he
is. However you

in
his
hig
cisi
wo

in
sco
abo
me
dec
nar
vol
day
ma
hav
of
slav

Alonzo Bailey. A laborer whose peonage case went twice to the U.S. Supreme Court. From Ray Stannard Baker, "A Pawn in the Struggle for Freedom," *American Magazine* 72 (Sept. 1911), 608.

Fred S. Ball and Edward S. Watts. Two young Alabama attorneys who took the case of an illiterate black laborer, Alonzo Bailey. From Ray Stannard Baker, "A Pawn in the Struggle for Freedom," *American Magazine* 72 (Sept. 1911), 609.

Charles Wells Russell. He battled immigrant peonage and discovered that, in the North as well as in the South, men of wealth sanctioned slavery. Compliments of Georgetown University Archives.

Robert Gallagher. A foreman who introduced immigrants to Southern peonage. From "The Life Story of a Hungarian Peon," *Independent* 63 (Sept. 5, 1907), 563.

Mike Trudics. A Hungarian immigrant who became a peon. From "The Life Story of a Hungarian Peon," *Independent* 63 (Sept. 5, 1907), 557.

"Caught!" An artist's conception of fleeing peons. From Richard Barry, "Slavery in the South To-Day," *Cosmopolitan Magazine* 42 (Mar. 1907), 485.

Negro Who Confessed Slaying

Clyde Manning. A peon who faced awful choices on the Williams plantation. From *Atlanta Constitution*, Mar. 29, 1921, p. 2.

John Williams, As He Heard His Sentence

John S. Williams. The fell lord of peonage. From *Atlanta Constitution*, Apr. 10, 1921, p. 2.

Scenes in Jasper Tragedy

Williams home and some of the weights used to drown peons on the plantation. From *Atlanta Constitution*, Mar. 31, 1921, p. 3.

Principals in "Murder Farm" Trial at Covington

LEFT: John Williams arrives in Covington for his trial. RIGHT: One of Williams's daughters watches the courtroom proceedings. From *Atlanta Constitution*, Apr. 6, 1921, p. 1.

Tense Scene in Covington Courtroom as Clyde Manning Tells His Gruesome Story

Clyde Manning testifying before a packed courthouse in Covington, Georgia. From *Atlanta Constitution*, Apr. 7, 1921, p. 1.

Leading Legal Characters in "Murder Farm" Trial

(1) Greene F. Johnson, Williams's lawyer; (2) Judge John B. Hutcheson; (3) W. M. Howard, and (4) Solicitor-General A. M. Brand, for the state; (5) Sheriff B. L. Johnson of Newton County; (6) Graham Wright, assisting the state. From *Atlanta Constitution*, Apr. 6, 1921, p. 1.

Dr. Sidney D. Redmond. A Mississippian who revealed peonage during the 1927 Mississippi River flood. From Green P. Hamilton, *Beacon Lights of the Race* (Memphis, 1911), p. 134.

Robert Russa Moton. President of Tuskegee who missed an opportunity to strike out at peonage. Courtesy of Tuskegee Archives.

The Colored Advisory Commission. From The American National Red Cross, "The Final Report of the Colored Advisory Commission: Mississippi Valley Flood Disaster, 1927," p. 9.

Mother of nine refugees does laundry in Red Cross camp. From The American National Red Cross, "The Final Report of the Colored Advisory Commission: Mississippi Valley Flood Disaster, 1927," p. 22.

Flood refugees waiting for boats to Red Cross camp. From The American National Red Cross, "The Final Report of the Colored Advisory Commission: Mississippi Valley Flood Disaster, 1927," p. 15.

Paul D. Peacher. He saw nothing wrong with mixing law enforcement and slavery. From "Races, Slavery in Arkansas," *Time* 28 (Dec. 7, 1936), 17. Courtesy of Wide World Photos.

William Henry Huff. He led the fight against William T. Cunningham. a planter who wanted to take peons from Illinois back to Georgia. From *New Masses*, Oct. 27, 1942, p. 20.

Some of the slaves who testified against Paul Peacher. From "Races, Slavery in Arkansas," *Time* 28 (Dec. 7, 1936), 17. Courtesy of Photo-world.

it is all right with me, if you don't want to, it means your neck or theirs," Williams told him, "if you think more of their necks than you do of your own it is all right."[18]

The killings started less than a week after the special agents left Williams's farm. Ironically, the first to die bore the name of Johnny Williams. Manning and John S. Williams went to the pasture where Johnny Williams was working, and the planter ordered Manning to kill the black peon. Johnny Williams "kept backing around," Manning related, and "I didn't want to hit him, he was begging and going on, and I didn't want to kill him." But the planter told Manning that if he would not do it to give him the ax, so "I was afraid to give him the ax and so I hit him with the ax, hit him one lick on the back of the head, sort of side of the head with the back of the ax, and then we dug a hole there." Two other peons, "Little Bit" and "Red," were bound, weighted, and tossed from Water's Bridge over the Alcovy River. "Big John," Johnnie Green, and Willie Givens were also murdered with an ax.[19]

On February 26, several days after the killing began, Williams went to his sons' plantation five miles away and told three of the stockade Negroes that he would take them to the train that night. He instructed them to drive the hogs down to his home place, and that after supper he would free them. After the meal five blacks and John S. Williams got into his car. A few miles down the road Williams stopped the car and with the help of Manning and Charlie Chisholm bound three blacks with trace chains and hung hundred-pound sacks filled with rocks around their necks. "Lindsey Peterson and Will Preston, they didn't think we were going to do anything to them, until we got to the river," Manning remembered. There, with Williams giving the order, Charlie Chisholm and Manning lifted the two men to the bridge railing "and they were scuffling and trying to keep back, to keep from going over, and he told us to push them over.... and we throwed them over and then we got in the car and left there." Williams then drove several miles to a bridge across the South River. Harry Price, the third of the peons who left the Williams plantation in the car, pled with Manning, "Don't throw me over, I will get over." Then Price "crawled up on the ban-

---

[18] Statement of Manning, p. 139, *Georgia* v. *Manning*, Newton Superior Court.
[19] Testimony of Manning, pp. 36–40, *Georgia* v. *Williams*, Newton Superior Court.

nister, set up on the bannister, he set there just a little while, and he says 'Don't throw me,' He says, 'Lord, have mercy,' and went right on over."[20]

Earlier the same day Williams had asked Artis Freeman, another of the stockade blacks, if he wanted to go home, and as Manning recalled, "took him to Jackson, that is where he said he was going and he come back with the automobile." The next day Fred Favors, after a conversation with Williams, left the home place for Huland Williams's farm five miles away. Manning related that "I never seen him from the time he left out of Mr. Johnny's yard since, I have never seen him anywhere at all since." A week later Williams and Manning threw Charlie Chisholm into the Alcovy River because the planter feared that he would talk.[21] Finally, Williams shot Fletcher Smith with a shotgun, and Manning helped bury him. "After we got him covered up we plowed over him again and he says, 'Clyde, I don't want to hear nothing from this. There is nobody knows about this but just me and you. If I ever hear it come out I will know where it come from." Manning assured him, "I aint going to say nothing about it to nobody."[22]

Only after being promised protection by law enforcement officials would Clyde Manning talk about the gruesome murders. Secure in the Fulton Tower in Atlanta he confessed on March 24 that he and John S. Williams had murdered eleven peons.[23] Williams, never caught without an alibi, claimed that he had been framed by a neighbor who had a feud with him.[24]

The local reaction to the murders was uniformly one of horror and embarrassment, but also of curiosity to discover all the gory details. Sheriff B. L. Johnson of Newton County promised that he would get to the bottom of the murders and would not sidestep his responsibility. Though it was Johnson who led the investigation, on March 26 he took occasion to praise Sheriff W. F. Persons of Jasper County and said that "there isn't a man in Jasper or Newton county more determined than he is to bring the whole truth to the surface and clean up Jasper county."

20 Ibid., pp. 27, 30.
21 Ibid., pp. 40–41, 54. See also testimony of Lessie May Benton [Whitlow], p. 60; Clyde Freeman, p. 61, ibid.
22 Testimony of Manning, p. 43, ibid.
23 *Atlanta Constitution*, Mar. 25, 1921, p. 1; *Savannah Morning News*, Mar. 25, 1921, p. 1; *New York Times*, Mar. 26, 1921, p. 3.
24 *Atlanta Constitution*, Mar. 26, 1921, p. 1; *New York Times*, Mar. 26, 1921, p. 5.

Sheriff Persons needed some public relations help, for he was a cousin of John S. Williams, the suspected murderer. Moreover, he had only recently been indicted for peonage, casting doubt on his professions of sincerity regarding a genuinely honest investigation.[25]

After the discovery of the first two bodies on March 13, the people of Newton and Jasper counties took an active if morbid interest in discovering the bodies of the other murdered blacks. With hundreds of local citizens flocking behind, Manning led officials on a grim trip about the county pointing out the graves of the victims. Two days later, on March 28, rumors spread throughout the area that the blacks of Jasper County were gathering along the river bank, and reports of black insurrection quickly spread. Suddenly the roads were clogged with automobiles bearing armed white men, racing toward the river. There they discovered the blacks holding a prayer meeting.[26]

James Weldon Johnson, executive secretary of the National Association for the Advancement of Colored People (NAACP) and editorial writer for the *New York Age*, quickly pointed out the similarity of this reaction among the whites with that two years earlier in an incident at Elaine, Arkansas. Blacks in that area of Arkansas were organizing to protest peonage conditions; the riot had begun at a Negro church when several white men attempted to ascertain why the blacks had gathered. Firing started and rumors spread that the blacks were beginning a race war.[27] The Georgia whites, however, sheepishly returned to their homes. Suspecting some deeper reason for the rumor, a Newton County grand jury heard additional evidence while investigating the murders. Floyd Johnson, a young white man, testified that anonymous letters had been sent to white planters in the area warning them of "black vengeance." Further investigations revealed that the notes actually had been

[25] *Macon Daily Telegraph*, Mar. 27, 1921; *Chattanooga Times*, Mar. 27, 1921; clippings in NAACP Papers, Box C 387; *Atlanta Constitution*, Mar. 16, 1921, p. 1.

[26] *Macon Daily Telegraph*, Mar. 27, 1921; *Jackson* (Mississippi) *Clarion*, Mar. 29, 1921; *New York Times*, Mar. 29, 1921; clippings in NAACP Papers, Box C 387.

[27] Press release by James Weldon Johnson, n.d. [Mar. 1921?], NAACP Papers, Box C 386. See also Arthur I. Waskow, *From Race Riot to Sit-in* (Garden City, 1966), pp. 121–36. Though the Elaine riots occurred allegedly because of peonage, the cases quickly became an effort to defend the victims from injustice. Unfortunately, the conditions that led to the original complaints and organization of a union remained uninvestigated and uncorrected. The same area of Arkansas proved fertile soil for the Southern Tenant Farmers' Union efforts in the 1930s. See David Eugene Conrad, *The Forgotten Farmers* (Urbana, 1965).

sent by Huland, Julius, and Marvin Williams. The jury concluded that
the men had sought to bring about a race war in an effort to shift the
attention from their father and to create a climate of opinion that would
discredit the testimony of Manning. As James Weldon Johnson wrote
in the *New York Age,* "Here we have the same sort of thing that happened in the Arkansas cases, only in that instance the ruse succeeded."
Johnson concluded that in the entire history of peonage the Williams
affair was "the most flagrant and savage case. The details are more hor-
rible than anything that was disclosed in the atrocities in the Belgian
Congo."[28]

While Georgia Governor Hugh M. Dorsey deplored the murders and
a Georgia church organization claimed that "Christ . . . is using the
murder of the eleven negroes . . . to wake Georgia to the need for justice
to the negro," the NAACP launched a massive publicity campaign.
James Weldon Johnson sent telegrams to Governor Dorsey, President
Warren G. Harding, and Attorney General Harry M. Dougherty,
while Walter White, assistant secretary of the NAACP, sent some
twenty letters to congressmen, state representatives, and local NAACP
leaders. White asked that petitions be drawn up and that state legislatures pass resolutions calling for a thorough investigation of peonage.[29]
Several state legislatures did pass such resolutions. Herbert J. Seligmann,
press secretary of the Negro rights organization, appealed to labor
unions to make statements condemning peonage.[30]

Hoping to gain credit and publicity for the exposé of peonage in
Georgia, the NAACP asked the Justice Department "if there is any
connection between the facts which we presented last September on
peonage conditions in Georgia with the later statement by Hooper
Alexander of Georgia and the investigation and prosecution of Jasper
county, Georgia peonage cases." The Justice Department replied that it
had "carefully investigated" all the complaints of the NAACP but could

28 *New York Call,* Mar. 31, 1921, clipping in NAACP Papers, Box C 387; *New York Times,* Mar. 30, 1921, clipping in ibid., Box C 388; *New York Age,* Apr. 2, 1921, p. 4.
29 Dorsey to Johnson, Mar. 31, 1921, NAACP Papers, Box C 387; *Atlanta Geor-gian,* Apr. 5, 1921, clipping in ibid. See numerous letters in ibid., Box C 388.
30 Frederick M. Roberts to White, May 5, 1921; Harry E. Davis to White, Apr. 26, 1921, ibid., Box C 386; White to Arthur H. Day, Apr. 27, 1921, Box C 388. See Seligmann to E. N. Nickels, Apr. 7, 1921, and numerous other letters in ibid., Box C 388.

not reveal the results of the investigations "owing to the confidential nature of the work." In another letter regarding the *Williams* case the Justice Department explained that it "may interest you to know that the facts in connection therewith were discovered by agents of this Department." Expressing impatience with the NAACP, the Justice Department denied that it needed help from the Negro rights organization, adding that many cases the NAACP had uncovered were not peonage but some other crime.[31] Perhaps the Justice Department was getting touchy as a result of a *New York World* report that appeared just before the Williams trial began. A correspondent reported that the federal agents had been impressed with Williams's "frankness" and desire to reform, and they "returned to Atlanta convinced of his innocence."[32] While the Justice Department was anxious to claim credit for the investigation, it was silent as to why no charges were ever brought against Williams, and no satisfactory explanation of this failure ever emerged.

The general reaction of disgust at the grotesqueness of the crimes was not restricted to Northern whites and blacks, as in other cases; it was also felt among Southern whites—rural whites who were usually reluctant to admit the existence of sin in their midst. It was the brutal nature of the drownings, the publicity, the convincing testimony of Clyde Manning, the apparent lack of a motive ("There wasn't even a remote phase of the 'usual crime' involved," one Southern newspaper admitted),[33] the insatiable curiosity to discover who committed so enormous a crime, and probably the Newton County natives' desire to assuage their wounded local pride that led to Williams's indictment and trial.

The federal agents' investigation became the key to the state's prosecution as the trial of John S. Williams opened in Covington, Georgia, on April 5. Williams was on trial for the first-degree murder of one of the peons, Lindsey Peterson, whose body had been discovered in Newton County. The county courthouse was packed with observers, and there were numerous law officers on duty to preserve order as blacks and whites mingled in the overflow crowd or strained to catch each word

[31] White to William C. Herron, Mar. 29, 1921; R. P. Stewart to White, Mar. 31, 1921; Stewart to Johnson, Apr. 15, 1921; Stewart to White, Apr. 15, 1921, ibid., Box C 388.
[32] *New York World*, Apr. 4, 1921, clipping in ibid., Box 387.
[33] *Atlanta Georgian*, Mar. 21, 1921, clipping in ibid.

from their segregated vantage points within the courtroom. And Williams would certainly be judged by his peers, for there were seven farmers, four merchants, and one druggist on the jury.[34]

Over the objection of Williams's lawyers, Judge John B. Hutcheson allowed the two agents to testify. The state claimed that Williams's motive for murder was to silence the peons in the event he had to stand trial for peonage. Agent George W. Brown took the stand first. He gave an account of the investigation and told of Williams's openness and earnestness. He had examined the partitioned houses and admitted that they could have been used for keeping prisoners. Williams had admitted that he had "worked some stockade negroes on his place and while he had worked them he instructed them that they must not leave his place until they had paid him back what he had paid out for them." Brown stated that it was his impression that most of the stockade Negroes had left by the time of the investigation. At this point his testimony began to blur and obfuscate.[35] The special agent appeared to stop short of telling all he knew.

The defense attempted to show that the agents had found no peonage on the Williams plantations and that Williams did not need to murder the men for fear of federal prosecution. When cross-examined, Brown admitted that he had talked to Doyle Campbell, solicitor of the Ocmulgee Circuit, but he denied that he told Campbell he found nothing objectionable there. "I stated they looked better cared for than the negroes on Mr. Harvey J. Person's place," he said. The prosecution then asked why Williams had not been arrested if there was something objectionable about the place. "I don't make cases," Brown replied. He added that he had made his report to the attorney general and to the district attorney in Atlanta. "I found enough there to issue a warrant on," he added. "As to why I did not swear one out, Mr. Williams stated that he might have technically violated the law, but he was doing better and the case was still under investigation." The last statement conflicted with the report that Williams had duped the agents into dropping the case. Brown never revealed what he learned from the peons—only that

[34] *Atlanta Constitution*, Apr. 6, 1921, p. 1.
[35] *New York Tribune*, Apr. 7, 1921, clipping in NAACP Papers, Box C 388; Testimony of Brown, p. 9, *Georgia* v. *Williams*, Newton Superior Court.

he "didn't go into details with them."[36] A U.S. attorney reported later that the agents "were unable to obtain any material information," but exactly what the report contained remains a mystery, for those investigatory files are yet unopened.[37]

Agent Wismer gave much the same testimony as Brown, excusing his failure to prosecute Williams with the identical words that Brown used: "I don't make cases." Wismer described the house where locks were on the windows and the doors, the talks with the laborers, Manning's lies, and the talk with Williams about the meaning of peonage. Wismer hinted that he had heard things on the plantation that led him to believe that Williams practiced peonage, but he did not elaborate at this trial. Wismer told Williams that the fact that his son Leroy was carrying a gun looked bad. Yet in this trial neither Brown nor Wismer told exactly what they heard at the Williams plantation. Two months later, testifying in Manning's trial, Wismer did go into more detail; by then Brown no longer worked for the government. Wismer then related that "the only information I got while I was on the place that day that had any bearing on the entire situation by any one, I got from Johnny Williams, he was the only negro on the place that told anything." Wismer explained that the complaints of Gus Chapman and James Strickland, who claimed that they were held in peonage and had witnessed murders there, spurred the investigation.[38]

Nothing could have substantiated the complaints more than what Johnny Williams told them and what they saw. "Johnny Williams told us that Clyde Manning acted as guard over the hands on the John S. Williams place, he looked after them at night and he was made to tote a pistol." That was the only information that they got, he said, "except as to the quarters, I inspected the quarters on the Huland Williams place." Wismer added that from the "general attitude" of the Negroes, he concluded that "they were afraid to tell anything for fear they would tell the wrong thing and would get into trouble and be punished there on the plantation." The government agent also revealed that, when he

---

[36] Testimony of Brown, pp. 12–14, *Georgia* v. *Williams*, Newton Superior Court.
[37] W. A. Bootle to Attorney General, June 24, 1930, file 50–05–19, Dept. of Justice, NA, RG 60.
[38] Testimony of Wismer, p. 20, *Georgia* v. *Williams*, Newton Superior Court; Wismer, p. 49, *Georgia* v. *Manning*, Newton Superior Court.

checked back at the jails where Williams had secured the peons, the records did not even show who had paid the fines.[39]

The attitude of John S. Williams—his frankness, his apparent eagerness to reform—offset the fact that Johnny Williams admitted he was being held, that they found barracks with locks, and that Leroy Williams carried a gun. The agents explained that they made their reports to the proper authorities, but John S. Williams testified that the agents told him, "I don't think you need to have any fear of any case before the Federal Grand Jury."[40] And though Williams's word was not to be trusted, the fact remains that no charges were brought against him. Obviously, something broke down in the process of bringing charges for peonage. If such conditions as Brown and Wismer saw habitually led to no charges, the Justice Department simply ignored the existence of peonage, or they hoped that by investigation alone they could discourage the practice. The vague and evasive evidence given by Brown and Wismer indicated that they were telling as little as they could about conditions on the farm. What they did tell showed that even the most brutal and open peonage could escape prosecution.

Next Clyde Manning took the stand. Asked where he was born, the illiterate Manning replied, "When I first remember myself, I was in Jasper County." Sitting in the "splint bottomed witness chair," Manning calmly told of each murder in gory detail. The only humor of the trial came when Manning, with an unintended stroke of paradox, referred to the special agents as "United States protectors." The "coal black, short, stockily built man" impressed the spectators with his iciness on the stand. From the time he took the stand, they reported, his voice did not show any emotion nor did he "twiddle a finger of those folded black hands, or shuffle a foot." Williams, they noted, "listened with an inscrutable face."[41] They were a grim pair. Williams's lawyers tried to shake Manning's testimony by implying that the black was trying to place the entire blame on Williams in order to save himself. "As to my

[39] Testimony of Wismer, pp. 51, 53, *Georgia v. Manning*, Newton Superior Court.

[40] Statement of John S. Williams, *Georgia* v. *Williams*, Newton Superior Court, p. 79. Until the Federal Bureau of Investigation opens its files to research, the content of the investigation and the reason for no further action will remain unknown. (See Critical Essay on Authorities.)

[41] *New York World*, Apr. 7, 1921, clipping in NAACP Papers, Box C 387.

expecting to get off lighter, I just expect to tell the truth, and take it just as it comes," he said. "I aint putting no more on Mr. Williams than his part and I aint telling any more on myself than my part."[42]

In such a case Georgia law permitted the defendant to give a statement, not under oath or subject to cross-examination. The next day Williams gave his statement, beginning by saying that he had "never had any kind of crime charged against me in my life." He was the father of twelve children, he added, four of whom had served in World War I, and "I have always tried to do the best that I could for my fellow man." His Jasper County plantation was not nearly so large as the newspapers reported, he complained. "Niggers, boll weevil and low price of cotton just about cleaned me up." Admitting that "like most farmers that I know" he had bonded blacks out of jail and worked them, he stressed that "in many instances" he paid them. One of the federal agents assured him, he testified, " 'I don't think you have any fear of any case before the Federal Grand Jury.' " He said that following the departure of the agents he called all his help together and told them they could leave. He gave them $5 each, and when they did not appear the next day, he asked Manning where they were. "They went on off last night," he quoted Manning as saying.[43]

Throughout his testimony Williams tried to make it appear that Clyde Manning had killed the peons. Manning had been offended, Williams charged, when he admitted to the agents that Gus Chapman had been chased, making a liar out of Manning. The sheriff and other officials "insisted on him telling something on me." Finally Williams charged, "He is a very cruel nigger to the niggers, the whole Manning crowd is." Manning had once threatened to kill his wife when she left him, Williams testified, "and he was a bad nigger." The planter concluded that he was innocent in this case, the murder of Lindsey Peterson. When the murders committed in Jasper County were tried he would "explain them to the satisfaction of the jury."[44] No witnesses took the stand in Williams's defense. Except for Williams's statement, the prosecution's testimony stood unchallenged.

Williams and his attorneys knew that it was rare that a jury would

[42] Testimony of Manning, p. 58, *Georgia* v. *Williams*, Newton Superior Court.
[43] Statement of Williams, pp. 76, 79, 81, 83, ibid.
[44] Ibid., pp. 83–85.

convict a white man for the murder of a black man, especially when the sole witness to the slaying was black. What the Jasper County planter could not have known was that he was the first Southern white man since 1877 to be indicted for the first-degree murder of a black—and he would be the last until 1966.[45] Having to stand trial for murder, Williams used the race issue shrewdly. It was primarily Manning's testimony against Williams's statement, black against white, and the planter shifted the blame from himself to the black man. On April 8 the jury was locked up, and Williams, "smiling and unconcerned, chatted with those around him." He had every reason to be confident as he "joined his family in a picnic lunch spread on counsel's table inside the bar."[46]

The next day the jury returned with the verdict of guilty and asked for life imprisonment. They might have asked for the death sentence, a Southern newspaper reported, but "there were some who felt rather strongly opposed to hanging a white man based upon the statement of a negro." James Weldon Johnson, reviewing the case in the *New York Age*, editorialized that Williams's lawyers "stacked all their chances to free their client on the belief that no jury of white men in Georgia would take away the life or liberty of a white man on the word of a Negro." Johnson hoped that the grotesque murders would spur a wide and thorough investigation of peonage so that "the Negro peons who lost their lives on Williams's plantation will not have died in vain."[47]

The immediate reaction throughout Georgia and the nation showed shock, disgust, and then relief when Williams received a life sentence. A Georgia newspaper, the *Madison Madisonian*, charged that the people of Jasper County had allowed a climate of opinion to reign which led to the murders. "So many negroes have been killed in that county in recent years with no protest from its pulpit, its press or its people," it charged, "that the perpetrators of the recent deeds had a feeling of security—that they could commit the crimes, and even if detected, could somehow

[45] See Mary F. Berry, "Do Black People Have a Constitutional Right to Life: A Consideration of Federal and State Concern about the Murder of Black People, 1877–1969," Paper delivered to Southern Historical Association Convention, November 12, 1970, pp. 22–28.

[46] *New York World*, Apr. 7, 1921, clipping in NAACP Papers, Box C 388.

[47] *Atlanta Georgian*, [Apr. ?] 1921, clipping in ibid.; *New York Age*, Apr. 16, 1921, p. 4.

'get away with it.' "[48] And perhaps Williams could have gotten off in Jasper County, but it was the trial in Newton County that decided his fate. It could well have been that Williams's only miscalculation was in disposing of several of the men in Newton County.

The *New Republic*, with a great deal of truth, pointed out that the "system of forced labor is essentially a continuation of the system of slavery. Neither war nor constitutional amendments abolished the essentials of slavery."[49] Echoing Progressive era thinking, historian Albert Bushnell Hart called for a "comprehensive congressional inquiry into peonage as a violation of federal law," adding that this "would furnish a basis on which the public could act with intelligence." Hart wrote that he had visited the South for the past five years and had constantly heard rumors of peonage, but that the ignorance of the victims and the terrorism of those who practiced it made it difficult to discover or prosecute.[50]

The most forceful attack on Georgia peonage came from Governor Hugh M. Dorsey. Having been recently defeated in a Senate campaign by the old Populist hero Tom Watson, Dorsey struck hard at the rural conditions in Georgia where Watson drew most of his support. On April 22 he released a pamphlet titled *The Negro in Georgia*, a catalog of lynchings, peonage, organized lawlessness, and cruelty. Among the others, ten cases of peonage added to a dismal picture of the conditions in rural Georgia.[51] Seeming to follow the advice so recently offered by Hart in calling for evidence, Dorsey quickly discovered that more than evidence was needed to change the sentiment supporting forced labor.

Judge W. E. H. Searcy, Jr., of the Flint circuit condemned the entire pamphlet in general as "gratuitous, unwarranted and untrue," and he specifically bore in on a particular case that involved his integrity. Searcy denied that he had agreed to send a black to the chain gang because the laborer had demanded that a warrant be read to him before he would enter jail. Searcy not only defended his own integrity but also

[48] *Madison Madisonian*, Apr. 15, 1921, clipping in NAACP Papers, Box C 387.

[49] "The Fruits of Peonage," *New Republic* 26 (Apr. 20, 1921), 224. See also "Georgia's Death Farm," *Literary Digest* 69 (Apr. 16, 1921), 13–14; "Peonage in Georgia," *Independent* 105 (Apr. 16, 1921), 400; "Peonage, a Mere Symptom," *Review of Reviews* 63 (June 1921), 575–76.

[50] Albert Bushnell Hart, "Peonage and the Public," *Survey* 46 (Apr. 9, 1921), 43–44.

[51] Hugh M. Dorsey, *The Negro in Georgia* (Atlanta, 1921).

went beyond the call of duty and defended the citizens of the eight counties in the Flint district.[52] Organizations quickly sprang up throughout Georgia, outraged that Dorsey would reveal such stark conditions. One case of brutal treatment was exceptional, even permissable—but Dorsey's pamphlet hinted that the Williams farm was typical. And Southerners who prided themselves on their race relations could not tolerate such a charge. Following publication of Dorsey's pamphlet, public opinion quickly reversed. In Macon a group called the "Guardians of Liberty" asked for the impeachment of Dorsey, charging that no "living man will stand by while a villain defiles his mother. Georgia—our mother—is being defiled before the world." The *Macon Daily Telegraph* likened Dorsey to Benedict Arnold, while other groups condemned the pamphlet as one of the "vilest slanders ever heaped upon the people of Georgia." James Weldon Johnson saw the pamphlet in a different light. "There are cases cited which are sufficient to drive colored readers to despair or anarchy," he wrote.[53]

If it was the guilty verdict of a white man that made the *Williams* case most unusual, it was the ordeal of Clyde Manning that made the case most instructive in understanding peonage, in understanding how a man could become completely encased in a brutal system. Manning stood trial for murder in May, 1921, and the jury found him guilty and sentenced him to life imprisonment. But his case was appealed successfully because the trial judge omitted the charge that first-degree murder had to be committed with malice.[54] At Manning's second trial on July 26 and 27, 1922, his defense rested on the nature of the compulsion that the Williams family used. The issue then was not that Manning had murdered the men, but that he had been compelled to murder for fear of his own life.

The witnesses, those black men and women who had survived, revealed the hopeless desperation, the terror, and the ignorance that characterized the vertiginous world of peonage. They knew little of the world beyond the Williams plantations. The farm existed seven miles from Monticello, twenty miles from Covington, and only five miles

[52] *Macon Daily Telegraph*, May 11, 1921, clipping in NAACP Papers, Box C 387.
[53] *New York Times*, May 16, 1921; *Macon Daily Telegraph*, May 23, 1921, clippings in ibid.; *New York Age*, May 7, 1921, p. 4.
[54] See *Manning* v. *Georgia*, 153 Ga. 184.

from Polk's store. Claude Freeman, one of the overseers on the plantation, testified that he did not even know where nearby Polk's store was.
He had heard people say it was five miles from the farm, "but I don't
know where Polk's store is." Lessie May Whitlow, a cook on the place,
made much the same statement, "I don't know, sir, where Polk's store
is at." When a lawyer asked her if she understood his question containing the words "general report and rumor," she answered, "I don't know
what you are talking about." Except for the stockade Negroes who
came from the outer world, most of the blacks had spent their adult lives
on the Williams farms. They knew vaguely that some white people
lived nearby, but they had no dealings with them. When the state attempted to show that Clyde Manning could have fled at any time and
reported the murders, Emma Freeman answered, "I mean to say he
couldn't get away. I was there, we couldn't get away."[55] From the point
of view of the men and women there, the situation was hopeless; they
were peons, and peonage on the Williams place was the only life they
knew.

Williams's revealing statement that most of the neighboring planters
were also guilty of peonage perhaps explained why no whites complained. His neighbors evidently approved or acquiesced. Those sparsely
settled river-bottoms were still frontier-like in their customs and seclusion, and strong men were their own law. Black laborers living in
that area were at the mercy of the whites; there was no savior.

Clyde Manning, like Williams, made an unsworn statement to the
jury. "The crime what I have done, I done to save my own life," he
began, and that was the theme of his defense. After the killings began,
all the fear and anticipation, all the harrowing history of the farm, fo-
cused on Manning, for he better than the others knew the nature of
John S. Williams. "After these killings started, he would call me all
through the night," Manning related. "He would call me during the
night to see if the cows were in the wheat or in the oats and he would
say he heard a noise with the mules and for me to see if any of them
were hung, and I figured it he was calling me to see if I was off the
place." Had he fled, Manning continued, Williams would have "found
me and he would have brought me back there, and would have killed

[55] Testimony of Claude Freeman, p. 103; Lessie May Whitlow, pp. 123–24, 130;
Emma Freeman, p. 121, *Manning* v. *Georgia*, Newton Superior Court.

me." He had not wanted to kill. "It was against my will to do it, but it was against my power not to do it and live."[56]

He told the jury that he had wanted to flee the place, to tell someone of the murders, but he was unfamiliar with the surrounding countryside. "I was raised around there and been kept right there and never been away, never had been but a little ways from the farm, never had been up here to Covington." Some of the stockade men, he said, had been over the world, and yet Williams had caught them. "I didn't know anything about going nowhere." Even had he known where to go, there was the added responsibility of his family. "I had a family, I had my wife and my baby and there was my mother and sister and brothers, I couldn't run off with my whole family." Had he left and told of the murders, "my wife and sister and mother would all have been killed right there." He asked the jury to understand his situation, that he had no choice. "Anybody on that place, white folks, that he said to do it, would tell them it had to be like he did me they would have done it." Though Manning's situation had been desperate, hopeless, he maintained the same natural and unaffected manner that had characterized his entire ordeal. "I am not crying for mercy, just give me justice," he concluded.[57] And the jury sentenced him to life imprisonment.

Three of Williams's sons remained fugitives for several years; they faced federal peonage and state murder charges. By 1927 Huland, Marvin, and Leroy Williams had surrendered and made bond. Yet they never stood trial for either state or federal offenses. A U.S. attorney explained in 1930 that "less than half of the witnesses could be located," that Clyde Manning, the key witness, had died on the chain gang several years before. Further excusing his failure to bring the peonage cases to trial, the attorney explained that John S. Williams had been "the real moving spirit of the entire offense." Meanwhile, the three sons had moved to Florida where "each of them is running a store and filling station and is no longer employing or working labor of any kind." This apparent good behavior, like their father's success in duping the federal agents in 1921, evidently convinced the attorney that a trial was unnecessary. The surviving witnesses could have certainly linked the men to the peonage system, but the attorney argued that such a trial would

56 Statement of Manning, pp. 139–40, ibid.
57 Ibid., pp. 140–43.

be a "hopeless task" and convinced the attorney general to drop the cases.[58] The final ironic twist of the case occurred years later at a Georgia prison farm where John S. Williams had earned a trustee position. He was killed while attempting to prevent a jailbreak.[59]

[58] W. A. Bootle to Attorney General, June 24, 1930, file 50–05–19, Dept. of Justice, NA, RG 60.
[59] S. M. Hay, Clerk of Newton Superior Court, to author, Aug. 26, 1969.

CHAPTER VII

Weary Blues

The dread of peonage stretched beyond the Williams farm, for in the 1920s many Southern blacks continued to live in bondage. Complaints from the South resembled those of twenty years before, as the same patterns of exploitation continued. The migration of thousands of blacks to the North, the impact of World War I, and the beginning of agricultural mechanization had little effect on the lives of many rural laborers. The Justice Department continued to pay scant attention to peonage complaints, and federal apathy, local customs, and community acquiescence allowed peonage to exist almost as unhindered in the 1920s as it had a generation earlier. Peonage was so deeply rooted that it could not be dislodged by the efforts of either the NAACP, U.S. attorneys in the field, or the victims. For the Southern peon, life ground on inexorably, filled with pain. Far removed from the excitement of Garveyism, the Harlem Renaissance and jazz, these black Southerners had their own sad theme, the weary blues.

At the beginning of the 1920s, Hooper Alexander, a U.S. attorney in Georgia, recorded one of the most complete accounts of an attorney's fight to bring a peon-master to justice. His letters revealed the constants of peonage—the power of the masters, the corruption of local law-enforcement officials, the ignorance of black victims, the apathy of the Justice Department, and the terrorism aimed at potential witnesses. Born on October 6, 1858, in Floyd County, Georgia, Alexander taught elementary school, college, and finally began a law practice. He represented DeKalb County in the Georgia legislature for eight years, and when the Democrats came to power in 1913, Alexander sought the post of U.S. attorney. He received glowing endorsements from Senator Hoke Smith of Georgia for his legal talent, and reformer Alexander J. McKelway praised "the blue-eyed, tow-headed gentleman" for his fight against high rail rates.[1]

Since August, 1919, Alexander had been pushing a case involving Cornelius Alexander, a black agricultural worker. The first time attorney Alexander saw the black laborer, he had entered his office with head encased in bandages to tell a story of brutality. Cornelius Alexander had cranked ice cream all one morning at the house of Robert Connell, a wealthy Pike County farmer. That afternoon the owner's young son appeared at Alexander's house and asked why he had left the job. Alexander said that "he was tired of freezing ice cream, as none was given to him." The word quickly got to an older Connell brother, who appeared and asked what Cornelius Alexander meant "by sending such a big word to the house, and thereupon beat Cornelius over the head with the butt of a pistol injuring him severely." The attorney was about to tell the farm hand that this case did not fall within the jurisdiction of the federal government when Cornelius Alexander stated that Willard Connell, a son of the planter, had bought him from Franklin Huff, a man who had been convicted of peonage several years before; Connell had paid $175 and Alexander was working off the debt. The attorney advised the black worker to remain in Atlanta, but several months later Willard Connell found Cornelius Alexander in Douglas County and took him back to Pike County.

Hooper Alexander then decided that he could successfully prosecute Willard Connell for returning a worker to peonage, and he issued subpoenas for witnesses to appear before a grand jury in Atlanta on March 8, 1920. The day before the scheduled appearance the sheriff of Pike County telephoned the U.S. attorney, asking that the appearance be postponed for three days. On that date all the witnesses appeared except Cornelius Alexander. Despite the absence of the star witness, the grand jury ascertained that the sheriff of Pike County had accompanied Willard Connell to Douglas County, arrested Cornelius Alexander, and carried him handcuffed to Pike County jail. Several days later Phillip Moore, a black worker from Connell's farm, had appeared at the jail,

---

[1] Alexander J. McKelway to Attorney General, Sept. 20, 1913; Hoke Smith to James C. McReynolds, Sept. 23, 1913; Alexander to Charles B. Sornborger, Sept. 26, 1913; Appointment and Credentials Files, Dept. of Justice, NA, RG 60.

befriended Alexander, and assumed the $175 indebtedness, telling Alexander that the $22.50 per month he would earn should be applied to the debt. "It is believed in this office that the whole arrangement was collusive between Connell and Phillip Moore," Hooper Alexander surmised. Moreover, no one had seen Cornelius Alexander since the night of March 6, despite several investigations by federal agents.[2]

Two months later a body washed up in the Flint River in Spalding County near where Alexander disappeared. "Inquiries of persons who saw the skull developed the fact that it had a hole in it, possibly made by a pistol bullet and that one of the left front teeth had a gold crown," Alexander reported to the attorney general. Thinking that he could positively identify the body if he could locate the dentist who had made such a crown for Cornelius Alexander, the attorney ordered the body exhumed. But it turned out, as in a William Faulkner novel, "that unknown persons had already exhumed the body and had taken the skull away." The skull-snatchers had not been thorough, however, for the attorney found letters in the dead man's clothes that proved he was the missing worker. Alexander reported that he had continued Cornelius Alexander's case beyond the July 6 trial date to September because Willard Connell's lawyer had to attend the legislature. Alexander warned the attorney general that Willard Connell "is rather an attractive young man and will make a favorable impression on the jury." The attorney also suspected that Phillip Moore, the Negro who bailed Cornelius Alexander out of jail, knew more than he had told. Hooper Alexander asked whether he could offer Moore immunity if he revealed incriminating evidence. Meanwhile, the trial was again postponed.[3]

By November, 1920, Alexander noted a sharp increase in the number of peonage cases, and he complained that it was "difficult—indeed, it is practically impossible—to obtain indictments for peonage in the Eastern Division of this District."[4] The oppressive racism continued, as two months later he reported that a former employer took a Meriwether County black laborer and tied him to a tree and "deliberately" shot him to death. He speculated that the laborer's attempt to escape from peonage had been the motive for the murder, just as he suspected that an

[2] Alexander to Attorney General, Apr. 15, 1920, file 50–259, ibid.
[3] Alexander to Attorney General, June 25, 1920, ibid.
[4] Alexander to Attorney General, Nov. 5, 1920, ibid.

arrest in Atlanta and return of a black to McDuffie County without a warrant had been simply a return to peonage. While he had been dictating his letter, six blacks from nearby Gwinnett County had entered his office and complained of whitecapping, of being run out of their homes. "Within the past two weeks all the negroes have been run out of the northern part of Hall County in this state," he continued.[5] Because he thought publicity might prevent other abuses, Alexander issued a press statement that vigorously attacked racism in rural Georgia. "If the people of Georgia were told the details of crimes that are constantly being committed in this state against helpless negroes they would be entirely incredulous," he announced. "It is almost impossible to realize the utter meanness and barbarity to which some men are lending themselves." He charged that "proper officers" made scant effort to contain the violence. "If the people of the state permit the continuance of conditions that now prevail," he prophesied with uncanny accuracy, "sooner or later, and in some way, we will suffer a dreadful retribution."[6] Six weeks later John S. Williams began disposing of human evidence after special agents investigated his farm.

Coincidentally, Willard Connell's peonage trial took place simultaneously with that of John S. Williams. On April 4, the day the *Williams* case began, Alexander called the attorney general's attention to his earlier press statement revealing conditions in Georgia, and he explained that white Georgians had not believed him. Later he noted that the *Williams* case horrified both the press and the white citizens of Georgia. That case, he grimly complained, "is more atrocious than others only in this, that I know of no other case where more than one peon has been put to death to prevent his testifying." To further illustrate the interlocking power of peon-masters, the attorney reported that, when Cornelius Alexander's body had washed up, the coroner's jury had been headed by Franklin Huff, "whom I once convicted of peonage and sent to the penitentiary for a year." Huff had been the very man who had sold Cornelius Alexander to Connell for $175. Moreover, the presiding judge showed no sympathy with peonage prosecutions, as he had told Alexander a year before "that he had little or no confidence in the stories that are told about peonage." Alexander noted that the judge was a large

[5] Alexander to Attorney General, Jan. 14, 1921, file 50–415, ibid.
[6] *Atlanta Journal*, Jan. 14, 1921; clipping in ibid.

landowner and "while he is a most honorable gentleman and an excellent lawyer, I am confident that his beliefs incline his mind to such an attitude as will make him prove very unsympathetic." Another crucial difficulty, he reported, "is the fact that peonage in this State is practiced chiefly by people who stand high socially and politically and who are people of wealth and influence as a rule." On the other hand, his side of the case was hamstrung by the "utter unreliability of the negroes and their terrible fears."[7]

On April 7, as John S. Williams testified fifty miles away, Alexander complained that his chances for conviction were bleak. He discovered that his black witnesses contradicted themselves on the stand. Not all black witnesses had Clyde Manning's presence of mind. Hoping to preserve interest in peonage though the case might be lost, he called for a "sweeping and complete investigation, long continued, by a skillful investigator." Alexander then bleakly prophesied to the attorney general: "I say to you very earnestly that I find myself unable to look into the future and see one solitary ray of light falling upon the relations between the races in this territory." This did not come from any moral lapse on the part of the people, he wrote. "There is abundance of protest, but it is all futile, because of the keen competition and acute demand for labor. The man who attempts, as I have done for seven years, to interpose authority and effort between the greed of the powerful and the suffering of the helpless, accomplishes little except to bring upon himself powerful and relentless enmities." Two days later the jury brought in a not-guilty verdict in the Connell case after a five-minute deliberation.[8]

But Alexander's worries were not over, for Phillip Moore, the black worker who had collaborated with Connell to secure Cornelius Alexander, had finally told a great deal about Connell's role in the murder. Connell's alibi got him off the peonage charge in spite of the testimony, but Alexander thought Moore could tell enough to put many Pike County planters in jail for peonage, and though Moore had earlier moved away from the Connell plantation, the attorney feared for his

[7] Alexander to Attorney General, Apr. 4, 1921, file 50–442, ibid.

[8] Alexander to Attorney General, Apr. 7, 1921, file 50–260, ibid.; *New York Herald*, Apr. 9, 1921; clipping in NAACP Papers, Box C 387.

safety. Pike County had given him much trouble, the attorney noted, and he suspected that "a general conspiracy exists among the planters in that neighborhood to defy the Government in the matter of peonage, and to cooperate in defeating justice." As a threat to Moore, night-riders "left a small paper coffin on his door-step, and a warning to leave the country." Later, night-riders shot up his house. On June 11 the sheriff of Pike County (Alexander described him as "one of the most unscrupulous men in the United States") arrested Moore on what attorney Alexander considered trumped-up charges and took him back to Pike County. "I think it may be regarded as certain that this arrest and prosecution is intended to terrorize the negroes of Pike County, and to make it appear to them that the United States is powerless to protect its witnesses." He asked for a court stenographer to record the case so that it could be appealed, and then he warned that the "situation in certain counties in Georgia is so grave as to be incredible."[9]

Three weeks later Alexander reported that he was unable to obtain a stenographer, for several of the judges were reluctant to interfere with the case. Also, one of the other witnesses in the *Connell* case had narrowly escaped a similar arrest by the Pike County law officers. Yet another witness who had been in Atlanta since the trial had letters from his relatives in Pike County warning that the law officers and planters made threats "that they will get him if he stays on the top of the earth." Alexander explained that black laborers were being harassed, not because they had broken any laws, but because they had testified to peonage in a federal court.[10]

For two years Hooper Alexander had battled to bring justice in the *Connell* peonage case, but success escaped him. It seemed by the summer of 1921—despite the publicity given in the *Williams* case, numerous investigations by special agents, and much tiring work on Alexander's part—that the adverse reaction to Governor Dorsey's pamphlet had erased any hope of cleaning up peonage in Georgia. As had been the case twenty years earlier, the momentary excitement of a sensational exposé quickly waned as people interpreted one successful case to sym-

[9] Alexander to Attorney General, June 20, 1921, file 50–260–9, Dept. of Justice, NA, RG 60.
[10] Alexander to Attorney General, July 8, 1921, file 50–260–10, ibid.

bolize the defeat of the institution. Williams had been successfully convicted of murder, not peonage. Moreover, Alexander's suggestion for a long and sustained investigation did not materialize, just as earlier investigations had faltered.

After twenty years of peonage prosecutions the Justice Department found itself in much the same position as when Fred Cubberly stumbled onto the *Clyatt* case in 1901. The peonage statute had been tested and applied to many practices that proscribed Southern laborers. The decisions of the Supreme Court, however, simply did not touch the Southern peonage farms, and the custom of peonage had become so entrenched that even poor neighbors whom it affected economically would seldom complain. The race issue proved more than just a valuable tool to move the masses at election time; it also blinded them to the economic impossibility of successfully competing with peon labor. Though the peon-masters did not leave any ledgers behind, the system must have been more profitable than a regular tenant arrangement, for labor costs were trimmed to an absolute minimum.

Rural conditions in Georgia in the 1920s suggested that the South had changed little since antebellum slavery days. If there was a New South, one had to look to urban areas to catch a glimpse of it. As Hooper Alexander so perceptively put it, "Conditions in this District are bad . . . but I am sure that they are infinitely better than in the Southern District and I strongly suspect that there are many districts in which they are worse than they are here."[11] Complaints supported Alexander's statement, since peonage seemed as prevalent in 1920 as when it had been discovered in 1901. Though scant public evidence of peonage appeared during the Wilson administration, there is no reason to doubt the widespread existence of the institution, for it exhibited continuity. Indeed, the cases reported in the 1920s seemed typical of those that arose a generation before. As in the earlier cases the complaints in the 1920s often portrayed slavery, brutality, and peonage.

Though in the 1920s the Justice Department seemed more active than during the Wilson years, many files only contained the original complaint or occasionally a vague promise from the Justice Department that it would investigate. Few cases revealed any follow-up action. Often, for example, the NAACP forwarded complaints to the Justice Department.

11 Alexander to Attorney General, Apr. 4, 1921, file 50–442, ibid.

The complaints remained, according to the evidence contained in the files, uninvestigated and forgotten.[12]

In Georgia the *Williams* case represented only the most sensational instance of murder. The early 1920s furnished many examples of attitudes toward black labor that had survived from the nineteenth century. Some farmers professed ignorance of what peonage was, even after the publicity surrounding the *Williams* case, Alexander's press statement, and Dorsey's pamphlet. "I don't know what peonage is," one farmer related, "but I do know that no negroes have been murdered here at my instructions." There had been some blacks killed there, he admitted, "but their deaths were investigated."[13]

All too many planters in the 1920s, as during slavery days, continued to regard blacks as private property. Cornelia Brown, for example, lived on a plantation near Augusta. Her sister Jessie Crawford complained in September, 1920, that L. D. Hill, the owner of the farm, would not allow her to visit the plantation. Finding that Hill held her deaf-and-dumb sister against her will, Jessie tried to take legal action to free Cornelia—but this only ended in getting her sister beaten. The only pay that Cornelia had received in twenty years, her sister affirmed, was board, lodging, and some clothes. L. D. Hill threatened Cornelia with legal action if she attempted to "decoy" her sister off the plantation.[14]

Peonage dominated Oglethorpe County in the 1920s as it had a generation earlier, and the brutality among the planters there continued. Charles C. Echols of Crawford complained in 1921 that All Brightwell beat a black girl to death because "she would not work, or something to that effect." The day before she died, Echols reported, Brightwell "poored live coles down her neck and made her sit down in hot coles. I might be rongly informed," he concluded, "but I think that this was the fourth per that he had killed." The inevitable reply came back from the Justice Department: this was a matter for the state courts.[15] Investiga-

---

[12] See numerous complaints in file 50–622, ibid.

[13] *Atlanta Constitution*, May 2, 1921; clipping in NAACP Papers, Box C 386.

[14] Affidavit of Jessie Crawford, Wayne County, Michigan, Sept. 28, 1923, ibid.

[15] Charles C. Echols to Department of Justice, Aug. 3, 1921; H. S. Ridgely to Echols, Sept. 1, 1921, file 50–547, Dept. of Justice, NA, RG 60. See also John W. Crimm to George C. Taylor, May 20, 1922; J. T. S. to J. M. Towler, Mar. 27, 1920; W. T. Kennerly to Attorney General, Nov. 17, 1920; Hooper Alexander to Attorney General, Nov. 30, 1920; Kennerly to Attorney General, Jan. 22, 1921; Taylor to Attorney General, May 15, 1922; Grovie White to Calvin Coolidge,

tors made no attempt to discover the particulars of the case. Oglethorpe County, bearing the name of the philanthropist whose utopian colony in the new world would end debt slavery, ironically became the center of peonage two hundred years later.

Fred Cubberly, the man most responsible for uncovering peonage in 1901 and father of the *Clyatt* case, a quarter century later reported that peonage still abounded in Florida. Holopaw, he reported, "is located in the Southern District of Florida and in a very thinly settled country in which the timber has recently become available and I have had related to me a number of accounts of alleged peonage conditions." He observed that some of the sugar companies practiced peonage. Florida also needed labor for the booming citrus groves. A veteran of World War I, writing from jail, reported "the Shanghighing of men here, without Just cause—by the Local Police, to receive free Labor." He argued that the federal government should not allow this, and he lamented that if it persisted "I fel sorrey i every carried a gun, to defend my country."[16] Probably the most spectacular case of peonage in Florida during the 1920s concerned Governor Sidney J. Catts, a former Baptist minister, who was acquitted in 1922.[17]

Perhaps Fred Cubberly thought rural conditions in Florida had remained unchanged as he successfully pursued another case that closely resembled the *Clyatt* case. Mood Davis, owner of two turpentine stills in Calhoun County, Florida, hired George Diamond and Galvester Jackson in June, 1924. Two weeks after they began work, both left, promising that they were only leaving to get their families from nearby River Junction. Later Davis tracked them down, had them arrested for stealing a total of $8.50 from his place, and then threatened that unless they pled guilty to the charge he would get them eight months in jail. On August 8 the judge allowed Davis to pay their costs, and he included Henry Sanders, another black facing charges for theft, in the deal. Davis paid

Feb. 25, 1926; O. H. Luhring to White, Mar. 5, 1926, file 50–259; Councell Allen to Justice Department, Nov. 29, 1921, file 50–0–2, ibid.; undated NAACP memo, 1921, NAACP Papers, Box C 386.

16 Cubberly to Attorney General, May 30, 1925, file 50–17–3–1; C. H. Robinson to Justice Department, Nov. 30, 1927, file 50–18–8–1, Dept. of Justice, NA, RG 60. See also Isaiah Johnson to Justice Department, Nov. 7, 1927, ibid.

17 John L. Neeley to Attorney General, Aug. 18, 1921, file 50–538, ibid.; *New York Times*, Nov. 21, 1922, p. 2; *Florida Times-Union*, Nov. 21, 1922, p. 4; Nov. 22, 1922, p. 4; *Washington Post*, Nov. 21, 1922, p. 1.

costs and assumed debts totaling $162.28. The three blacks joined De-Witt Stonan, also held at the Davis turpentine farm. On September 30, 1924, the four peons escaped from the still and hid in the woods, but the whites captured them as they attempted to cross the only access bridge in the area. Mood Davis, joined by four other whites, carried the four peons up the road and forced Stonan to beat the other three. Eventually they all ended up back at work. All five whites later served sentences for peonage.[18]

Complaints often hinted that attitudes toward black workers had not changed since slavery days. In South Carolina, N. B. Pritchard, outraged at the treatment of a "darkie," reported that two white men threatened a Negro on a public road. One of the men "threw gun on him and told him if he would not work for other man he would kill him, he was then struck in head with pistol and head split wide open, his cheek bone also was laid open with blow of pistol, he was then kicked around and make to drink Castor Oil and allowed to leave after being warned not to say anything about same." The complaint also pointed out that there was much bootlegging in the area. The Justice Department replied to Pritchard that "this does not appear to be in violation of the peonage statute or other Federal law, and is a matter for the State courts." The Justice Department did take interest in the suggestion that there was a violation of the liquor laws, and it sent the complaint to the prohibition director.[19]

Some complaints were such classic statements of peonage that Justice Department neglect was inexcusable. V. C. Badman, president of the Dorchester Lumber Company in Charleston, South Carolina, complained in 1925 that Leroy Martin, one of his former laborers and "a first-class man," was being held in Florida. Martin had moved to Florida a year before and worked there for five or six months. He bought some furniture while in Florida and stored it there when he returned to South Carolina. On May 14, 1925, a man from Greenville, Florida, accompanied by a South Carolina constable, called on Badman and demanded

[18] *Davis v. United States*, 12 Fed. 2nd 254–55; Brief for Defendant, *Davis v. United States*, copy in file 50–802; Lucius Pickett to Attorney General, May 13, 1920, file 50–261, Dept. of Justice, NA, RG 60.
[19] N. B. Pritchard to Department of Justice, July 11, 1921; Department of Justice to Pritchard, July 15, 1921; Attorney General to Roy A. Haynes, July 19, 1921, file 50–542, Dept. of Justice, NA, RG 60. For another case from South Carolina, see NAACP Press Release, Nov., 1920, NAACP Papers, Box C 386.

that Martin be arrested, stating that he was charged with "buying goods under false pretense." The constable took Martin to a small town nearby to await a hearing the next day. When the superintendent arrived at the town he discovered that the man from Florida had taken Martin back south to work out his debt; there had been no extradition proceedings. Badman wrote that he "would willingly send Martin $85.00, but I do not believe that the criminal side of the courts should be used as collecting agencies." Though the case clearly violated the peonage statute (it paralleled the *Clyatt* case) and the man complaining was a white Southerner, the Justice Department file apparently ended with no action taken.[20]

In the Tennessee hills construction companies were still occasionally resorting to peonage. One case in 1921 involved seventy-five blacks who were allegedly held until they paid their board bills.[21] Nick Chiles, black editor of the *Topeka Plaindealer*, complained in 1921 that a Tennessee laborer had left his job and that his former employer had subsequently had him arrested on a trumped-up charge and then bailed him out of jail. After three years the black "is still working for this man under the pretence he is under bond." Chiles concluded that black Americans had "never received absolute freedom as was intended by Abraham Lincoln" and called on the Justice Department to "bring about an abolition of slavery."[22]

Across the Mississippi River in Arkansas complaints abounded. From the little town of Peace, Rev. W. H. Booker complained of injustice. "If a negro commits a crime against the State [and] if he promise the white man that he will work for him in the cotton field that Settles that case." When men attempted to leave the employ of a planter, the black preacher continued, "their account is run up so high until the next man will not pay it off." Booker painted a bleak scene of oppression, writing of beatings and fraudulent dealings with black property-owners. "One big white man rules the east half of the county," he concluded, "and

20 V. C. Badman to J. D. Myer, May 25, 1925, file 50–18–5, Dept. of Justice, NA, RG 60.
21 W. T. Kennerly to Attorney General, Apr. 19, 1921, file 50–452, ibid.; *New York Times*, Apr. 13, 1921; *Knoxville Sentinel*, Apr. 18, 1921; clippings in NAACP Papers, Box C 387.
22 Chiles to Attorney General Daugherty, Apr. 25, 1921, file 50–479, Dept. of Justice, NA, RG 60. See also C. J. Henderson to W. E. B. Du Bois, May 26, 1921; R. P. Stewart to Walter White, June 7, 1921, file 50–509, ibid.

what he says go law or no law."[23] An Arkansan from Crittenden County documented some of the harshness mentioned in Booker's letter. Attempting to get a Negro to admit he robbed a peddler, a party identified as Mr. Buck and some of his friends took a Negro named Slim to the Mississippi River in 1921 and "tied him Hand and Feet and let him down and strangled him several times untill he told them what they wanted to here and then notified the county officers and they come and got him and carried him to Jale." Walter White, assistant secretary of the NAACP, had learned that such cases of brutality did not fall within the rubric of peonage, so he noted on the letter, "Not a case for D of J from facts cited." Evidently it was not a case for the NAACP either, for it was not mentioned again.[24] There was still no appeal from the brutality of the rural South.

Victims of Southern oppression complained to the Justice Department or to the NAACP, and their complaints commonly revealed not only peonage but also brutality. From Longview, Texas, Hallwood Hardy complained that his sister's husband had fled to Oklahoma and wrote his wife asking her to join him. This news outraged "Mr. Eddie and Ogie Heitt" who "through their pistol down on her and made threats to blow her brains out theay have been kicking and beeting up the other hands on his place making Slaves out of them[.]" She had appealed to the local sheriff for help, but that was futile, Hardy wrote. He asked the Justice Department for aid. "Unless such mistreatment amounts to holding in involuntary servitude for debt," came the reply, "or carrying away into slavery, no action can be taken by the Federal authorities in the matter."[25]

Methods of intimidating black labor to keep them at work were anything but subtle. An unidentified writer from Lone Wolf, Texas, complained to the NAACP in 1923 that Isiah Sanders had refused to work on a Saturday afternoon because he wanted to play baseball. He went to the game, and later that afternoon his bosses, the Green family, turned up at the game also. One of the white men asked to have a turn at bat, hit a ground ball, and ran to first base where he clubbed

[23] Rev. W. H. Booker to NAACP, Feb. 2, 1922, NAACP Papers, Box C 386.
[24] S. B. Argain to J. E. Spingarn, June 1, 1921, ibid. See also Josie Coleman to NAACP, June 12, 1922; H. L. Henderson to J. E. Spingarn, Aug. 26, 1922, ibid.
[25] John W. H. Crim to Hardy, Sept. 26, 1921, file 50-0-12, Dept. of Justice, NA, RG 60.

first baseman Sanders. Then "the other three Greens and Jimm Holmes all whites, took him unconscious and strip his clothing off, and in turn Whip him to death. One Mr mckay white prevail with them on to stop, his daughter fantd, at the groans the agony of a dying man." Though there were some hundred people present at the game, the writer revealed, they dared not testify unless they were given protection.[26] Such terrorism of labor was common throughout the South, according to complaints sent to the NAACP and to the Justice Department. But because there was no federal law prohibiting such abuses, nothing was done.

Inevitably, some complaints were fictitious or exaggerated. The El Paso chapter of the NAACP complained that their investigator had found a massive peonage plantation near Wellborn, Texas. "Once on the plantation they can never leave as free men and women," the complaint charged, for they were "killed and whipped." The Justice Department investigated and labeled the NAACP investigator "a stupendous liar." The agents could not even find the plantation complained of.[27]

Complaints of peonage in Louisiana increased during the 1920s. In the north Louisiana cotton country Joe Hardy raised a large crop and hoped to get out of debt in 1925. At settlement time he still owed John S. Glover $60, and he decided to move to a neighboring plantation whose owner agreed to pay his former boss the $60. As Hardy began packing his belongings, Glover appeared and told him that he could not move. A fight ensued, and Hardy killed his boss. Walter White of the NAACP complained to the Justice Department of peonage, and he wrote that Hardy had almost been lynched following the shooting. Since the man who was attempting to keep Hardy in peonage had been killed, the Justice Department reasoned accurately that there was no federal case; Hardy sought justice in the state court.[28]

Another Louisiana tenant, Emmanuel Williams, made a good crop in

[26] Unsigned letter to NAACP, Nov. 4, 1923, NAACP Papers, Box C 386. For other typical peonage complaints, see Maria Johns to Secretary, NAACP, Dec. 9, 1920, ibid.; Edwin Lacy to Attorney General, Apr. 8, 1926; affidavit of Colonel Pickering, Apr. 8, 1926; Lacy to Attorney General, Apr. 14, 1926, file 50–75–1–1; Dept. of Justice, NA, RG 60.
[27] L. W. Washington to James Weldon Johnson, May 2, 1921; Lewis J. Balry to Walter White, June 17, 1921, NAACP Papers, Box C 386.
[28] White to John G. Sargent, Jan. 26, 1926, file 50–33–2–1, Dept. of Justice, NA, RG 60.

1925 and "vexed" his boss because he calculated his yearly earnings and discovered he had gotten out of debt. Williams decided to hold the remainder of his cotton off the market a day so that he could sell it himself and insure getting a fair settlement. Outraged at Williams's independence, Tobe Gill, the owner of the farm, confronted his tenant and boasted that he was the "boss of this place." Williams's wife took offense, defended her husband, and when Gill drew his pistol she practically dared him to shoot. Gill killed them both, and then he successfully claimed self-defense despite the testimony of a sixteen-year-old witness.[29] These cases graphically illustrated the difficulty in establishing peonage in such circumstances. When blacks took initiative to break the system, their efforts were usually crushed by violence. Release from peonage required an escape or a plea for outside help; escape proved difficult, and the plea for outside help often went unheeded. Those who remained silent remained invisible, and only such intense investigations as those conducted in Alabama in 1903 and in Georgia in 1921 gave any indication of the extent of peonage.

Though peonage complaints continued to emerge from Alabama, the incidence fell off abruptly after the *Bailey* case. After the series of successful prosecutions, there emerged an awareness of what constituted peonage and a desire to prevent it. Nevertheless, R. L. Thornton, a mail carrier, reported that he saw a great deal of peonage but was afraid that revealing it would mean the loss of his job. Through his contact with the NAACP and its forwarding the letters to the Justice Department, several peons obtained freedom.[30] Alabama also had its tales of mistreatment and forced labor. A mother complained in 1926 that her thirteen-year-old daughter Carolina Dixon had been falsely arrested and bound out to Tom Couch at Robjohn for over five years. She could not visit her daughter or get any aid from law enforcement officials nearby. Another statement filed by Carolina Dixon after she escaped revealed that she was beaten "unmerciful" by the Couches, made to "marry against her own will," and that "Mr. Tom Couch & Mr Guy Couch by deathly threats forced me to be used personally for emoral purpose." When

[29] Joe Williams to Dr. John H. Frank, n.d. [1924?], NAACP Papers, Box D 3. See also press release, May 25, 1923, ibid., Box C 386; *Crisis* 26 (July 1923), 128.

[30] R. L. Thornton to Johnson, Sept. 25, 1923; White to Thornton, Sept. 29, 1923; Thornton to Johnson, Oct. 16, 1923; White to Burns, Oct. 29, 1923; Burns to White, Nov. 3, 1923, NAACP Papers, Box C 386.

the case finally went before a grand jury, it failed to find a true bill.[31]

Occasionally, local incompetence or bias emerged as it had earlier. A Justice Department official complained in 1923 that an Alabama case failed simply because "neither the alleged peon nor the two principal witnesses were subpoenaed." McDuffie Cain, U.S. marshal at Montgomery, replied that his deputies simply served with warrants those witnesses who were the most available, arguing that they saved money this way. Another reason for not serving a warrant on the victim, Cain argued, was that the deputies believed the victim "to be about half crazy and concluded that if he appeared before the commissioner confronted with three defendants who had terrorized him his testimony would not strengthen the case against the defendants." W. J. Burns, director of special agents, advised administrative assistant George E. Strong that the two marshals should be dismissed. Strong disagreed, arguing that they should be "advised." Strong then warned Cain that he did not want economy to interfere with justice, and he instructed him to advise the deputies "to ascertain in advance those witnesses who can furnish the best evidence and serve subpoenas on them."[32]

Complaints drifted up from Mississippi with increasing regularity. Three complaints in 1921 showed the conditions there to be as bleak as a generation before. A black woman from Sunflower County complained that "a mean Negro, and straw boss" would not allow her to get her children from a neighboring farm. The Justice Department promised an investigation.[33] Another person from the same county complained of much the same treatment, adding that even though Justice Department investigators had been to the farm, the workers had been so terrorized that they did not tell what they knew.[34] But not all peonage cases in Mississippi failed. A court fined W. D. Moore of Mc-

[31] Affidavit of Rebecca Jones, July 26, 1926; affidavit of Carolina Dixon, July 26, 1926, file 50–1–2; Nugent Dodds to Oscar DePriest, July 25, 1932, file 50–1–3, Dept. of Justice, NA, RG 60. For a successful prosecution, see Thomas D. Sanford to Attorney General, May 6, 1921, file 50–20–2, ibid.

[32] Cain to Attorney General, Aug. 8, 1923; Burns to Strong, Aug. 18, 1923, and penciled note on this letter initialed GES; Strong to Cain, Aug. 23, file 50–624, ibid. For another such case, see Arthur Jackson to (?), Dec. 17, 1924, file 50–40–1, ibid.

[33] Lem E. Oldham to Attorney General, Aug. 8, 1921; Ridgely to Oldham, Aug. 29, 1921, file 50–550, ibid.

[34] W. R. R. Rogers to James Weldon Johnson, June 16, 1921, NAACP Papers, Box C 386.

Comb City $250 for taking a Negro from a Delta plantation and holding him in chains while working out a debt.[35]

Nor did all complaints concern blacks. In January, 1925, Congressman Alben W. Barkley revealed an unsigned letter complaining that a white man in Mississippi had been held in peonage. William Huffman had walked off a job after he had been sold to a new employer for his debt. When he returned from Louisiana to Mississippi a year later, the sheriff arrested him because he had not repaid the debt. "This state has a contract law that may be or may not be just," the informer wrote. "But the fact that it is twisted to hold laborers in slavery is a well known fact." In June of the same year George Forrest McMurphy, presumably the unidentified correspondent, reported that Huffman remained in slavery. "This is the most damnable case of involuntary servitude for debt I ever heard of," he complained to Barkley. Barkley insisted that the Justice Department push the case, but he received the news that the facts of the case had been presented on May 5 to a grand jury in Jackson, Mississippi, and it had returned a no bill.[36]

Southern whites who reported peonage were sincerely outraged by its continued existence. Robert L. McLendon of Sebastopol in southern Mississippi reported in 1924 that a planter held two blacks on a nearby farm. When they tried to escape, the owner captured and returned them. He noted that much peonage continued, but that people did not complain about it. "Slavery was abolished during the year four of my uncles died on the battlefields in 1865," he protested, "and I really see no need for its local continuation now here and yonder when we have a law and a Constitutional Law against it." The Justice Department assured McLendon that it would investigate the complaint. The investigation did not come quickly enough to suit McLendon, however, and on May 4 he complained of other abuses. If the investigator would visit one of the victims, he insisted, he could "get the book full of peonage, slavery and involuntary servitude."[37]

[35] *New York Tribune*, May 10, 1921; clipping in ibid.
[36] Enclosure in Alben W. Barkley to Attorney General, Jan. 9, 1925, file 50–41–1; George Forrest McMurphy to Alben Barkley, June 30, 1925; Barkley to Attorney General, July 9, 1925; B. M. Parmenter to Barkley, July 15, 1925, file 50–41–1–2, Dept. of Justice, NA, RG 60.
[37] McLendon to General Stone, Apr. 11, 1924; Darl J. Davis to McLendon, Apr.

How much peonage existed in the 1920s remains impossible to determine. Complaints were fewer than they had been twenty years earlier, yet those who investigated the rural areas stated that it was widespread. The action of one concerned man such as Hooper Alexander failed to end peonage—partly because he received no help from local officers and little aid from the Justice Department, but also because he ran head-on into entrenched custom. Moreover, a mood of apathy as pronounced in the 1920s as it had been twenty years earlier existed from Washington to the depths of the forlorn South, where peon-masters ruled their domains unmolested. Community support of the planters, both in keeping the abuses quiet and in forming sympathetic juries, continued to hinder prosecution. Forced labor with its inevitable brutality persisted as it had a generation earlier. The corruption of local law-enforcement officials, their false arrests and their pursuit of fugitives, continued. The South clung to its anachronistic heritage of violence and forced labor.

16, 1924, file 50–632; McLendon to Department of Justice, May 4, 1924, file 50–41–3–1, ibid.

CHAPTER VIII

Two Old Men

Like Mississippi River floods, the incidence of peonage rose and fell, unpredictable, violent, inexorable. The mighty 1927 flood baptized the land along the river, flushing out not only living things but stagnant customs as well. As refugees came dripping to the high ground, peonage—still flourishing in the poverty and authoritarianism of the Delta—bubbled to the surface, revealing an antediluvian labor system. The treatment of black laborers, the attitude of planters, and the bureaucratic indifference of the federal government and the Red Cross were instructive in understanding how Southern society could contain covert and suppressed customs that appeared only in an emergency.

Secretary of Commerce Herbert Hoover, who was in charge of administering relief to hundreds of thousands of refugees, received numerous complaints that blacks were held in peonage behind fences and guarded by soldiers. These complaints forced Hoover to appoint a "Colored Advisory Committee" to investigate the refugee camps. The 1927 flood emergency offered this handful of black leaders an unprecedented opportunity to attack peonage in the Mississippi valley. The public reaction to the massive enslavement of black sharecroppers, had the Negro Flood Commission released the story, might have unleashed a tide of protest that would have forced the federal government to intercede and alter the relationship between tenant and landlord. The crisis revealed, however, that the black man, whether in a refugee camp along the river or in a Negro college, dared not challenge the whites who controlled him. As the landlords of the Mississippi valley suppressed the protests of flood victims, so the Red Cross and the U.S. Department of Commerce quashed blacks' efforts to publicize the conditions that could have altered the lives of black peons in the valley. As usual the Justice Department stood to the side, interceding halfheartedly only when persistently requested—and then, as always, belatedly, wanly, ineffectually.

The discrimination and exploitation that followed the 1927 flood did not exemplify the first time that blacks had been abused during such a crisis, nor would it be the last. Natural disasters had a way of exposing the unnatural caste system of the South. In 1917, for example, a hurricane hit Texas City, Texas, flooding the area. Two days later the local police, with the aid of the Texas National Guard, rounded up the black citizens of the town, put them in a detention center, and used their labor to clean up the white section of town. Five days later they were allowed to return to their homes and clean up the black section of town. Persistent complaints by these blacks eventually led to financial compensation for the five days' work. Similarly, following a hurricane in the fall of 1926, black residents of Miami were forced to work under guard to clean up the white section of town.[1]

What happened along the Mississippi River in 1927, then, was but one case among many. "Some years ago," the *Memphis Commercial Appeal* remarked in 1927, "somebody wittily said that God created man and gave him dominion over everything except the Mississippi River." There was little humor along the valley, however, for by this time the river had announced that it would test the levees—indeed, it had already broken through them in Tennessee. "The Old Man," as novelist William Faulkner called the river, had issued his unsettling challenge, giving men their puny chance to prevent the torrent from breaking the man-made barricades. After successive floods the Army Corps of Engineers had raised the levees along the river ever higher, and in 1927 it announced that the river was restricted to its channel.[2] But the terrible 1927 flood

1 Interview with General J. F. Bell, n.d.; J. F. Bell to War Department, Sept. 25, 1915; Bell, Memorandum, Sept. 30, 1915; unidentified clipping, ca. Mar. 6, 1916; Petition to Henry Cabot Lodge and Philander C. Knox, Feb. 23, 1917, Adjutant General's Office, file 2325295, National Archives, Record Group 94. See the series of letters concerning the 1926 hurricane in file 50–18–7, Dept. of Justice, NA, RG 60; correspondence in NAACP Papers, Box C 387.

2 *Memphis Commercial Appeal*, Mar. 23, 1927, p. 6. Faulkner wrote a vivid story of the 1927 Mississippi flood, "The Old Man," in *The Wild Palms* (New York, 1939); Major D. H. Connolly calmly announced on April 10, 1927, "We are in condition to hold all the water in sight" (*Jackson Clarion-Ledger*, Apr. 10, 1927, p. 1).

proved that man had failed to contain either the river or peonage. It revealed that seventy-five years after emancipation white Southerners continued to hold black laborers in bondage.

Though the river crept ever higher, many inhabitants along the valley seemed to trust the fatuous pronouncements of the Army Corps of Engineers. Yet the water ascended steadily, and finally men frantically piled sandbags atop the crumbling levees. At Stopps Landing north of Greenville, Mississippi, thousands of men battled to contain the river, but by April 20 the water was "splashing over the levee." The next day the levee collapsed even as the men stood atop it, and "several hundred negro plantation workers lost their lives."[3] Rescue efforts around the Stopps Landing crevasse were typical of those in other areas of the valley. Nothing could be done for the livestock caught away from high ground, and some 400 mules and hogs perished near the break. At Scott, a small town near the crevasse, white women and children escaped in automobiles while black women and children fled in railroad boxcars. But 400 black men were reportedly abandoned atop the levee.[4]

Because the people had foolishly clung to the hope that the levees would hold, relief agencies had made scant preparation to care for the refugees. Those who escaped from the flooded area sought high ground away from the river, while those not so fortunate fled to the levees (still the highest ground available) or to Indian mounds. Feeding and clothing the refugees, who often fled with only the clothes on their backs, presented an awesome challenge. Secretary of Commerce Hoover, a veteran of such relief tasks, took over on April 22 as the coordinator of the relief effort, aided by the Red Cross and other relief agencies.

Caring for so many refugees would have been a gigantic problem under any circumstances, but the racial customs of the South complicated the problem along the Mississippi River. The Delta, that strip of rich land that stretched along the river from Memphis to Vicksburg, had survived as a tangible link with the antebellum South. Both in Mississippi and across the river in Arkansas the planters jealously guarded their black labor from agents who infiltrated from the North and tempted the black men to desert their agrarian life. Under normal con-

[3] *Memphis Commercial Appeal*, Apr. 21, 1927, p. 1; *Jackson Clarion-Ledger*, Apr. 24, 1927, p. 1.
[4] *Memphis Commercial Appeal*, Apr. 22, 1927, pp. 1, 15.

ditions the planters could handle most of their labor problems, but during the flood, when all black laborers fled from the land, owners expressed concern lest the lures of the labor agents or of native planters not affected by the flood leave them with no tenants.[5]

Since Justice Department investigator Mary Grace Quackenbos had invaded the Sunnyside plantation in 1907 and reported peonage among Italian immigrants, rumors of peonage had continually drifted from the Delta area. But plantation owners had successfully kept their labor under control by debt, by coercion, or by giving ample settlements. On April 3, 1927, for example, the *Jackson Clarion-Ledger* reported that two Sunflower County men had been charged with peonage.[6] Whether peonage had been universal along the Delta or not, the planters insisted that their laborers be returned to the plantations after the flood.

Along the river numerous refugee camps sprang up. Blacks and whites huddled in public buildings or in tents, ate what food was available, shared clothing provided by concerned Americans throughout the country, and waited captively for the waters to subside. In Memphis, for example, the fairgrounds which served as a refugee camp were also in effect a labor prison. "The camp is closed to the public," reported the *Memphis Commercial Appeal*. "No one will be permitted to enter or leave the grounds except on passes from headquarters." In Mississippi, General Curtis Green of the National Guard stated that it "is our duty to return these people to their homes, and every camp under our control will handle the situation in this manner."[7] The sanitation problem, officials announced, necessitated the closing of the fairgrounds, but the closed gates in the camps served several functions. They contained disease within the camp; they kept the workers in one place; and they kept the labor agents out. As other refugees were plucked from atop barns, snatched from trees, or taken from crumbling levees, the camps grew, complicating relief. While animals that were natural enemies formed a temporary truce and shared available dry land, refugees

[5] William Alexander Percy, *Lanterns on the Levee* (New York, 1953), pp. 257–58. See also unpublished paper by James P. Woods III, "Herbert Hoover, Black Refugees, and the Mississippi Valley Flood of 1927: A Case Study in 'Bureaucratic Conservatism,' " pp. 9–10. Copy in possession of author.

[6] *Jackson Clarion-Ledger*, Apr. 3, 1927, p. 1.

[7] *Memphis Commercial Appeal*, Apr. 24, 1927, p. 6; Apr. 28, 1927, p. 4; *Jackson Clarion-Ledger*, Apr. 24, 1927, p. 9.

had to be sorted out according to color, deposited in the assigned camp, and cared for.

At first, as prominent Greenville planter William A. Percy recorded in *Lanterns on the Levee*, men seemed to rise to the disaster, forgetting for the moment their Ku Klux Klan heritage. Even bootleggers from the White River region near Greenville appeared and aided in rescue efforts. But the river did not fall quickly; indeed, in Greenville the waters did not completely subside until late August.[8]

The yellow waters spread out to distances of fifty miles on both sides of the main Mississippi River channel, and in some areas it became obvious that no cotton crop would even be planted in 1927. Planters became increasingly agitated about their laborers, as labor agents from other parts of Mississippi and from the North approached the idle farmworkers. Mississippi Governor Dennis Murphree audaciously warned of "the serious result which can be brought about if refugees are allowed to be taken from the refugee camps for selfish interests," nicely ignoring the human interests of the mass of black laborers who were systematically being denied the right to search for a new job.[9] Since most of the laborers were indebted to their employers, the official policy of returning them to the plantations constituted peonage. Thousands of black laborers remained involuntarily behind locked gates, waiting for the waters to recede so they could go back and work out their contracts.

On April 30 Sidney Dillon Redmond complained to President Coolidge that peonage was being practiced on a massive scale. Redmond, a fifty-five-year-old physician, lawyer, and businessman, was a native black Mississippian who had graduated from Rust College in 1894 and pursued his medical education in Northern schools. "These people are hurdled in camps of 5000 or more and soldiers from the National Guard are used to let none out of these camps and to keep people on the outside from coming in and talking with them." Redmond explained other hardships suffered by the refugees. Whites were taken from levees, he complained, and blacks left. In other cases planters "hold their labor at the point of a gun for fear they would get away and not return." Most debasing of all, he pointed out, "mules have been taken on board

[8] Percy, *Lanterns on the Levee*, pp. 251–52, 259–60.
[9] *Memphis Commercial Appeal*, Apr. 28, 1927, p. 4. See also *Jackson Clarion-Ledger*, May 8, 1927, p. 1.

and Negroes left in peril."[10] Several days later black politician Perry Howard, a native of Mississippi and Republican national committeeman, informed the attorney general that "colored refugees, who are employees of landlords in the Mississippi valley, particularly in the States of Mississippi, Louisiana and Arkansas, are being held in a state of peonage in certain refugee camps."[11] Despite the complaints, no action was forthcoming from the Justice Department.

As if the flood were not enough hardship, earth tremors hit the region on May 7. Then tornadoes swept through the area, along with terrifying electric storms. During the flood concerned Americans joined in the relief effort, sending money, food, and clothing to the refugees. The press carried stories of the work being done throughout the Mississippi valley, and Herbert Hoover and the Red Cross received numerous tributes.[12]

Still the reports of peonage grew louder. On May 16, Walter White of the NAACP reported from Memphis that black laborers were "closely guarded especially from Negroes who might help them go somewhere else." Red Cross supplies, he warned, were being given to the planters for distribution, and it was "certain that these landlords are going to use this means of sticking the Negroes into debt." White stated that the Red Cross did not go along with these practices but much of the relief was "in the hands of these Crackers." The next day he reported that Dr. William R. Redden, then directing much of the Red Cross activity, had promised to investigate the problems. White, struck by the disaster, noted that though many of the horror stories

10 Redmond to Calvin Coolidge, Apr. 30, 1927, file 50–637–2, Dept. of Justice, NA, RG 60. For a sketch of Redmond, see Green P. Hamilton, *Beacon Lights of the Race* (Memphis, 1911), pp. 133–38. See also Turner E. Campe to Attorney General, Apr. 29, 1927, file 50–637–1, Dept. of Justice, NA, RG 60.
11 Howard to Attorney General, May 4, 1927, file 50–637, Dept. of Justice, NA, RG 60. See also J. B. Brown to Senator Charles Curtis, June 22, 1927, Commerce Department Files, 1–I/435, Herbert Clark Hoover Papers, Herbert Hoover Presidential Library, West Branch, Iowa. (Hereafter cited Hoover Papers.) I am indebted to James P. Woods III for photocopies of the Hoover material and for his insights in an unpublished paper (note 5). Wood cites complaints of peonage on pp. 24–25 of his paper.
12 See list of flood donors; also press release, "American Red Cross Now Caring for Needs of 323,837 Refugees in Mississippi Valley," file 84076, Box 615, Dept. of Commerce, National Archives, Record Group 40; L. C. Speers, "The Red Cross Takes up Titanic Task," *New York Times*, May 8, 1927, VIII:1; *New York Times*, May 15, 1927, IV:6, 20; Herbert C. Thompson, "Red Cross Ever Ready to Give Aid in Disaster," *New York Times*, May 22, 1927, IX:14.

were undoubtedly true, "they are the inevitable occurrences during a catastrophe like this."[13]

Even as White made his investigation, Robert R. Moton, president of Tuskegee Institute, sent Thomas M. Campbell, field director of the Negro Agricultural Extension Service, to the flood area. Moton had become head of Tuskegee Institute in 1916 after Booker T. Washington's death, and he maintained some of his predecessor's political power. Like Walter White, Thomas Campbell was struck by "the intense excitement and fear caused by this terrible catastrophy." At Baton Rouge on May 19 Campbell observed the presence of National Guard troops. He noted what was to become a critical element in the peonage charges: "The whole question seems to have been whether guards were stationed there to keep the refugees in or to keep the public out." Though the Vicksburg camp seemed clean and comfortable, Campbell reported that one refugee complained that had he been allowed to pack some of his belongings he would have been much more at ease. "They made us work on the levees down in the delta, up to the last minute," the refugee stated, "tellin' us that the levee wasn't goin' to break and then when it did break, we didn't have time to do nuthin' but save our families."

As to the question of holding refugees against their wills, Campbell reported the gist of conversations with leading Negro Mississippians. When the flood struck, the planters advised the blacks to go to the camps. "In the event the Refugee goes to the Camp, he must register, and then he can not get out unless some outside person makes application for his release with the promise of giving him a home and seeing that he is not a Public Charity Ward." Because labor agents could not get into the camps and planters could, Campbell wrote that most refugees had no choice but to return to the plantations.[14] Campbell did not label the restrictions on black laborers as peonage, but, because most of the tenants were indebted to their employers, the label would have applied.

Upset at the continuing reports of peonage, Herbert Hoover on May 24 telegraphed Moton to suggest a Negro committee to assure "the proper treatment of the colored folks in the concentration camps and

---

[13] Report from Walter White, May 16, 1927; report from Walter White, May 17, 1927, NAACP Papers, Box C 77.

[14] Report of Thomas M. Campbell, n.d. [May 1927?], Robert R. Moton Papers, Tuskegee Institute Archives, Tuskegee Institute, Alabama, Box GC 48. (Hereafter cited as Moton Papers.)

with view to inquire into any complaints." Two days later Moton sent a list of eleven Negroes, four of them located in Tuskegee and only two from the North. No representative from the NAACP was on the list. Several days later Moton agreed to serve as chairman of the committee.[15] Though the peonage complaints had led to the formation of the committee, its duties went beyond investigating peonage.

Hoover was but one step ahead of the NAACP, however, for on May 28 the press carried White's report on the refugee camps. "I was told of negroes eluding guards and escaping," he warned, "preferring to forego food, shelter, clothing and medical attention rather than go back to the plantations from which the flood waters had driven them." Hoover quickly "denounced" White's report, saying that it was "without foundation." The instant denial of poor conditions became the standard tactic used by Hoover and the Red Cross. "The only thing necessary to prove how baseless is such a charge," Hoover countered with an impossible invitation to the skeptical, "is to visit any of the negro concentration camps in Mississippi, Arkansas, or Louisiana." He also announced the formation of the Negro committee.[16]

Though the average American citizen could not visit the camps, Moton's Colored Advisory Commission did. The sixteen members met in Memphis on June 2.[17] The committee divided into five groups and set off for Arkansas, Mississippi, northern, central, and southern Lou-

[15] Hoover to Moton, May 24, 1927; Moton to Hoover, May 26, 30, 1927, ibid. The members of the commission were: Bishop Robert E. Jones, in charge of southwestern district of the Methodist Episcopal Church; Albon L. Holsey, secretary to Moton and secretary of the National Negro Business League; Dr. J. S. Clark, president of Southern University; Eugene K. Jones, executive secretary of National Urban League; Jesse O. Thomas, southern field secretary of National Urban League; Mrs. John Hope, director of Atlanta Neighborhood Union; Miss Eva D. Bowles, executive secretary of National Y.W.C.A.; Claude A. Barnett, director of Associated Negro Press; Dr. Roscoe C. Brown, assistant secretary of National Medical Association; Miss Mary E. Williams, public health nurse under Tuskegee chapter of American Red Cross; Robert R. Taylor, vice-principal and director of mechanical industries at Tuskegee Institute; Dr. L. M. McCoy, president of Rust College; Dr. J. B. Martin, regional director of National Negro Business League; Bert M. Roody, vice-president of National Negro Business League; Dr. S. D. Redmond, a Mississippi doctor, lawyer, and real estate dealer; Thomas M. Campbell, field representative, U.S. Department of Agriculture. (*The Final Report of the Colored Advisory Commission* [Washington, 1929], pp. 9–10.)
[16] *New York Times*, May 28, 1927, p. 7; May 29, 1927, p. 10.
[17] *The Final Report of the Colored Advisory Commission*, pp. 11–12. See also Moton to Mrs. John Hope, May 30, 1927; Moton to Hoover, June 2, 1927, Moton Papers, GC 48.

isiana. Even as the investigators crossed the wastes of flooded territory, interest in the presence of peonage increased. On June 4 the *New York Age*, a widely circulated Negro weekly, printed Walter White's story about peonage and invited the Justice Department "which has investigated peonage conditions in Georgia and Florida and prosecuted these modern slaveowners, to institute similar investigations in the flooded area." At about the same time the *Chicago Defender*, long an advocate of Negro emigration from the South to the North, reprinted a story from Greenville to the effect that William A. Percy, who was in charge of flood relief there, had ordered that unless there was a man in the household black families could not get Red Cross rations. Though Percy later explained that the confusion came from a newspaper misprint, the *Defender* continued its attack, charging that waste was dumped in the Negro section of Greenville and that dead bodies of Negroes were slit, loaded with sand, and sunk in the river. Percy naturally denied these accusations, but he did admit that pressure from the local planters who had laborers in the levee camp forced him to risk their health by keeping them there instead of sending them to a better camp.[18] What emerged from Percy's admission and from other reports which came to light was the fact that local custom approved of confining the black laborers. The tragedy of the policed concentration camps was not so much the willingness of the National Guard to prevent movement or even of the planters to demand closed camps, but that almost all white Mississippians had become so accustomed to controlling black laborers by force that such proscription seemed appropriate and necessary.

In the face of increasing charges of peonage, Gen. Curtis T. Green of the Mississippi National Guard denied on June 8 that laborers were held involuntarily. "Refugees go and come at will," he stated; "there are no camp restrictions and the National Guard is doing only sanitary, police and guard duty incidental to the care and preservations of Government property and the enforcement of necessary sanitary regulations"[19] Green's statement contradicted not only the reports of Walter White and Thomas M. Campbell but also Green's own earlier press reports that all laborers, white and black, would be held in the camps

[18] *New York Age*, June 4, 1927, p. 4; Percy, *Lanterns on the Levee*, pp. 257–58; *Chicago Defender*, n.d. [June 4, 1927?], clipping in Moton Papers, GC 48. See also Percy to Mrs. John Hope, June 7, 1927, Moton Papers, GC 48.
[19] Green to J. H. Noonan, June 8, 1927, file 50–637, Dept. of Justice, NA, RG 60.

until they could return to the plantations. To add to the woes of white Mississippians, Hoover decided to appoint Dr. Sidney D. Redmond, one of the first men to report peonage, to the Colored Advisory Commission. Governor Murphree complained that Redmond's appointment would be a "mistake" and informed Hoover that it would "tend to nullify the good work you have already done in this state." Hoover stood behind his appointee, however, and on June 6 Moton informed the black physician that he was "authorized to join party."[20]

With Hoover and Red Cross vice-chairman James L. Fieser present, the commission met in Baton Rouge on June 10 to assemble its report. The observations of the committee transcended peonage, revealing an all-encompassing pattern of discrimination. The report covered 14 of the 154 camps operated by the Red Cross. Bert M. Roody and Dr. L. M. McCoy reported that in Arkansas the relief work was generally well-administered. They did ask that the Red Cross investigate some of the practices in distributing seed and supplies to the refugees. The Red Cross gave supplies to the planters, they charged, and the planters then billed the tenants for the goods.[21]

Four members of the committee, T. M. Campbell, Mrs. John Hope, Dr. J. B. Martin, and Mary E. Williams, complained of the same conditions in Mississippi. At the Deason camp the Negro group noted hostility from the planters, reporting that the planters "were jealous of their Negro labor and did not want any outside interference." Both white and black labor, they discovered, objected to the presence of soldiers around the camps. At Greenville they again heard complaints about armed guards. At Vicksburg refugees reported that when twenty-five blacks had attempted to leave the camp in order to escape work on the waterfront, they were "severely whipped by National Guardsmen." In a separate report Redmond revealed more oppressive conditions. He found soldiers stationed at the camps at Vicksburg, Yazoo City, and Natchez. He also complained that carloads of clothing had stood on the tracks for several weeks, though the refugees were in desperate need of garments.[22]

20 Unidentified clipping, file 50–637, ibid.; Moton to Redmond, June 6, 1927; Redmond to Holsey, June 21, 1927, Moton Papers, GC 48; *New York Age*, June 25, 1927, p. 4.

21 Report of Roody and McCoy, Moton Papers, GC 48.

22 Report of Mrs. Hope, Martin, Williams, and Campbell; S. D. Redmond to

While the Baton Rouge camp got good notice, some of the camps in lower Louisiana were unacceptable to the committee. In the Lafayette camp Negro nurses complained that they were not being paid while the white nurses were. White guards were stationed around the camp, but "they appeared to be friendly." At Opelousas the committee recommended that the thirty soldiers, "each one carrying on his side a pistol," be removed. "The camp at Opelousas," the group reported, "impresses one more as being a prison camp than a refugee camp which probably accounts for the fact that so many of them want to leave." The white guards came in for general criticism, as Robert R. Taylor and Albon L. Holsey, both from Tuskegee Institute, complained that the guards at Opelousas "have been too free with a few of the colored girls."[23] The report revealed that throughout the area the blacks had no choice but to remain in the camps.

Two of the committee, Claude A. Barnett and Jesse O. Thomas, stumbled into one camp unannounced, and they reported that they saw this camp "in what was a normal rather than a prepared setting." Barnett, director of the American Negro Press Association, and Thomas, field secretary of the National Urban League, approached the camp and saw a dozen white military men with rifles who "lounged about Red Cross headquarters." They confronted a white man who greeted them with laughter and said, "You boys don't need anything here, not with all those clothes you have got on. What do you want us to give you?" Then the two blacks presented their credentials and the man exploded. "What in the hell do you think of this," he shouted to the loungers about the camp. "Isn't this the damest thing you ever saw? What G—D—S— of a B— do you suppose signed this letter," he asked, retreating into the offices. Immediately the tone became more subdued as a subordinate returned and sent the two men to find a Lt. Clark. Suddenly the whites about the camp disappeared. The two investigators started for Clark's tent, but a subordinate told them that he had gone riding with a lady. They spotted him watching them, however, and though he started walking off, they hailed him. He told them to find a man called the "Deacon" and "then rode off in his auto with the lady." They were pleased to have

Hoover, n.d., ibid. This letter was incorporated into the official flood report submitted to Hoover.

[23] Report of J. S. Clark and Roscoe Brown; Report of Taylor and Holsey, ibid.

the opportunity to talk with the refugees with no whites present. "There had been all along the suspicion in our minds," they revealed, "that the refugees to whom we had talked had at other times expressed the opinions which they thought our guides wanted them to express rather than what they really felt."

In addition to the guards about the camp, the investigators discovered that 90 percent of the refugees there were black and that they suffered from privations. For example, the men did not find a single tent or cot among the black refugees. One woman had nine children and had one "tick filled with rags." "They were indescribably dirty with a dozen flies eating at the baby's nasty face." Though the whites had cots, they discovered that the blacks had been afraid to ask for bedding. "The Negroes got white salt meat while the whites got smoked bacon and ham," they discovered. Moreover, the white women got first choice of all provisions that came into the camp. Some of the refugees, though still unable to leave the camp because of the high water, had their provisions cut off. These conditions, they concluded, came from "the sodden apathy and lack of sympathy of those in charge."[24]

On June 11 Moton met with the committee; two days later they sent Hoover a preliminary report. The report substantiated the rumors of peonage, but its focus widened to include other conditions in the area. From what they learned, Moton said, the better camps reflected the participation of the blacks in running them. In the well-organized camps such as at Baton Rouge, blacks were placed in responsible positions. In Sicily Island, on the other hand, the whites had shown a disrespect for the wishes of the blacks. The recommendations of the committee sought to correct the abuses. The committee recommended recreational activities, better cafeteria arrangements, cots (of the fourteen camps visited, only one supplied blacks with cots), better distribution of clothing, and trained black personnel. The committee also asked that "as far as possible the Negro refugee camps be relieved of armed white guards-

[24] Report for Louisiana, ibid. Though unsigned, the report is probably that of Thomas and Barnett. Bruce Alan Lohof in "Hoover and the Mississippi Valley Flood of 1927: A Case Study of the Political Thought of Herbert Hoover" (Ph.D. diss., Syracuse University, 1968), stated regarding the committee's findings: "Their findings were predictable. Conditions for the Negro had not changed substantially as a result of the flood. . . . In short, racial conditions in the flood zone were precisely what one would have expected" (pp. 157–58).

men except those who are stationed at the entrances to the camps."[25]
It was obvious to the committee that the guards were placed at the
camps to keep the blacks inside until they could be returned to the
plantations.

Besides the report to Hoover, which would be complete, Moton asked
that the committee consider "a report to the public which would give
an account of our stewardship as leaders in our group." The restrictions
placed on black laborers during the flood epitomized a way of life. "We
were interested in a song that these people sang in the levee camps—
that the flood had washed away the old account." Moton said. "They
felt that the flood had emancipated them from a condition of peonage."
Though he held the national Red Cross leaders blameless, Moton nevertheless noted that on the local level there were "rank discriminations,"
noting that in Arkansas the planters received the supplies free and then
charged the tenants for them. "We were face to face all the time not
only with emergencies but one of the greatest labor questions of America, which found itself in the relation between the planter and these
tenant farmers," Moton observed. Evidently Moton was shocked by
the conditions in the Delta. The people "lived not only in a state of
fear but a state of abject poverty although they work from year to
year." And though it was tragic that they lost their homes in the flood,
"they were hardly homes," for like the schools and churches they were
"mere shacks." Somehow he wanted his investigation to help "relieve
the hopeless condition under which these people have lived for all these
years." The blacks should not be sent back "into this hopeless situation
that face them in the future." He desired that the Red Cross, by its rehabilitation work, create "a sense of freedom and hope."[26]

While Moton's proposed public statement lay dormant, Hoover answered the committee's report. The conditions complained of had been
corrected, he assured them. Though the camp at Opelousas had not been
closed, it had been put "on an acceptable and sanitary basis." The National Guard was being "demobilized as rapidly as possible although it is necessary to maintain some police authority in order to protect people in the
camps from petty thieves and bad men." Despite the damning evidence

[25] Moton to Hoover, June 13, 1927, Moton Papers, GC 48.
[26] Memorandum for the committee, n.d., ibid. Perhaps Moton got the idea from
Hoover. See Lohof, "Hoover and the Mississippi Valley Flood of 1927," pp. 210–12.

uncovered by the commission, Hoover informed the White House, which had received many complaints of peonage, that the report was "highly flattering to the Red Cross."[27]

Meanwhile, Walter White urged Hoover to break up the concentration camps. White reiterated that black sharecroppers who were under contract were treated as slaves, not as free men, and he quoted a Mississippi newspaper to support his contention that the refugee camps were in fact slave labor camps. White gave Hoover and the Red Cross credit for the relief work in the disaster but urged Hoover to give the black refugees "full freedom of movement as American citizens" and to stop "the efforts by selfish persons to use the Red Cross towards retention of Negroes as though they were chattels."[28]

Hoover, with the Moton report then before him, stated on June 21 that "I am sure that neither the Red Cross nor any other decent person would stand for unfair practices of the type you suggest toward the colored refugees." After saying that "decent" people would not stand for such conditions, Hoover explained that "the National agencies have no responsibility for the economic system which exists in the South or for matters which have taken place in previous years." Of course the Justice Department, which had by then received numerous complaints, did have the responsibility to investigate peonage, but Hoover apparently did not pass White's letter along to the proper federal agency. Hoover shifted his reply away from specific complaints of ill treatment to the general nature of the relief work, its magnitude, and its success. Hoover's staff had already been warned about the "fanatic" Walter White. One staff worker explained that "White is literally the nigger in the wood pile and if anything can be done to placate or squelch him I think there will be no more trouble."[29] Yet Hoover and the Red Cross refused to accept the responsibility for discriminatory conditions and blamed longstanding customs of the South. They would not take action to relieve refugees who were held in camps, as White said, "as though they were chattels."[30]

[27] Hoover to Moton, June 17, 1927, Moton Papers, GC 48; Hoover to E. T. Clark, June 15, 1927, Hoover Papers, Box 1–I/435.
[28] White to Hoover, June 14, 1927, Hoover Papers, Box 1–I/435.
[29] Hoover to White, June 21, 1927; Lawrence Richey to George Akerson, June 9, 1927, ibid.
[30] White to Hoover, June 14, 1927, ibid. See also White to James L. Fieser, July 12, 1927, ibid.

By late June Moton's report that would have substantiated White's charges appeared to have died, but on June 22 the *Nation* carried White's story on the flood. He charged that "the most significant injustice is in the denial to Negroes of the right of free movement and of the privilege of selling their services to the highest bidder." At the same time new complaints of peonage appeared.[31] The National Equal Rights League, led by long-time black militant spokesman Monroe Trotter, passed a resolution in Boston condemning the "barbaric cruelty in a catastrophic flood" and urged that the people there were "lower than any civilized people." Though Moton may have been alarmed that his proposed public report might be grouped with the militant Trotter protest, more likely he had come to believe that the best hope of the blacks in the Delta lay in the promised rehabilitation. As long as Hoover knew of the plan to report to the people, Moton could use the peonage stories as leverage to get more rehabilitation from the Red Cross. On June 28 Hoover and Red Cross vice-chairman Fieser came up with an elaborate plan to bring relief to the refugees as they returned to their homes. Two months later Fieser apparently shelved this plan, arguing that the Red Cross funds should go for levee repair, not to help the people make a fresh start.[32]

Though complaints of peonage had spurred the investigation, the conditions in the flood area suggested a way of life not very different from slavery days. The flood emergency had simply washed the system into the open. If the Red Cross plan promised a better day for laborers in the Delta, the previous conditions must have been abysmal. The plan called for "a cabin of simple construction" to replace those destroyed by the flood. The cabins were to be built as much as possible from "lumber which has been flood stained" and "will not cost more than $150.00 per cabin." Also a stringent set of rules had to be met before the cabins could be constructed. The Red Cross authorized $100,000 to supply the materials.[33] It had come to the point in the Delta that during the

[31] Walter White, "The Negro and the Flood," *Nation* 124 (June 22, 1927), 689. See Myron S. McNeil to Attorney General, June 27, 1927, file 50-41-4-1; A. G. Wolff to President, June 25, 1927, file 50-0, Dept. of Justice, NA, RG 60.
[32] Enclosure in Wolff to President, file 50-0, Dept. of Justice, NA, RG 60; Memorandum of Hoover and Fieser, June 28, 1927, Moton Papers, GC 48; Fieser to Hoover, Aug. 27, 1927, Hoover Papers, Box 1-I/435.
[33] Memorandum of Hoover and Fieser, June 28, 1927, Moton Papers, GC 48. See also "Memorandum of Conference between Officials of the American Red Cross

prosperous 1920s a $150 shack built of stained lumber was progress for black laborers. If Moton staked his dream of changing the Delta on roughly 700 such cabins, the conditions before the flood must have been wretched. Combined with this home-construction project, Moton probably hoped to play a game that he had played previously: he would cooperate closely with the government, pushing them along with the militant reports from the NAACP and other radical groups, while seeming to offer wise counsel to avoid race friction.[34]

Redmond, unlike Moton, possessed little patience and even less ability to take insults. By July the Justice Department, with characteristic slowness, finally sent a special agent to talk to Redmond about the peonage he had complained of in April. J. H. Noonan of the Federal Bureau of Investigation called on Redmond, and the black later complained to the attorney general that the agent "did not seem to possess an open mind on the matters stated in my letter to the President." Rather, Noonan struck Redmond "more as one who came to defend the planters and to disprove everything I said, than otherwise." The irate Redmond told Noonan that the information that he had used in the letter to President Coolidge in April had been taken from the *Memphis Commercial Appeal* and the *Jackson Daily News*, and if the FBI man wanted to see peonage for himself, he should visit the camps. Redmond revealed that he had traveled to Vicksburg to confirm rumors of peonage. "These guards, U.S. soldiers, with rifles on their shoulders, were stationed only a few feet apart around all Negro camps in this state," he reported to the attorney general. "This was not true around the white camps." As his car approached the entrance to the Negro camp at Vicksburg, a guard held up his rifle and told him to "move on." A short distance further he got the same order from another guard. He finally "got over behind the camp" and there interviewed some of the people inside. The inmates told him "they were not allowed to leave camp without a special permit and that outsiders were not allowed to come into the camps, nor to talk with them without special permission."

Instead of lashing out at the practices, Redmond carefully explained

---

and members of the Colored Commission on Flood Rehabilitation at National Red Cross Headquarters," July 8, 1927, Hoover Papers, Box 1–I/435.

[34] See article by author, "Black Power in the 1920s: The Case of Tuskegee Veterans Hospital," *Journal of Southern History* 36 (Aug. 1970), 368–88.

them to the attorney general. The laborers probably thought they were legally held because most of them had been in debt to their masters. The Mississippi statute that allowed that kind of peonage had been declared unconstitutional, he reminded the attorney general. The custom prevailed, though, and men were arrested and jailed for attempting to leave the plantations. The custom of restricting the movement of blacks had become so common that it was generally accepted. Because many of the guards were from the same area and especially because the press had reported that no movement was allowed, the victims thought that their imprisonment was legal. Redmond enclosed a newspaper story of the advisory committee report about the good camps (Baton Rouge and Lafayette, Louisiana, and Natchez, Mississippi) and the bad ones (Greenville, Mississippi, Crowley and Sicily Island, Louisiana), reminding the attorney general that the Negro group "was made up of some of the most conservative men of the country."[35] The attorney general answered that both Gen. Green and Henry M. Baker of the Red Cross had "filed letters denying the conditions alleged to exist." Nor had the FBI found such conditions; the case was closed.[36] Officially there was no peonage. For some reason the Negro committee did not challenge the official conclusions of the Red Cross and the FBI. Yet another instance of peonage remained officially invisible.

On July 11 the committee met in Washington, D.C., to develop a rehabilitation plan. They scheduled no more work until fall, when another investigation would be carried out to check on the progress of rehabilitation. It emerged on July 23 that Hoover "requested of Dr. Moton to arrange for a check-up on the rehabilitation program early in September, and that the Commission's report not be published until then." Albon Holsey, a member of the commission and secretary to Moton at Tuskegee, admitted that he had typed but three copies of the eighty-five page report, but he hoped that each member of the commission could eventually secure one.[37] And in August, to further add to the myth that all was and had been well in the Mississippi valley, *Opportunity*, the organ of the Urban League, carried a story praising the

[35] Redmond to John Sargent, July 5, 1927, file 50–637–5, Dept. of Justice, NA, RG 60.
[36] O. R. Luhring to Redmond, July 18, 1927, ibid.
[37] *The Final Report of the Colored Advisory Commission*, p. 23; Holsey to Jesse O. Thomas, July 23, 1927, Moton Papers, GC 48.

work of the Red Cross, just as Moton in June had promised Hoover that the journal would "present to the readers ... the correct attitude of the American Red Cross towards Negro refugees."[38] Moton confidently supported Hoover and the Red Cross, hoping that they could reconstruct the Delta. But, by not publicizing the peonage conditions, Moton had missed a chance to use his most powerful argument for rehabilitation.

By September Moton realized that he had erred. Thomas M. Campbell wired him that conditions were so bad in the flood area that Hoover should "inaugurate colonization" for the refugees and have them settle in Macon County, Alabama, near Tuskegee Institute. L. M. McCoy reported the lack of proper housing, clothing, and food among "the impoverished people."[39] Moton urgently appealed to Hoover, telegraphing that there was "great suffering and much want in certain flooded areas. Reports alarming." He desired a house-to-house canvass to determine need so that the "tenants not become restless and start moving from South." Seeing that his dream for significant changes in the Delta would not come true, he added that a colonization plan should be inaugurated, though he probably knew that the planters would never agree to allow their black laborers to move. Throughout the autumn reports of suffering and discrimination mounted.[40]

If some black committee members had reservations about the Red Cross's administration of relief, such doubts were realized in November, 1927, when another group of investigators "invaded" the flood territory. White landlords, as had been reported earlier, were continuing to acquire free Red Cross supplies and to charge black sharecroppers for them; black landowners could not even obtain such supplies. But the committee members' main concern was the incredible conditions in the Delta. Not only were Red Cross programs aborted by local of-

38 Jesse O. Thomas, "In the Path of the Flood," *Opportunity* 5 (Aug. 1927), 236–37; Moton to Hoover, June 25, 1927, Moton Papers, GC 48.

39 Campbell to Moton, Sept. 2, 1927; McCoy to Moton, Sept. 2, 1927, Moton Papers, GC 48.

40 Moton to Hoover, Sept. 6, 1927, ibid. For reports on the continuing discrimination, see unsigned report, Sept., 1927; Clark to Moton, Oct. 3, 1927; C. C. Neal to Kathryn B. Monroe, Oct. 7, 1927; Clark to Moton, Oct. 14, 1927; J. S. Jones to Clark, Oct. 24, 1927; Redmond to Moton, Oct. 25, 1927; Report on the flood conditions in Louisiana; Moton to Lester A. Walton, Nov. 17, 1927; Barnett to Moton, Nov. 19, 1927; Jones to Clark, Dec. 1, 1927; Elijah Thompson to Clark, Dec. 3, 1927; Moton to Clark, Dec. 16, 1927, ibid.; Confidential report sent by Moton to Hoover, Oct. 1, 1927, Hoover Papers, Box 1–I/435.

ficials, but "we found a class of people who were lacking in schools, who were living in homes scarcely worthy of the name, who existed in unhealthy conditions under an economic status unsound and unfair." The committee labeled this "a semi-peonage system," but it met all the legal requirements of peonage. "Some of the colored people who had been on the plantations attempted to leave," the report revealed. "Those who were caught, were whipped and at times threatened with death if they left the plantation again." The entire black population, the report continued, lived in dread; they would "tell you frankly that they are afraid that if they tell the truth, and somehow it is discovered that they have 'talked too much', that they would be killed." The report concluded by making much the same recommendations that the commission had made in June. Hoover admitted that administration of the relief might not be perfect, but again he shifted his argument to the people who had been helped, forgetting those who continued to suffer despite his earlier promises.[41]

Perhaps feeling a bit guilty about his unfulfilled promises regarding rehabilitation, Hoover formally defended the work of the Red Cross on December 16. Noting that both whites and blacks complained of being served last, he asked Moton to look at the broader picture of flood relief. "In the large sense, we must remember that 400,000 colored people were rescued from the flood, with the loss of scarcely two lives after our organization was initiated; that the present conditions among them, as reported by the health units established through the aid of the Rockefeller Foundation, is better than before the flood, and this is borne out by all statistical evidence as to illness and death." Hoover's statistics glossed over the continuing discrimination. As one of the flood committee wrote in the margin of the report of better conditions after the flood, "that may not mean much."[42]

Because Moton settled for the statistical victory over the flood, it was left to the NAACP (too late to really gain better conditions or treatment for the black refugees) to publish what it could gather concerning the flood. *Crisis*, the organ of the NAACP, ran three installments, "The Flood, the Red Cross, and the National Guard" in January, Feb-

[41] Moton to Hoover, ca. Nov. 1927; Hoover to Moton, Dec. 16, 1927, Hoover Papers, Box 1–I/435.
[42] Hoover to Moton, Dec. 16, 1927; Report on flood conditions in Arkansas, Moton Papers, GC 48.

ruary, and March, 1928. Incorporating material similar to what Moton had refused to publicize, *Crisis* painted a dismal picture of the flood refugees as well as of the Red Cross and the National Guard. "By far the majority of the Negroes were share-croppers, held in perpetual peonage by the planter," the first installment reported.[43] Once in the camps, the workers were not permitted to leave. "The work on the Vicksburg levee was entirely the enforced labor of Negro refugees, superintended by armed guardsmen."[44] The two other *Crisis* installments covered the story of the refugees as they went back to the flood-swept land. Yet the opportune time to expose such conditions had passed. Few people, even in an election year when Hoover was running for president, were excited by a report of peonage during the flood.

By stressing the new $150 shacks as an improvement, the Red Cross and Hoover had managed to disguise the main problem presented by the flood. With either short crops or none at all in 1927, black laborers fell even more into debt. Planters, on the other hand, used the provisions given by the relief agencies to run their plantations, often charging the blacks for them. Rather than an improved attitude as a result of rehabilitation, which Moton had hoped for, one investigator in November, 1927, reported that "we found much difficulty in getting facts on account of a fear among the people."[45] Instead of improving the lives of black sharecroppers in the Delta, the flood experience had immersed them even deeper into debt. More was done to contain the river than was done to end peonage.

As a fitting conclusion to the public account of the flood story, the Red Cross in 1929 published a pamphlet, *The Final Report of the Colored Advisory Commission.* Filled with photographs, statistics, and a history of the commission's work, it included only enough references to discrimination to justify the existence of the committee. The booklet reported that the "commissioned officers of the National Guard have been as courteous and sympathetic as essential discipline would permit,"

---

[43] "The Flood, the Red Cross and the National Guard," *Crisis* 35 (Jan. 1928), 5.

[44] Ibid., p. 6. See also *Crisis* 35 (Feb. 1928), 41–42, 64; (Mar. 1928), 100, 102. For an excellent account of the NAACP's work on the flood, see "An Open Letter to the Colored Flood Rehabilitation Commission," 1928, Arthur Spingarn Papers, Manuscript Division, Library of Congress, Washington, D.C., Box 27.

[45] Flood conditions in Arkansas, n.d.; Sub-Committee report, n.d. [Nov. 1927], Moton Papers, GC 48.

a statement that remains open to interpretation. "It is not possible in this report to cite individual cases, favorable or otherwise, with specific names and incidents," the Moton report continued, "as this would tend to reduce the report to a mass of detail."[46] The report made only vague allusions to camp guards, discrimination, and peonage. The published report read more like a eulogy to Hoover and the Red Cross than a report on peonage and discrimination. The flood commission's unpublished manuscript that did reveal peonage joined the list of previous reports and investigations of peonage which were left moldering, neglected. Peonage remained invisible, improbable, but real. It lay hidden by the inability of most Americans to believe that peonage could exist, and by the willingness of those who knew to allow it.

[46] *The Final Report of the Colored Advisory Commission*, p. 20.

CHAPTER IX

The Dark Side of the Moon

On April 6, 1936, Congressman Braswell Deen of Georgia, alarmed that the stage version of Erskine Caldwell's *Tobacco Road* was playing in Washington, D.C., during the Cherry Blossom Festival, attacked the drama and the author of the novel. Typical of so many Southern politicians, journalists, and New South boosters who preferred to dream of the plantation legend, Deen charged that *Tobacco Road* was "based on a condition that never existed." He explained that the drama contained "filth, debauchery, vulgarity, and flirtations with immorality." Deen did admit that some Southern tenants were bad off, but he defended them as fine people.[1]

Erskine Caldwell, whose preacher father had stated that *Tobacco Road* "bordered on the mild when compared with the actual, raw conditions under which thousands live,"[2] went beyond defending his work; he attacked Deen and all he stood for. Writing to Deen "as one Cracker to another," Caldwell explained that the people in Georgia and throughout the South were yet hungry and miserable when he made his Cherry Blossom speech. "Stretching from South Carolina to Arkansas its [the South's] stench is a complacent nation's shame." The miserable conditions affected both black and white, and for a half century the churches had sent missionaries to far lands while "its own people were being subjected to the economic blood-sucking of the land-lord-elders and the politician-deacons." The author took a cue from his father's

[1] U.S., Congress, House, *Congressional Record*, 74th Cong., 2nd sess., 1936, 80, pt. 5: 5010.
[2] *New York Post*, Apr. 8, 1935; clipping in Schomburg Collection, New York Public Library, Sharecropping folder. (Hereafter cited as Schomburg Collection.)

profession as he preached on the treatment of the Southern poor, denounced the violence, and with an eye to the Jeeter Lesters of the world explained that his novel showed that the South "has not only produced a coolie serfdom but, more than that, has turned around and deliberately kicked it in the face."[3] A year later Caldwell co-authored a book, *You Have Seen Their Faces*, again showing that he understood the ugly side of the Southern economic system. "Peonage, like lynching, is not condoned in theory; but conditions, usually best described as local, are sometimes called upon to justify it in practice." He contended that the black tenant farmer "is still a slave."[4]

Such statements as those of Caldwell had been heard earlier and disregarded. Indeed, one reason that peonage and involuntary servitude seldom gained national attention rested on the inability of Americans to believe that anything akin to slavery could continue to exist in the United States. The idea was unbearable and consequently unthinkable. Its stench of medieval bondage or Latin American oppression created security for it. Though peonage complaints diminished during the early years of the Depression, cases increased in the middle and late 1930s.[5] That peonage had declined during the preceding seven years is doubtful,

[3] *New York Times*, May 10, 1936, X: 1, 2.

[4] Erskine Caldwell and Margaret Bourke-White, *You Have Seen Their Faces* (New York, 1937), pp. 10, 11. Compare with Caldwell, *Tobacco Road* (New York, 1963), pp. 101–2. See also Charles S. Johnson, Edwin R. Embree, and W. W. Alexander, *The Collapse of Cotton Tenancy* (Chapel Hill, 1935); Arthur F. Raper, *Preface to Peasantry* (Chapel Hill, 1936); Charles S. Johnson, *Shadow of the Plantation* (Chicago, 1934).

[5] Despite the disruption of the Depression and the glut of labor throughout the country, peonage complaints continued. For example, see C. W. Houston to Department of Justice, Jan. 18, 1930; B. E. Leroy McKalop to Department of Justice, May 1, 1930; Nellie Jones to Attorney General, Jan. 3, 1931; E. C. Folkes to Herbert Hoover, Nov. 25, 1931; C. J. Ivy to Department of Justice, Feb. 24, 1932; W. M. M. Harper to Department of Justice, Apr. 4, 1932; Hartford Traylor to Department of Justice, May 16, 1932; Mingo Norfleet to Attorney General, Aug. 29, 1932; M. H. Hardesy to Frank M. Parrish, June 20, 1933; W. J. Young to Mr. Cummings, July 17, 1933; A. L. Hurst to Department of Justice, Nov. 20, 1933; Nathan Williams Youngblood to Department of Justice, Feb. 10, 1934; Cleveland Baldwin to Franklin D. Roosevelt, July 7, 1934; John Delooch to Joseph B. Keenan, July 21, 1934; Walter White to Homer S. Cummings, Aug. 17, 1934; Rev. Curlee Johnson to Theodore [*sic*] Roosevelt, Jan. 9, 1935; Levi Wilkerson to Dept. of Justice, Jan. 22, 1935; Charles H. Houston to Frances Perkins, Sept. 23, 1937, file 50–0, Dept. of Justice, NA, RG 60. These complaints were usually dismissed by the Justice Department as beyond federal jurisdiction; in other cases an investigation was promised, but no evidence remains of prosecution in the above cases.

though the surplus of unemployed labor would seemingly make peonage unnecessary, as men were begging for work at any wage. Most likely so many other people had been pulled down to the living level of the peons that there was a numb acceptance of the democracy of poverty and oppression. Though Caldwell could remind his congressman of the continuing misery in the South, local customs continued to rule the isolated rural areas.

A case in Arkansas in 1936 showed vividly how the old factors of peonage were surviving the Depression, but the case also offered a new departure in peonage prosecutions. Paul D. Peacher, town marshal of Earle, Arkansas, secured a contract from the Earle Special School District in Crittenden County to clear some land, sell the timber, and put the land under cultivation. On May 13, 1936, eight days after securing the contract, Peacher, described as "a typical small-town bully," began rounding up blacks to take to his newly acquired project. Peacher's search for laborers coincided with a strike called by the Southern Tenant Farmers' Union. Seeing Powell Willis, a black worker, sitting on his porch, Peacher called, "Come here, boy." Willis got into Peacher's automobile, as did eventually some nineteen other blacks, and Peacher took them to the Earle jail, charging them with vagrancy.[6]

The next day, after failing to give the prisoners any food, Peacher carried them before Mayor T. S. Mitchell, who served as local justice of the peace. At first the blacks refused to plead guilty, and Peacher sent them back to their cells. Impatient, he returned to their cells and shouted, "All you God damned niggers come out of here." Mitchell, without asking if they had jobs or money, found them all guilty of vagrancy, and he gave them thirty days at hard labor on Peacher's farm. There the men found armed guards, and their accommodations resembled a "chicken house and had bars over the windows—and dogs."[7]

On September 24, 1936, Peacher appeared before a grand jury in Little Rock. Lawyer Gordon Dean and U.S. District Attorney Fred A.

[6] Record of the Proceedings before the Grand Jury at Little Rock, Arkansas, Sept. 24, 1936, Western Division of the Eastern District of Arkansas, pp. 5, 35, Box 2084, Dept. of Justice, NA, RG 60. (Hereafter cited as Proceedings before Grand Jury.) For the role of the Southern Tenant Farmers' Union in the Peacher case, see Donald H. Grubbs, *Cry from the Cotton: The Southern Tenant Farmers' Union and the New Deal* (Chapel Hill, 1971), pp. 114–18.

[7] Testimony of John Curtis, pp. 14, 21; Statement of Gordon Dean, pp. 5–6, Proceedings before Grand Jury.

Isgrig presented the government's case. Instead of relying on the peonage statute, Isgrig based his case on the slave-kidnapping law of 1866, relying on the construction of the law in Judge Thomas G. Jones's charge to the jury in the 1903 Alabama peonage cases. The Justice Department had allowed the law to remain largely dormant since the 1908 fiasco when Charles W. Russell and Mary Grace Quackenbos had lost the case against Francesco Sabbia. But for no apparent reason the Arkansas attorneys dusted off the statute and again attempted to use it to prosecute for the offense of slavery, where debt was not a factor. The men were not vagrants, Dean noted, and the job of clearing the land for the school district was not part of Peacher's law-enforcement duties. In essence Peacher had "held them in involuntary servitude for his own private benefit."[8] The witnesses bore out the accusation. John Curtis swore that he was on his way to work when Peacher forced him into the car. Another laborer had a job but was observing the STFU strike. Fifty-one-year-old Winfield Anderson had a $10 monthly income from an insurance company, for he was partially disabled. The government's case supported the contention that Peacher had simply rounded up the most available black laborers, charged them all with vagrancy, held a kangaroo trial, and taken them to his newly acquired farm as a slave labor force. The grand jury agreed and found a true bill.[9]

In December, 1936, Peacher stood trial for slavery. Peacher's lawyer N. F. Lamb gave a classic statement on white attitudes toward black labor. "All Negroes, like some white men, are different from the rank and file of the good class of our citizens. . . . These Negroes were vagrants. Earle was full of loafers. Why not clean up the town? Loafers, leeches, and gamblers have no right to lie around."[10] Throughout the trial Peacher sat "sneeringly confident of acquittal." The jury went out and returned after an hour and a half, undecided. Judge John E. Martineau further charged the jury. "Every circumstance in this case points to the guilt of this man," he said. The jury went back to debate, and Paul Peacher boasted, "He don't scare me none. That jury will turn me loose." Later Peacher understandably said, "I don't want to talk to

[8] Statement of Dean, ibid., p. 4. See 14 Stat. 50.
[9] Testimony of Curtis, p. 14; Powell Willis, p. 33; Winfield Anderson, p. 83; B. L. Damron, p. 85; Statement of Dean, ibid., p. 1.
[10] " 'Slaves': Civil War Statute Catches 'De Law' in Arkansas," *Newsweek* 8 (Dec. 5, 1936), 18–19.

nobody," for he had received a two-year suspended sentence, a $3,500 fine, and had lost his marshal's badge.[11]

Making a relevant comment about slavery or peonage convictions did not come easy in 1936, but *Christian Century* tried. Only one precedent could be found, the Old South. "Slavery was too integral a part of the social life of the South and too vital to the interests of certain classes to be suddenly eliminated by a mere constitutional amendment," it stated, "although the amendment did make necessary the finding of new ways of perpetuating the Negro's enslavement."[12] The war to end slavery had ended seventy-one years previously, a long enough time to eliminate slavery. Despite the success of this case the Justice Department continued to use the peonage law (except in rare cases) until the U.S. *Code* was revised in 1948. Again the Justice Department neglected to follow up on what was certainly a major departure in trying involuntary servitude cases. Unless a complaint specified debt, it was usually dismissed as being outside federal jurisdiction.

Peonage in the 1930s bore characteristics of the earlier two waves of peonage during the first and third decades of the twentieth century. Francis H. Inge, a U.S. attorney in Alabama, echoed the same frustrations that had haunted peonage prosecutions for forty years when he complained in 1940 that a case originated in an area of Alabama "where there is strong and widespread sentiment, even among the better citizens, against prosecutions under the Peonage Statute in the absence of marked and inexcusable brutality." Custom, he explained, had taught the black laborer that he "should not leave the employ of the landlord until the debt is paid." Inge managed to have men indicted in one peonage case plead nolo contendere and receive light fines. He, like so many before him, feared that his case would have failed before a sympathetic jury.[13] Southern whites of all classes united to coerce black laborers in 1940, even as they had since the days of slavery.

Typical of the earlier cases, the brutality that existed in the desolate areas continued. On July 10, 1937, for example, Sheriff Harry H. Dogan of Tallahatchie County, Mississippi, investigated a complaint made by

11 "Races. Slavery in Arkansas," *Time* 28 (Dec. 7, 1936), 17. A similar case arose in 1943, *U.S.* v. *Skrobarcek*. See file 50–74–6, Dept. of Justice, NA, RG 60.

12 "Slavery Seventy Years After," *Christian Century* 53 (Dec. 9, 1936), 1645.

13 Francis H. Inge to Attorney General, Mar. 29, 1940, file 50–663, Dept. of Justice, NA, RG 60.

a black worker. The complaint charged that Joseph S. Decker held the laborer's wife in slavery. Sheriff Dogan called at Decker's house and, after persuading Decker to put away his pistol, went to the black woman's cabin. There he found Ethel Lee Davis "fastened by a trace chain, one end of which was looped around her neck and fastened by a padlock connected to two links of chain, the other end of the chain being secured to a bed in the cabin." Decker freed the woman and when Dogan asked why he locked up the woman he answered, "The s—o—b— are running away on me and I'm getting G—D— tired of it." The chaining incident was but the culmination of a series of abuses that the black couple had suffered. Decker had chained and beaten them previously, had attempted to sell them to another planter, and had allowed them nothing for the crop they had made the previous year. Decker received a three-year jail sentence and a $1,000 fine.[14]

A Georgia case in 1939 seemed a century misplaced. Indeed, this significant case contained many of the ingredients of the fugitive-slave ruling which *Prigg* v. *Pennsylvania* decided in 1842. William T. Cunningham, an Oglethorpe County planter, pursued four of his indebted laborers to Chicago and persuaded the Chicago police to aid in rounding them up, but he ran into trouble before he could return the fugitive peons. William Henry Huff, a native of Oglethorpe County who traced his black lineage to Revolutionary times, interceded on behalf of the peons. Although he had worked for several years for the National Medical Association, he employed his experience as a lawyer to halt extradition

[14] Lester M. Sack to Attorney General, Sept. 10, 1937, file 50–679, ibid. During the late 1930s and early 1940s there were numerous reports of peonage. See the excellent article by Charles Rowan, "Has Slavery Gone with the Wind in Georgia?" *Crisis* 47 (Feb. 1940), 44–45. See also "Peonage in the South," June 21, 1938, typescript in Peonage file, Schomburg Collection; J. A. Hackworth to U.S. District Attorney, Aug. 26, 1937; Francis H. Inge, Disposition of a criminal case, *U.S.* v. *Thomas Jefferson Blair*, Mar. 23, 1938, file 50–3–2; Jim C. Smith to Attorney General, May 10, 1938, file 50–767; T. Reese Watkins to Attorney General, Oct. 13, 1939, file 50–740; Julian Hartridge to Attorney General, Jan. 12, 1940, and other correspondence in file 50–790; John P. Cowart to Attorney General, Sept. 25, 1941, file 50–816; Inge, Report of Disposition of Criminal Case, Oct. 27, 1941, file 50–745; Frank H. Patton, Memorandum for Mr. George McNulty, (n.d.) 1941, file 50–30–2; Toxey Hall and Stewart C. Brown to Wendell Berge, July 29, 1942, file 50–14–13; Berge to Malcolm E. Lefargue, Oct. 31, 1942, file 50–33–5; J. O. Day to Attorney General, Dec. 28, 1942, file 50–40–5; Maconolia Wilder to Justice Department, Mar. 3, 1943, file 50–1–9; Hall to Berge, Mar. 19, 1943, file 50–41–9; Hall to Clark, Sept. 2, 1943, file 50–41–4; Albert J. Tully to Clark, Nov. 9, 1943, file 50–1–10, Dept. of Justice, NA, RG 60.

proceedings against four blacks: Doc and Otis Woods, Solomon Mc-Cannon, and Ed Raines. The case appealed to Huff, who hated peonage "with all my heart, soul, and mind," remembering from his childhood the peon-masters of Oglethorpe County, their beatings, bloodhounds, and the other brutalities which he labeled "Hitlerized bestiality." Before planter Cunningham could push through his fraudulent extradition proceedings, Huff exposed him and then appealed to Governor Henry Horner of Illinois. Recognizing the seriousness of the charges, Cunningham fled to neighboring Indiana to await the outcome of the case.[15]

Meanwhile realizing that the peons might yet end up in Georgia, Huff and others in Chicago and New York formed the Abolish Peonage Committee of America. This committee, formed with the organizational help of the International Labor Defense (ILD), became the first public organization to combat peonage. The ILD, organized in 1925 by the Communist party, had fought against the Ku Klux Klan, participated in the effort to save Nicola Sacco and Bartolomeo Vanzetti, and helped defend the Scottsboro boys.

The Abolish Peonage Committee quickly gathered information and began pressuring the Justice Department to indict Cunningham for peonage.[16] Sensing that federal authorities were reluctant to push the case, the committee began a publicity campaign. Early in 1940 historian Herbert Aptheker lent his energy and ability to the crusade, writing several articles on peonage and finally visiting Oglethorpe County with transportation money to rescue some of the peons who remained.[17] Previous efforts to send money to victims had failed, the committee believed, because Cunningham controlled the post office and the money orders had been intercepted. Twenty-five years old at the time, Aptheker met with black prostitutes in order to appear as a white with "legitimate" business in the black community. By this subterfuge he

[15] Harold Preece, *Peonage—1940 Style Slavery*, n.p., n.d., copy in Schomburg Collection, p. 15; William Henry Huff, "Peonage or Debt Slavery in the Land of the Free," *National Bar Journal* 3 (Mar. 1945), 47–48. See *Prigg* v. *Commonwealth of Pennsylvania*, 16 Peters 539. For a sketch of Huff, see *Chicago World*, Nov. 18, 1939, p. 8, clipping in Box 2083, Dept. of Justice, NA, RG 60.

[16] Huff to Wilda Gunn, Feb. 8, 1940; Huff to Herbert Aptheker, Feb. 8, 1940; Gunn to Aptheker, Feb. 17, 1940; Huff to Aptheker, Feb. 14, 1940, Herbert Aptheker Papers, in his possession, New York.

[17] Bob Wirtz to Aptheker, Feb. 24, 1940; Helen Kay to Aptheker, Mar. 29, 1940; Aptheker to Kay, n.d., ibid.

managed to get the money to the peons on the Cunningham plantation. The peons then slipped away, bought bus tickets to Atlanta and then to New Orleans, for had they bought tickets to the North they would have been stopped. In New Orleans a couple in a bookstore took the peons in, gave them directions on how to proceed to Memphis and then to Cincinnati and Chicago. Perhaps thirty persons escaped on this modern version of the underground railroad.[18]

Despite repeated complaints about Cunningham, supported by affidavits, the Justice Department announced on February 10, 1940, that the case was closed. Unable to persuade the Justice Department of the validity of the case, the Abolish Peonage Committee turned to American Labor Congressman Vito Marcantonio of New York.[19] Robert Wirtz, secretary of the ILD, appealed to Marcantonio, writing that the word from the Justice Department "proves conclusively that D of J and FBI are prepared to quash whole thing." Wirtz then prepared to break the story, pointing out to Attorney General Robert Jackson that the Negro press had already carried several interviews that showed beyond a doubt that peonage was the issue in this case. Wirtz warned Jackson that the powers of the Southern bloc of congressmen should not interfere "when hundreds of thousands and millions of American people are compelled to continue in conditions of peonage for failure of Federal investigations and prosecution." He also suggested that "we can use it in our campaign to raise the question of peonage to the level of a real national issue."[20] The elevation of peonage to a national issue might have been the best prescription for its cure, but unfortunately the issue did not get that far.

The Abolish Peonage Committee did continue to pressure the Justice Department, and in March, 1940, several persons interested in the case, including Huff and two of the peons, met with O. John Rogge of the Justice Department to describe conditions in Georgia. Not satisfied with Rogge's response to their complaints, the committee sponsored a mass rally in Washington. The Justice Department was meanwhile subjected

[18] Interview with Herbert Aptheker, Nov. 5, 1970.
[19] J. Edgar Hoover to Huff, Feb. 10, 1940; W. S. Devereaux to Wirtz, Feb. 16, 1940, Vito Marcantonio Papers, Manuscript Division, New York Public Library, Box 3. (Hereafter cited as Marcantonio Papers.)
[20] Wirtz to Marcantonio, memo dated Monday, 9 a.m. (probably Feb. 19, 1940); Wirtz to Jackson, Feb 17, 1940; Wirtz to Marcantonio, Feb. 21, 1940, ibid.

to a barrage of sympathetic letters to reinforce the committee's continuing interest in the *Cunningham* case.[21]

At long last this pressure did cause the Justice Department to reopen the case. While Attorney General Jackson persisted in his view that there was no violation of the peonage statute, the Justice Department eventually indicted Cunningham on a conspiracy charge, but the case ended when a federal judge in Georgia refused to approve extradition of the principals. The government's case rested on conspiracy between Cunningham and a local officer who accompanied him to Chicago, but the federal court argued that the officer was only doing his duty, not engaging in a conspiracy.[22] Why the Department of Justice did not indict Cunningham on a peonage or slave-kidnapping charge remains a mystery. With the well-publicized *Peacher* case only four years in the past, certainly the attorneys in Washington realized the utility of the 1866 law. Huff continued in his role as head of the Abolish Peonage Committee throughout 1942, but he was frustrated. "I deeply regret to say," he wrote to a friend, "that it seems to me that the Department of Justice as now constituted just simply does not intend to prosecute white persons for anything they do to Negroes!"[23]

Not everyone shared Huff's gloom. According to NAACP counsel Thurgood Marshall, by December, 1941, the Justice Department was "moving swiftly" on peonage.[24] The energetic backing of the *Cunningham* case by the Abolish Peonage Committee probably spurred the lethargic Justice Department into acting more vigorously on civil rights. Yet other dangers forced even more action. In August, 1942, the Justice

[21] Herbert Aptheker, "America Has Her Peons, Too!" *New Masses* 35 (May 28, 1940), 11; "Notice of Mass Rally," Mar. 19, 1940; "Memo of meeting at YWCA"; John P. Davis to O. John Rogge, June 12, 25, 1940; Rogge to Davis, July 20, 1940, National Negro Congress Papers, Schomburg Collection. See also William L. Patterson to Hugo Black, Feb. 21, 1940, Box 3, Marcantonio Papers; Patterson to Franklin D. Roosevelt, Oct. 22, 1940, file 50–0, Dept. of Justice, NA, RG 60.

[22] Jackson to Marcantonio, Mar. 9, 1940, Box 3, Marcantonio Papers; *U.S.* v. *Cunningham*, 40 F.S. 399 (D.C., M.D. Ga., 1941). See also U.S. Dept. of Justice Press Release, May 29, 1941, Justice Department Library, Washington, D.C.; "Peonage Probe," *Newsweek* 17 (June 2, 1941), 15; William Henry Huff, "The New Charter of Slavery," *National Bar Journal* 2 (June 1944), 65–69. For a similar case, see statement of David Williams, Aug. 31, 1942; John L. McMillan to Hoover, Jan. 9, 18, 1943; and other documents in file 50–67–2, Dept. of Justice, NA, RG 60.

[23] Huff to General W. Smith, Oct. 15, 1942, file 50–837, Dept. of Justice, NA, RG 60.

[24] Marshall to Huff, Dec. 16, 1941, Box 3, Marcantonio Papers.

Department took a quite different stand on matters pertaining to civil rights; the prod came not from their concern with those held in peonage, but from a foreign propaganda threat. Writing to a Texas U.S. attorney about a peonage case that had been dropped, Assistant Attorney General Wendell Berge warned, "Enemy propagandists have used similar episodes in international broadcasts to the colored race, saying that the democracies are insincere and that the enemy is their friend." The president ordered that "lynching complaints shall be investigated as soon as possible," and that the investigations be fully publicized. "The Attorney General has requested that we expedite other cases relating to Negro victims," he instructed.[25]

From evidence in the Justice Department files the FBI had been very slow in responding to complaints. In July 1941, for example, a Mississippi U.S. attorney sent a clipping from the *Waco Messenger* complaining of peonage in the Yazoo River Delta. Five months later another attorney noted that no investigation had been made.[26] Japanese propaganda created the necessity for U.S. counterpropaganda. There were numerous cases to act upon, for the early 1940s were filled with peonage complaints. Whether the activity came from an increase of peonage during those years or from more vigorous prosecution because of the Japanese challenge, cases increased.

With the age-old consistency of the institution, peonage seemed unchanged since its first exposé in 1901. A Florida case suggested abuses of immigrant labor by the Florida East Coast Railway thirty-five years earlier. The United States Sugar Corporation of Clewiston, Florida, found it necessary to recruit black laborers in other states, principally Tennessee, due to the wartime shortage of labor. They sent labor agents to neighboring states, told the prospective employees that they were a government corporation, promised high wages, and furnished transportation to Florida.[27]

In Clewiston the laborers were assigned to one of the eleven com-

[25] Berge to Steve M. King, Aug. 8, 1942, file 50–74–4; Berge to Clinton R. Barry, Aug. 8, 1942, file 50–9–5, Dept. of Justice, NA, RG 60.
[26] See Wendell Berge to Hoover, July 5, 1941; Toxey Hall to Berge, July 10, 1941; J. J. Lyman to Victor Rotnem, Dec. 19, 1941; Berge to Hoover, Dec. 20, 1941; *Waco Messenger*, undated clipping in file 50–817, ibid.
[27] One laborer, for instance, remembered that "he was going to work on a government-owned farm and that it was a national defense job." Notes on statement of Cornelius Long, file 50–18–15, sec. 1, ibid.

pany camps. They were held, beaten, and threatened, and they complained that their mail was censored. After the conditions were exposed, a Tennessee investigator reported that the camps were "above average," and the *Tampa Morning Tribune* suggested that the complaints probably originated from "a group of disgruntled negro laborers, probably agitated by negro organizations which pretend to be devoted unselfishly to safeguarding the interest of the colored race."[28] Introspection seemed impossible; the habitual cry of innocence, the instant denial of wrong, the charge that an outside group of agitators were behind any racial troubles continued to characterize white public opinion in the South. As had been the case with Cunningham, the charges against the U.S. Sugar Corporation remained unsettled.[29]

Similarly, reflecting the false optimism that so often permeated the Justice Department, Assistant Attorney General Wendell Berge wrote to FBI director J. Edgar Hoover in March, 1943, that peons often looked to the FBI and the Justice Department attorneys "as the only practical sanctuary from this type of abuse." That much was accurate enough. "Only in a few remote areas, particularly in turpentine camp localities," he continued, losing sight of reality, "do there still exist flagrant conditions remindful of practices three decades ago." Berge likened peonage to a skin disorder that had been brought under control.[30]

The optimism seemed fatuous, not only because complaints still poured in but also because it came between major Supreme Court cases which illustrated precisely how little progress had been made combating peonage. Though Alabama had purged its contract labor law in the *Bailey* case in 1911, not all Southern states followed the decision. Georgia and Florida maintained their contract-labor laws, complete with the prima facie restrictions, and the Justice Department allowed the laws to stand for thirty years uncontested.

Taylor v. *Georgia* went to the U.S. Supreme Court in 1941 and chal-

[28] Notes on statements of Vernon Lawhorn, Robert Mitchell, John Lee Alsobrook, Williard Jones, James Maddox, Clara E. Kitts of Tennessee State Employment Service, ibid.; *Tampa Morning Tribune*, Apr. 29, 1943, clipping in ibid.
[29] See Herbert S. Phillips to Attorney General, Jan. 1, 1943; Berge to T. D. Quinn, May 25, 1943, ibid. A federal grand jury indicted the corporation and certain individuals in 1942, but in April, 1943, it dismissed the indictments "for certain legal reasons." Another grand jury, convened in 1943, returned a no bill (Warren Olney III to Vernon J. Lawhorn, Feb. 17, 1955, ibid.).
[30] Berge to Hoover, Mar. 4, 1943, file 50–73–1, ibid.

lenged the Georgia law of 1903 that forbade a laborer to break a contract after receiving an advance. To it the Georgia legislature had attached the "presumptive evidence" restriction similar to that in the *Bailey* case.[31] As in the *Bailey* case, the Justice Department, bestirred by a just cause, filed a brief amicus curiae. "Recent federal investigations in Georgia," the brief explained, "have disclosed that involuntary service of debtors has been coerced in whole or in part by the threat of prosecution under the state statute."[32] The Justice Department's brief also introduced evidence that peonage continued to be widespread in the South, quoting a resolution of the Georgia Baptist Convention in 1939 which declared that "there are more negroes held by these debt slavers than were actually owned as slaves before the War between the States." After stating the legalities of the case, the lawyers concluded that it was "a strange anomaly that Georgia, colonized as a protest against the English custom of imprisonment for debt, has itself legalized the same custom."[33]

After defending Georgia's position and countering the Justice Department's arguments, the Georgia authorities concluded their case. "So even if we presume that this statute is conducive of peonage, imprisonment for debt, and involuntary servitude," the argument ran, "it is manifestly evident that very few wicked people in Georgia are taking advantage of it when it appears that during the last fifteen years in a state of three and one-half million population only ten of such cases have reached the Appellate Courts of Georgia."[34] As Erskine Caldwell had pointed out only a few years before, local custom prevailed; previous Georgia legal rulings had obviously stifled the incentive to appeal cases involving labor contracts.

The U.S. Supreme Court in 1942 overturned the ruling of the Georgia Supreme Court, and Justice James F. Byrnes, a South Carolinian, read the unanimous decision. "There is no material distinction between the

[31] Georgia *Laws*, 1903, pp. 90–91. The law passed on Aug. 15, 1903. For a statement of the facts, see Brief for Appellant, p. 6, *Taylor* v. *Georgia*, 315 U.S. 25. See also Georgia *Code*, 1914, vol. 6, p. 384, secs. 715, 716. A study of the judicial history of this one law would be a major undertaking, and it would doubtless reveal much of the social history of Georgia's tenant class.

[32] Memorandum for the United States as Amicus Curiae, *Taylor* v. *Georgia*, 315 U.S. 25.

[33] Brief for Appellant, pp. 11–12, ibid.

[34] Brief for Appellee, p. 6, ibid.

Georgia statutes challenged here and the Alabama statute which was held to violate the Thirteenth Amendment in *Bailey* v. *Alabama*." The Court struck down both the prima facie and the substantive parts of the law.[35]

The case ending the contract law in Florida would have been merely a footnote to the *Taylor* decision had not Justice Robert Jackson, recently having moved from the attorney generalship to the Supreme Court bench, written such a significant decision. Like Alabama and Georgia, Florida had passed a contract-labor law complete with the prima facie section early in the twentieth century. In 1919 the Florida legislature, after previously striking the law from the books, repassed the provision. The Florida Supreme Court, like its Georgia counterpart, had insisted that the law was constitutional.[36] Mann Pollock, an illiterate black laborer, obtained an advance of $5 in October, 1942, and he could not pay his fine and went to jail. But Pollock somehow filed a writ of habeas corpus, and the Circuit Court of Brevard County held the 1919 statute unconstitutional and freed Pollock. The state supreme court reversed the lower court's decision, and the case went to the U.S. Supreme Court. The state of Florida, with the *Taylor* case so recent and so conclusive, argued that the statute was constitutional because in this case the prima facie part of the law had not been utilized. The government argued that the case should be reversed because of the Taylor precedent and because a fair reading of the law clearly illustrated that the intent of the law was "to establish, maintain and enforce, directly or indirectly, the voluntary or involuntary service of labor of peons, in liquidation of debts or obligations."[37]

Associate Justice Robert Jackson, who as attorney general so recently evaded the protests of the Abolish Peonage Committee, delivered the opinion. After reviewing the 1867 statute he stated, "Congress thus raised both a shield and a sword against forced labor because of debt." He

[35] *Taylor* v. *Georgia*, 315 U.S. 29. The prisoner according to this law could offer an unsworn statement to the jury. See also "State Peonage Law Held Violative of Thirteenth Amendment," *Bill of Rights Review* 2 (Winter, 1942), 142–43; Waite, "The Negro in the Supreme Court," p. 288.

[36] Florida *Laws*, 1907, p. 182; Florida *Laws*, 1919, p. 286; *Williams* v. *Pollock*, 14 So. 2nd 700.

[37] Brief for appellant, pp. 3–5, 18–19; Brief for appellee, pp. 12–13, *Pollock* v. *Williams*, 322 U.S. 4.

then reviewed the major Supreme Court decisions regarding peonage. In the *Clyatt* case the federal act had been "used as a sword and an employer convicted under it." In the *Bailey* case the act and the Constitution "were raised as a shield against conviction of a laborer under an Alabama act substantially the same as the one before us now." In the *Reynolds* case the act "was sword again," and in the *Taylor* case "the Federal Act was again applied as a shield, against conviction by resort to the presumption, of a Negro laborer, under a Georgia statute in effect like the one before us now."[38]

Yet as Jackson reviewed the history of peonage he fell into a trap that had ensnared many other unwary commentators on peonage. He accurately noted that most of the cases under the peonage statute had come from Florida or a bordering state. "This is not to intimate that this section, more than others, was sympathetic with peonage," he argued incorrectly, "for this evil has never had general approval anywhere, and its sporadic appearances have been neither sectional nor racial." With the exception of the immigrant cases, peonage had been both sectional and racial. Whether Jackson had been misled by the brief and misleading report on peonage in the immigration investigation or by the printed pamphlets of Charles W. Russell that concentrated almost entirely on immigrant peonage (he cited both), his analysis failed.[39]

Although his historical analysis of peonage was not definitive, Jackson's conclusion showed a grasp of the legal history of the institution. His indictment of the Florida legislature for ruling against the precedent-setting *Bailey* case showed impatience. "The Florida Legislature has enacted and twice re-enacted it since we so held," he charged. "We cannot assume it was doing an idle thing." The intent of the law had been obvious, he stated, and in each case the facts were similar. "In each there was the same story, a necessitous and illiterate laborer, an agreement to work for a small wage, a trifling advance, a breach of contract to work. In not one has there been proof from which we fairly could say whether the Negro never intended to work out the advance, or quit because of some real or fancied grievance, or just got tired." Unlike the *Bailey* and *Taylor* cases, the Florida law permitted the victim

[38] *Pollock* v. *Williams*, 322 U.S. 8–10.
[39] Ibid., pp. 11, 18n, 24n.

to offer his sworn word against the presumptions. "These distinctions," Jackson concluded, "we think are without consequence."[40] The *Pollock* case held unconstitutional not only the prima facie provision but, like the *Taylor* case, the entire contract-labor law.

Chief Justice Harlan F. Stone concurred in a dissent by Stanley F. Reed. The two dissenting justices argued that the two parts of the law should be judged separately. "We cannot conclude that a statute which merely punishes a fraud in a contract, as the first section does if considered alone, violates the provision of the Thirteenth Amendment against involuntary servitude or is null and void ... because it is an attempt to enforce compulsory service for a debt."[41] While the two dissenting justices reflected consistency with the earlier rulings of the Court, the majority began a new departure portending a greater concern for minority rights.

Thirty years since the *Bailey* decision had been pushed by Booker T. Washington and his small band of allies, no group such as the NAACP, the American Civil Liberties Union, or the Justice Department had challenged the obviously unconstitutional contract-labor laws. Peonage had been overlooked as usual, languishing in the backwater of state laws and the customs of another era. These cases, indeed none of the peonage cases, should have been necessary. The cases arose because of economic and social ills in the southern United States, conditions that grew out of the evils of a race system inherited from the days of slavery and the frontier. The two traditions blended to create peonage. Peonage constituted a system of forced labor run by men who thrived in the wilderness, whose manhood called for constant reaffirmation by subduing both environment and man. The peon-master personified Wilbur Cash's "savage ideal" as surely as the peon personified Ralph Ellison's "invisible man."

Even before the echo of the *Pollock* case had faded, Florida had again gained national attention for alleged practices of peonage. The Workers Defense League (WDL), an organization specializing in legal

---

[40] Ibid., pp. 15, 22, 25.
[41] Ibid., p. 30. For comment on the case, see "Constitutional Law-Prohibition against Involuntary Servitude," *New York University Law Quarterly Review* 20 (July 1945), 361–64; "Constitutional Law—Thirteenth Amendment," *George Washington Law Review* 12 (June 1944), 492–94; "Peonage," *Law Guild Review* 4 (1944), 29–30; Waite, "The Negro in the Supreme Court," pp. 290–92.

work and civil liberties, in January, 1945, investigated complaints against
the sheriff of Broward County, Florida. According to a WDL investigation, black workers were arrested and jailed, given no trial, and forced
to work in the fields. The WDL increased its pressure, but a grand jury
failed to find a true bill regarding the cases.[42] The old system of arresting
poor blacks, fining them, and then putting them to work to pay off
their debts had not died out. In the winter of 1946 Morris Milgram published an article listing many cases of such practices in Florida, a report
which described the inevitable beatings and other instances of brutality.
The Florida cases trailed off with threats by the victims to sue the local
law-enforcement officers for their offenses. As in many similar cases,
the Justice Department seemed reluctant to intervene.[43]

The Workers Defense League kept a steady barrage of cases before
the public. In 1946 the WDL reported a successful Texas case that ended
in the conviction of a sheriff and former sheriff. Three years later, to
dramatize the extent of peonage still existing in the United States, the
WDL appointed a commission to gather testimony concerning forced
labor. From Florida, Rev. Leroy Hacker testified that peonage still
pervaded the turpentine areas of his home state. Hacker, an army veteran
and Methodist minister, charged that peonage existed in nine Florida
counties and in parts of South Carolina and Tennessee. When the commission ended, it had heard 30 witnesses and collected 300 affidavits.[44]

With the United States entering an economic revolution following
World War II, peonage presented a gloomy juxtaposition to the bright
face of American technology. The changing nature of society made
peonage even more difficult to conceal. The availability of automobiles
made escape easier. A telephone call could arouse some form of legal
assistance, or might at least carry a threat to cause an employer to hesitate
about keeping laborers against their wills. Moreover, mechanization on
the farm, the cotton-picker and the tractor, drove even more workers
from agriculture. Nearly all factors had changed except the nature of
man and the customs of the area, and when a vulnerable laborer met an
employer who refused to accept a workman's freedom, involuntary

[42] Workers Defense League, News Service, Jan. 26, 1945, unbound leaflets in
New York Public Library. Hereafter cited as WDL News Service.
[43] Milgram, "Involuntary Servitude in Florida," pp. 408–15. See also WDL News
Service, May 3, 31, June 27, Sept. 6, 1945, Feb. 21, 1946.
[44] WDL News Service, Nov. 27, 1946, Mar. 9, 1949.

servitude resulted. The peons continued to exist because of ignorance, isolation, corruption among local officers, and the apathy of the Justice Department. Custom prevailed over technology.[45]

Technically, the Justice Department was better prepared to deal with peonage and involuntary servitude. Eighty years after slavery formally ended, a revision of the United States Code clarified the old slave kidnapping law of 1866, and the modification enabled the Justice Department to combat slavery.[46] Of course the *Peacher* case in 1936 had already demonstrated the efficacy of the slave-kidnapping law, but the new wording made the law more flexible. The 1948 codification gave the Justice Department three tools with which to prosecute: the peonage statute (1581 USC), the slave-kidnapping law (1583 USC), and the sale into involuntary servitude law (1584 USC).[47]

Following 1945, definite evidence of peonage becomes more difficult to obtain, for the Justice Department complaint files are closed to researchers, and one must turn to newspapers, periodicals, and legal cases to document its extent. Since 1945 these sources present a picture of the institution which suggests that peonage certainly diminished; but to what degree it persisted is impossible to determine. Reports of such abuses continued, and many of the reports came from outside the South.[48]

Quite by accident a Senate subcommittee on labor and labor management relations in 1951 heard testimony that peonage had yet to be obliterated in Georgia. Thomas W. Johnson, a Macon attorney, testified that a Negro, James Edward Day, Jr., had appealed to him to help free his four children from William Belote, a naval stores operator. Day, whose appeals to the FBI had been to no avail, fled the turpentine still after Belote threatened to kill him, but he had not been able to take

[45] See Arthur F. Raper, *Machines in the Cotton Fields* (Southern Regional Council, 1946).

[46] United States *Code*, sec. 1583. For the statute, see 14 Stat. 50.

[47] See Arthur B. Caldwell, "The Civil Rights Section, Its Functions and Its Statutes," Paper delivered to civil rights class of the summer session of the University of Pennsylvania, July 16, 1953, p. 26; Sydney Brodie, "The Federally-Secured Right to be Free from Bondage," *Georgetown Law Journal* 40 (Mar. 1952), 367–98.

[48] See *New York Times*, Aug. 29, 1948, p. 4; Aug. 20, 1949, p. 11; Sept. 10, 1949, p. 3; "Involuntary Servitude," *Newsweek* 29 (Mar. 10, 1947), 28–29; "Emancipation for Frank," *Newsweek* 33 (Feb. 14, 1949), 21.

his children with him. Attorney Johnson attempted to get the children back, but Belote told him bluntly, "I want that God-damned nigger to come down here because I want to put him in jail." To get the children Day took Belote to court, but there officers arrested Day on a trumped-up charge. He remained in jail for eight days as Johnson attempted to free him while Belote tried to entice him to return to work, promising that he would forget the alleged debt if Day would return. Day refused to go back, and eventually Belote dropped the charges.[49]

The committee became interested in the system that Johnson revealed. Though vague about the laws he was referring to, Johnson stated that the Georgia law that the Supreme Court struck down (presumably the *Taylor* case) was "still being used today and it is being used actually as a peonage statute. For instance," he testified, "sawmill people—and I think they are the worst offenders I know of—get Negroes in debt to them purposely." Johnson continued his startling revelation, admitting that peonage existed and that "it is rather prevalent." He had contacted the FBI and the Justice Department, but they had done nothing about it. When asked how prevalent the offenses were, he estimated that he knew of some dozen cases in the past year. For example, he testified, the Cordell Lumber Company in Dublin had found cheap labor by "a system of prisoners being released to employers on the payment of fines or the posting of bonds."[50] Yet the committee apparently did nothing to eradicate the conditions in the areas where they suspected peonage.

During the same year as the congressional investigation, Stetson Kennedy, a Floridian who had gathered much information on peonage, testified before a United Nations Forced Labor Committee in Geneva, Switzerland. While he no doubt exaggerated the extent of peonage, he correctly assessed the attitude of the Justice Department. "The official United States attitude toward charges of peonage in the South is that while some bad conditions exist efforts are constantly being made to improve them and these efforts are having a great deal of success."[51]

[49] U.S., Congress, Senate, Special Subcommittee on Labor and Labor-Management Relations, Committee on Labor and Public Welfare, *Labor Practices in Laurens Co. Georgia*, Hearing, 82nd Cong., 1st sess., Aug. 13, 1951, pp. 79–86.
[50] Ibid., pp. 87–88, 92, 104–8.
[51] *New York Times*, Nov. 8, 1952, p. 3. He claimed that 5,388,000 workers were held in involuntary servitude.

Kennedy's statement could have been given in 1901 as easily as in 1951, for the Justice Department had always used much the same words to describe its progress in halting peonage.

Despite the unfavorable publicity abroad, the Justice Department often dropped cases on the evidence in the complaint, choosing not to investigate. In March, 1952, Sydney Brodie wrote an article incorporating legal history and current statistics on peonage in which he revealed that in 1951 the Justice Department had received sixty-three complaints under the anti–forced labor statutes while investigating only thirty-six of them. There were two prosecutions, though some of the cases were settled out of court in favor of the complainants.[52]

In 1954—the same year that the Supreme Court struck down school segregation—two Alabama farmers went to jail for eighteen months for holding a man in slavery. "The defendants," reported the *New York Times*, "were charged with putting the Negroes in bondage by paying their jail fines and forcing them to work them out in the fields." One of the blacks who had been bailed out had later been beaten to death when he had attempted to flee.[53]

Reports of peonage decreased in the late 1950s, but it may be a mistake to assume that the lack of public awareness of peonage or slavery in 1960 was any more an indication of its extent than had been the lack of public reports in earlier days. The 1961 Commission on Civil Rights reported uneasily that though the Justice Department received sixty-seven complaints of peonage or slavery from January 1, 1958, through June 30, 1960, "no prosecutions were brought apparently because none of those complaints was deemed valid." But the commission warned that "the victims of peonage and involuntary servitude are even less likely than the usual victims of police brutality and private violence to be articulate in protesting—especially if local officials cooperate with their 'masters.' "[54]

According to statistics gathered by Harry H. Shapiro, from 1961 to 1963 the Justice Department received some 104 peonage or slavery complaints. From these complaints there were two prosecutions, one no bill

[52] Brodie, "The Federally-Secured Right," p. 373.
[53] *New York Times*, Sept. 10, 1953, p. 50; May 15, 1954, p. 16, Dec. 17, 1954, p. 55; *Time* 64 (Dec. 27, 1954), 13.
[54] *1961 Commission on Civil Rights Report: Justice* (Washington, 1961), p. 55.

by a grand jury, one case pending, one subject admonished, one referred to the local authorities, six still under investigation, and ninety-two closed on the face of the complaint.[55] Considering the nature of the complaints throughout the years and the constant Justice Department excuse that most cases did not fall within federal jurisdiction because there was no debt involved, the outright dropping of 92 of the 104 cases would seem unwarranted, especially in view of the code revision in 1948. The entire Justice Department peonage files available to researchers provide convincing evidence that the primary reason for not acting on such cases came not from lack of evidence that some crime had been committed but from doubt of federal jurisdiction. Yet at the height of the civil rights movement the Justice Department remained remarkably insensitive to peonage and slavery complaints.

Shapiro's state-by-state analysis from 1961 to 1963 revealed that the complaints came from thirty states. The most numerous cases came from (in order) California, Florida, Georgia, Alabama, Mississippi, Texas, and Arkansas.[56] Though there was no explanation of why California led the list, the abuses of migrant and Mexican labor probably were at the basis of the complaints, while the continuation of peonage complaints from Florida, Georgia, Alabama, and Mississippi doubtless stemmed from the local customs and attitudes that for centuries had sanctioned the abuse of poor laborers. The statistics, incomplete as they were, showed that in the long history of peonage only the magnitude had changed; most of the complaints came from the same area of the South. Despite occasional victories in the courts and accompanying publicity, peonage still lingers in the Southern hinterland as it has since the Civil War, defeated but not yet dead.

Planters continued to disregard honesty and came to deplore civil rights. In 1964 a student civil rights worker in Mississippi wrote that a black worker "secretly left the plantation to come and ask us for help." The laborer had borrowed $250 from the boss two years before, and "since then, his 'owner' has taken $10 a week out of his pay and hasn't stopped." When the debt should have been paid in full, the worker asked his boss how much he owed; "he was told $100, and got the same

[55] Harry H. Shapiro, "Involuntary Servitude: The Need for a More Flexible Approach," *Rutgers Law Review* 19 (1964–65), 85.
[56] Ibid.

answer ten weeks later (with the $10 a week still being deducted)." He must have annoyed his employer, the student continued, "because the next week, after his boss discovered that he attended citizenship classes, the boss came to him with a note saying he owed $650." Though there was no mention that the worker had been compelled to remain on the plantation, the student explained that protest against this practice to local authorities was useless, for the boss and a local deputy sheriff co-owned the plantation.[57]

In the same spirit, it was clear that the vicious pattern of immigrant peonage was still alive, luring hopeful foreign workers to a nightmare in the South. In 1969 Felipe Pagan Vidal, a Puerto Rican, complained that he had been recruited to work on a truck farm near Miami and ended in peonage. Vidal, like the immigrants from New York in 1906, received a glowing promise of high pay, a bonus, and low transportation fare. After a week on the job Vidal became dissatisfied and announced that he was leaving. The foreman told him he could not leave; when Vidal began walking off, the foreman "hacked him across the back and shoulder" with a machete. Afterward Vidal stated that the foreman refused him medical attention and guarded him. Other workers experienced the same fate, Vidal testified, and "had been threatened with death and beatings."[58]

Even a 1969 federal anti-poverty pamphlet cited what amounted to peonage. It noted that "semi-feudal conditions" existed in the turpentine camps of the South. Advances were given and were difficult to pay off, so tenants moved off in the middle of the night because they were instructed to remain on the farms until they had paid their debts.[59]

In the summer of 1969 Robert Coles and Harry Huge wrote "Peonage in Florida" for the *New Republic*. Though they did not define peonage, the authors painted a picture which revealed the continuing existence of the institution. Moreover, their story substantiates the hypothesis that where peonage had long existed little has changed since

[57] Elizabeth Sutherland, ed., *Letters from Mississippi* (New York, 1965), pp. 57–58. See also *New York Times*, Oct. 31, 1963, p. 1; May 2, 1964, p. 11; *Arlan (Bill) Bryant* v. *Billy Donnel and Jackie Donnel*, 239 F.S. 671 (U.S. D.C. Tenn., 1965).

[58] *Washington Post*, Dec. 18, 1968, p. A 16. See also ibid., Dec. 13, 1968, p. A 2; Dec. 15, 1968, p. A 2.

[59] *Continuity and Change in Antipoverty Programs*, 2nd annual report (Washington, 1969), pp. 2–3.

the day Fred Cubberly stumbled onto peonage in a Florida turpentine camp. Present-day peons suffer from the same vulnerability that their predecessors did. "They own people, that's what," a Florida peon complained, "unless they escape, like I did; but I'll tell you the truth, a lot of migrants—you know, they're Mexican-American like me, or black people, and a few white, yes, but not many—they're not aware of their rights, and they're scared, and they should be." Employers continued to use force. "The men will ride around with guns, and the crew leaders will herd the people into the trucks to go picking," a worker revealed.[60]

These peonage conditions existed only a short distance from Cape Kennedy, only scant miles from the shadow of the glorious moon rockets. "Meanwhile," the authors wrote, "Senators come and are horrified and ashamed. Tourists drive by and if they see anything, shake their heads and wonder how many miles to the next Holiday Inn." Nor was the Justice Department ignorant of the conditions. Workers filed complaints, but the Justice Department apparently took no action. One woman complained in an affidavit that the guards told her that she "could not go because I owed $25 to the company."[61]

Over 120 years since the United States acquired peonage from New Mexico and over a century after Congress passed a statute outlawing the practice, it continues. Concerned people on the local level who recognize the evil and try to crush it are continually frustrated now, as in the past. For peonage has been like the dark side of the moon; it existed, but only exceptional circumstances enabled one to see it. Nor was the average citizen concerned with such dark and dangerous places. So it remained largely unexplored, charted only in law books and statutes which remained regrettably removed from the reality, from the vertiginous but stagnant world of peonage.

Those who attempted to crush peonage in the South were surrounded by almost as many circles of futility as the peons. Local officials discouraged meddlers, and the Justice Department moved sluggishly on complaints or dismissed them outright. The press often glossed over the conditions, choosing to defend the landowners and their labor system rather than champion the often unattractive, inarticulate, and illiterate

---

[60] Robert Coles and Harry Huge, "Peonage in Florida," *New Republic* 161 (July 26, 1969), 19.
[61] Ibid., p. 20.

peons. And there were still isolated areas that offered sanctuary for diabolic men's passions—or apathy enough to create the same effect. As long as those conditions persisted, there would be the helplessness of the peons and the impotent frustration of their defenders. Such was the case in 1969, as the pleas of the peons were drowned out by the roar of the rocket. One labor organizer in Florida echoed the disappointments of Fred Cubberly in 1901, of Mary Grace Quackenbos and Charles W. Russell in 1908, of Hooper Alexander in 1921, and of William Henry Huff in 1942. "These people have nothing to fall back on but the conscience of the nation, and a lot of good that's done for them."[62]

[62] Ibid., p. 21.

Critical Essay on Authorities

The peonage collection in the U.S. Department of Justice files in the National Archives in Washington, D.C., furnished the primary documentation for this study. This collection in Record Group 60 contains complaints from laborers who considered themselves victims of peonage, correspondence between local federal attorneys and the attorney general, clippings, trial transcripts, briefs, and other miscellaneous material. This collection would have been of even more value were the investigatory records of the Federal Bureau of Investigation available. These reports, however, were screened out. A long and involved attempt by the author to gain access to these files, with aid from Senator B. Everett Jordan and his staff, was unsuccessful. The Deputy Attorney General cited 5 U.S.C. Sec. 552(b)(7) as the reason the files remain closed, but the flexibility of this law did not convince the writer that the entire file should be closed. The writer's request for definitive statistics on the frequency and result of peonage complaints since World War II were ignored. Yet the available documents are rich, revealing the hardships of poor laborers in the South. This collection was supplemented by the Appointment and Credentials Files of the Department of Justice, a collection of letters of recommendation that provided biographical information on federal officials. The Appealed Case Files of the Justice Department in Record Group 267 were of limited value. Of restricted usefulness in this study were the records of the Bureau of Freedmen, Refugees and Abandoned Lands in Record Group 105, the Adjutant General's office material in Record Group 94, the Correspondence of U.S. attorneys and marshals in Record Group 118, and the Department of Commerce material in Record Group 40. The Federal Records Center in East Point, Georgia, contained useful material on the Alabama peonage cases of 1903 and *United States* v. *Reynolds*, 235 U.S. 133 (1914).

The Booker T. Washington Papers in the Manuscript Division of the Library of Congress furnished an intimate look into Washington's efforts to crush peonage. These documents will eventually be available in Louis R. Harlan, ed., *The Booker T. Washington Papers* (Urbana: University of Illinois Press). The National Association for the Advancement of Colored People Papers (NAACP) has some material on peonage that was especially useful in the *Williams* case and the Mississippi flood of 1927. Unfortunately, the NAACP's interest in peonage did not continue. The Library of Congress collections of Theodore Roosevelt Papers, Ray Stannard Baker Papers, William H. Taft Papers, and Arthur Spingarn Papers were of limited use. The Booker T. Washington collections at Tuskegee Institute and at Howard University supplement the Library of Congress collection. The Robert Russa Moton Papers at Tuskegee Institute, a rich and practically unused collection, was most valuable in material relating to the 1927 flood.

In New York the Schomburg Collection of the New York Public Library contains useful information, especially in the clipping files on sharecroppers, the National Negro Congress Papers, and material relating to the *Cunningham* case. The Manuscript Division of the New York Public Library contains peonage material in the Gino C. Speranza Papers and the Vito Marcantonio Papers. The Workers Defense League press releases in the New York Public Library supplied some information on peonage in the 1940s.

The writer is especially indebted to Herbert Aptheker for both the use of his private correspondence and for an informative interview regarding the *Cunningham* case. S. M. Hay, clerk of Newton Superior Court in Georgia, revealed information on the fate of John S. Williams.

Though it would seem that Southern manuscript repositories would be rich in peonage documents, a survey of several collections proved disappointing. Peonage, it seems, escaped the notice or concern of men and organizations that should have been most interested in the practice.

Legal sources are rich in peonage material. The trial transcripts in the *Williams* and *Manning* cases were extremely valuable. The richness of the testimony in those cases invites greater utilization of such documents in writing legal and social history. State and federal reports, annotated codes, briefs and records of the Supreme Court cases also provide valuable insights into the legal problems of peonage.

Public documents used in this study were often unreliable. *The Annual Report of the Attorney General* occasionally commented on peonage, but often superficially and in sometimes misleading fashion. Charles W. Russell's *Report on Peonage* (Washington, 1908), however, gave a useful synopsis of the prosecutions involving immigrants. Some researchers unfortunately took his report to mean that there was little peonage among other classes of Southerners. Likewise, the peonage report in the *Abstracts of Reports of the Immigration Commission. Senate Documents*, 42 vols., 61st Cong., 3rd sess., 1910–11, no. 747, II:443–49, was brief and misleading, probably intentionally so. The *Congressional Record* contained speeches of Southern Congressmen either attacking the Justice Department or adding twentieth-century refinements to the states' rights defense of peculiar institutions. The *Register of the Department of Justice* was useful in tracing the dates of employment and the positions of federal employees. State legislative journals and congressional hearings were of limited use.

Throughout the twentieth century magazines reported spectacular cases of peonage. *Outlook* gave excellent coverage of the Alabama cases in 1903 and continued this coverage through the *Bailey* case in 1911, and *Nation*'s coverage was also useful during these years. Among the more useful articles relating to peonage were: Gino C. Speranza, "Forced Labor in West Virginia," *Outlook* 74 (June 13, 1903), 407–10; "Peonage in Georgia," *Independent* 55 (Dec. 24, 1903), 3079–80; Herbert D. Ward, "Peonage in America," *Cosmopolitan* 39 (Aug. 1905), 423–30; Richard Barry, "Slavery in the South To-Day," *Cosmopolitan* 42 (Mar. 1907), 481–91; Mike Trudics (as told to Alexander Irvine), "The Life Story of a Hungarian Peon," *Independent* 63 (Sept. 5, 1907), 557–64; Ray Stannard Baker, "A Pawn in the Struggle for Freedom," *American Magazine* 72 (Sept. 1911), 608–10; Walter White, "The Negro and the Flood," *Nation* 124 (June 22, 1927), 688–89; "The Flood, the Red Cross and the National Guard," *Crisis* 35 (Jan. 1928), 5–7, 26, 28; (Feb. 1928), 41–42, 64; (Mar. 1928), 100, 102; Morris Milgram, "Involuntary

Servitude in Florida," *Twice a Year* 14–15 (Fall–Winter, 1946–47), 408–15; Robert Coles and Harry Huge, "Peonage in Florida," *New Republic* 161 (July 26, 1969), 17–21.

Newspapers usually reported peonage cases of major importance. The *New York Times* was very useful in recent cases because of its index. The *New York Evening Post*, which gave a neo-abolitionist point of view, and the *Montgomery Advertiser*, which attempted to minimize the extent of peonage, were useful in the Alabama cases of 1903. The *Atlanta Constitution* gave excellent coverage of the *Williams* case in 1921. Other newspapers were used occasionally to give supporting documentation. The clipping collections in the NAACP Papers and the Moton Papers were useful in gaining an idea of newspaper reaction pertaining to the Mississippi flood and the *Williams* case. The clippings in the Justice Department files, though sketchy, were also useful.

Though many of the excellent state studies in agriculture and in black history were useful in understanding the context of peonage, few of these works touched at all upon peonage itself. Because such works are generally known and nearly all are cited in the *Harvard Guide to American History*, listing such tangential works here is unnecessary. Especially useful works are mentioned at specific points throughout the study, though with few exceptions such works were not dealing with peonage but with agricultural or social problems. Richard B. Morris's two excellent articles on peonage in the antebellum United States, "White Bondage in Ante-Bellum South Carolina," *South Carolina Historical and Genealogical Magazine* 49 (Oct. 1948), 191–207, and "The Course of Peonage in a Slave State," *Political Science Quarterly* 65 (June 1950), 238–63, were excellent in pointing out precedents of peonage. Dan T. Carter's "Prisons, Politics and Business: The Convict Lease System in the Post-Civil War South," (M.A. thesis, University of Wisconsin, 1964) helped establish the differences between peonage and the convict lease system. Mary F. Berry's "Do Black People Have a Constitutional Right to Life: A Consideration of Federal and State Concern about the Murder of Black People, 1877–1969" (Paper delivered to Southern Historical Association convention, November 12, 1970) gave the legal setting for the *Williams* case. James P. Woods III lent his paper, "Herbert Hoover, Black Refugees, and the Mississippi Valley Flood of 1927: A Case Study in 'Bureaucratic Conservatism,'" and he also lent the writer photocopies of documents from the Herbert Clark Hoover Papers, Herbert Hoover Presidential Library, West Branch, Iowa.

Hugh M. Dorsey's *The Negro in Georgia* (Atlanta, 1921) gave a revealing portrait of the violence that covered that state in the 1920s, though some of its investigations were called into question. *The Final Report of the Colored Advisory Commission* (Washington, 1929) reflected the optimistic and misleading attitudes of the Commerce Department, the Red Cross, and the Colored Advisory Commission and is valuable only for the factual material, not for its conclusions.

Harold Preece's *Peonage—1940 Style Slavery* (n.p., n.d.), located in the Schomburg Collection of the New York Public Library, utilized affidavits to give a vivid description of planter William T. Cunningham's domain in Oglethorpe County, Georgia. William Henry Huff's two articles in the *National Bar Journal*, "Peonage or Debt Slavery in the Land of the Free," 3 (Mar. 1945), 43–49, and "The New Charter of Slavery," 2 (June 1944), 65–69, give the view of a black man who had observed peonage as a youngster and his account of the *Cunningham* case.

There are several excellent legal studies of peonage. Robert K. Carr's *Federal Protection of Civil Rights: Quest for a Sword* (Ithaca, 1947) contains a brief survey of peonage cases. Edward F. Waite's "The Negro in the Supreme Court," *Minnesota Law Review* 30 (Mar. 1946), 219–304, reviews Supreme Court cases involving black Americans, and Arthur B. Caldwell's "The Civil Rights Section, Its Functions and Its Statutes" (Paper delivered to civil rights class of the summer session of the University of Pennsylvania, July 16, 1953, copy in possession of author) comments on the involuntary servitude laws and the activities of the Justice Department in prosecuting violators. Sydney Brodie, "The Federally-Secured Right to Be Free from Bondage," *Georgetown Law Journal* 40 (Mar. 1952), 367–98; Fred G. Folsom, Jr., "A Slave Trade Law in a Contemporary Setting," *Cornell Law Quarterly* 29 (Nov. 1943), 203–16; and Harry H. Shapiro, "Involuntary Servitude: The Need for a More Flexible Approach," *Rutgers Law Review* 19 (1964–65), 65–85, give excellent reviews of peonage and slavery and call for more vigorous prosecution.

William Delmer Wagoner, "The Non-Free Worker in Post–Civil War American History" (Ph.D. dissertation, University of Texas,

1961), is more a warning of the dangers of relying exclusively on published sources than a serious study of peonage. On the other hand, Howard Devon Hamilton, "The Legislative and Judicial History of the Thirteenth Amendment" (Ph.D. dissertation, University of Illinois, 1950), gives a useful review of peonage laws, state labor laws, and court cases.

Background reading for this study was extensive, yet to list books that have little or nothing to do with peonage would be distracting if not pedantic. Anyone working in the history of the South, however, must consult C. Vann Woodward, *Origins of the New South, 1877–1913* (Baton Rouge, 1951), George B. Tindall, *The Emergence of the New South, 1913–1945* (Baton Rouge, 1967), August Meier, *Negro Thought in America, 1880–1915* (Ann Arbor, 1963), and Wilbur Cash, *The Mind of the South* (New York, 1941).

Index